"Divided into well-defined sections for easy reading, this manual contains much researched material; useful and detailed case studies; wide-ranging perspectives, perceptions and myths; and good advice for any business to grow their brand. Witty and filled with anecdotes, these are certainly guidelines that are useful to anyone who is serious about their branding endeavours … a must-read for all brand owners and brand guardians regardless of the stage of their brand development."

Bryan Teh

CEO, Association of Small and Medium Enterprises (ASME)

"In an increasing globally competitive environment, company branding has become a critical challenge. This is not only for gaining mindshare of products and services, but even more importantly for talent attraction and retention. This is especially so for SMEs seeking to grow and secure a place in the global economy. The authors' latest book reflects their passion for the subject as well their many years of practical experience in helping to brand companies, both in Singapore and internationally."

Koh Juan Kiat

CEO, Singapore National Employers Federation (SNEF)

"Branding is very often misconstrued as slapping on a new label or creating a funky-looking logo, coupled with expensive advertising. It doesn't help that branding books in the market are often based on the experiences and tales of Western companies – many of which are already well-known names by the time they are highlighted in such literature. With Asia being the next growth story, it is only apt that there is a branding guide that draws inspiration from case studies in the region. What I like about the book is the inclusion of plenty of local examples and detailed descriptions of their branding journeys – from the circumstances that motivated those companies, most of them SMEs, to the eventual execution of their brand strategies. The authors are also unusually candid in their views on Singapore SMEs and the role that branding may play in their evolution. This book shows that branding is applicable not only for consumer products, but also B2B businesses."

Chen Hui Fen

Journalist, The Business Times

B2B

JACKY TAI
DR WILSON CHEW

10 Rules To Transform
Your Business Into A Brand

mc **Marshall Cavendish**
Business

First published by Marshall Cavendish Business
An imprint of Marshall Cavendish International
1 New Industrial Road, Singapore 536196

Other Marshall Cavendish Offices
Marshall Cavendish Limited PO Box 65829 London EC1P 1NY• Marshall Cavendish Corporation. 99 White Plains Road, Tarrytown NY 10591-9001, USA • Marshall Cavendish International (Thailand) Co Ltd. 253 Asoke, 12th Flr, Sukhumvit 21 Road, Klongtoey Nua, Wattana, Bangkok 10110, Thailand • Marshall Cavendish (Malaysia) Sdn Bhd, Times Subang, Lot 46, Subang Hi-Tech Industrial Park, Batu Tiga, 40000 Shah Alam, Selangor Darul Ehsan, Malaysia

Marshall Cavendish is a trademark of Times Publishing Limited

National Library Board Singapore Cataloguing in Publication Data
Tai, Jacky, 1970-
B2B : 10 rules to transform your business into a brand / Jacky Tai, Wilson Chew. – Singapore : Marshall Cavendish Business, c2011.
p. cm.
ISBN : 978-981-4328-32-6

1. Brand name products. 2. Branding (Marketing) I. Chew, Wilson, 1970- II. Title.

HD69.B7
658.827 – dc22   OCN704245997

Printed in Singapore by Craft Print International Ltd

To my wife Christine. Thank you, honey, for being my better half.
– Jacky Tai, 28 February 2011

To my best friends: Kai (wife) & Elizabeth (daughter).
– Dr Wilson Chew, 28 February 2011

CONTENTS

INTRODUCTION

THERE is one thing in life that we can take for granted and that is the fact that we live in a world where Sir Isaac Newton's Third Law of Motion – which states that "for every action, there is an equal and opposite reaction" – can be applied to everything that we do. We are not just talking about physics here. We are talking about the fact that for everything you say or do, there will always be someone who will say or do the opposite thing. Even if it is something for which you can produce irrefutable evidence, there will still be someone somewhere in the world who will say that the opposite is true.

Did you know that there are still people who believe that the world is not round despite all the scientific evidence to the contrary? And there are people who still say that the moon landing by Neil Armstrong did not happen and that it is simply propaganda by the US government. You can easily find these rather amusing views (and people) if you do a search on the Internet. There is nothing that you can do about this fact of life. After all, everyone should be entitled to his or her view on every single thing.

The same thing happens in the world of branding. We know because since the first publication of this book in 2007, we have had the opportunity to work on many interesting branding projects for small and big companies. We have enjoyed them all. We have also met many other business owners, chief executive officers (CEOs), marketing directors and even business students with whom we have had interesting conversations on the issues of branding. Therefore, we know that there will always be somebody who will take the opposite position.

Sometimes we come across people who were apparently born to take the opposite position. We are sure you have met such people who thrive on taking the opposite position on everything in life. A black cat can walk in front of you and if you say, "Look, there goes a black cat", they will say that it is not really a black cat but a charcoal grey one. But that is all right. Everyone is entitled to his or her opinion, regardless of whether we think it is right or wrong.

One of the opposing views that we have often heard from business owners is this: "Branding consultants like you people always say that branding is important. Of course you would say that because that is the business you are in. I don't think branding is important in order for me to build a successful business. In fact, I have built a successful business for the past 30 years without all this branding nonsense. What do you have to say to that?"

Although many of the business owners who have made such statements to us are people in their fifties or sixties, we have to qualify that statement by saying that we have also encountered many younger executives who have said the same thing so this is not just a cranky old businessman (or businesswoman) syndrome. Indeed, it is a valid question to ask and it is a question that we have to answer convincingly – at least to ourselves – if we are to continue to be effective in the work that we do as branding strategy consultants.

This may sound strange coming from two branding strategy consultants who have spent the better part of their careers promoting the art and science of branding but the answer to the question of whether branding is really necessary to build a successful business is no. For simplicity's sake, we define a successful business as being a business that is profitable – it doesn't matter if the net profit margin is less than 5 per cent, as long as the company is making a profit, we treat it as successful.

You don't need to have a strong brand to have a successful business. You need to be in the right place at the right time with the right product or service that people need or want. There is an element of luck – or fortuitous timing as some would call it – that is involved in building a successful business. That is of course not all there is to it. Your quality needs to be at least as good as your competitors. Your service levels must be acceptable to customers even if you sell really cheap to them. You must have people to help you run the business. Your price must also be competitive. Do all these things right and you could have a successful business – maybe even a world-class company. So why do you need to have a brand or pay attention to the branding strategy of the company?

THE EVOLUTION OF A BUSINESS

Before we answer the question of why you need a brand or why you need to pay attention to your branding strategy, let's take a look at how businesses evolve over time. A company might go through three phases in its life – from a start-up to a small- or medium-sized enterprise (SME) to a large multi-national corporation (MNC). Of course, there are many businesses that fail along the way and there are many that will not make it to the stage of large MNC but let's assume that your business goes through these three phases for the purpose of illustrating this process.

The Start-up Phase

At the start-up phase, a company is usually run and funded by its founders. Unless the founders have the backing of wealthy parents or inherited a fortune from some rich eccentric uncle as we so often see in the movies, the company will usually be run on a shoestring budget. There is never enough money to do all the things that the company needs to do but that is just the way it is with start-ups. It is always about compromise. If you want one thing, you must be willing to give up the other nine things that you also want. What a company does or does not do at this stage depends on what its founders can or cannot do. The scope is very limited.

For example, when Bill Gates and Paul Allen first started Microsoft, they probably wanted to do a lot of things but they had limited funds and manpower so they had to narrow the focus to the things that were within their personal circles of competence. As they were both excellent software programmers, they focussed on developing the world's first 16-bit operating system, which they pitched relentlessly to IBM. They didn't have a choice but to pitch to IBM because IBM was the de facto computing standard in those days. What went at IBM went in the world of computing.

You might have seen reports that show that the mortality rate of a start-up business is very high. Whether a start-up will be able to exit the danger zone – and that is the first three years – depends a lot on the founders' capabilities, drive, network and ability to juggle a hundred and one things without too many of them crashing to the ground. We have spoken to some 40 start-ups in the last four years. Sadly, many of them are no longer around today. Some of the start-ups that went bust were started by people who were extremely brilliant in their field but running a start-up is not just about how brilliant the founders are.

It is also about the ability to manage a business and the ability to sacrifice. Many of these start-ups simply tried to do too many things too soon and, as a result, they became overstretched and eventually collapsed.

The rule of thumb if you are running a start-up is this: What you do or don't do depends on what you can or cannot do. Figure that out and stick to what you can do given your limited time, money and resources.

The SME Phase

At the SME phase, a business has more money, more people and more resources but there are still limitations on what it can do. Usually at this stage, what a business does or does not do depends on the processes that it has put in place because once you are an SME, you are not as nimble as when you were a start-up. You have more clients to take care of and you need to put in place certain business, manufacturing or service processes to ensure that your company runs properly. So, at the SME stage, things are driven by processes.

One of our clients – Futuristic Store Fixtures International – is a very fast-growing SME that designs, manufactures and assembles store fixtures for its clients who are the who's who in the world of retailing. Futuristic is a very process-driven company. Its processes dictate that it can only serve clients with at least one hundred retail outlets. With anything less than one hundred stores, it becomes unfeasible for Futuristic to take on the business. Having these processes in place is a critical component in the success of an SME. These processes keep everything under control. They allow the company to become efficient.

The rule of thumb for ensuring that your SME can continue to operate profitably is this: Develop and implement processes throughout the company that will allow the company to run efficiently; and what you do or don't do will depend on these processes.

The MNC Phase

When a company reaches the MNC phase, what it does is very often driven by its values. For example, a company like The Body Shop might run its business based on the corporate values that it has put in place. The Body Shop takes an eco-friendly position and therefore what it does or does not do depends on whether the activity, product or business in question is eco-friendly. As long as an MNC sticks to its values and these values continue to be relevant to its customers, the business should continue to be successful.

These three phases were actually outlined in Clayton M Christensen's groundbreaking book titled *The Innovator's Dilemma*.[1] Now, everything else remaining constant, any company in any of these three phases should continue to do well if it sticks to the things that it is supposed to do. For example, a start-up should stick to what its founders are good at doing and walk that narrow path in order to have a chance of growing. An SME should just be driven by its processes and continue to refine and sharpen these processes along the way. An MNC should continue to live by its corporate values.

But things don't remain constant, do they? In business, there is one thing that will always upset the equilibrium and that is a pesky little thing that you would term as The Competition. Competitors are a way of life for any business. Just as they make life difficult for you, you also make life difficult for them. The need for a strong brand is driven by competitors and today, you have more competitors than you had five years ago and next year, you will probably have more, not fewer, competitors. Singapore is a small country of 704 square kilometres and around 4.8 million people but it also has 154,000 SMEs and over 7,000 MNCs housed here. The business landscape is a hypercompetitive one and it will only get even more so in the years to come.

COMPETITORS ARE USEFUL, UP TO A POINT

You need to have competitors. They are useful because they help to define your brand. They give you a reason to exist. And they keep you on your toes. Without competitors, you tend to become complacent and lazy because you have nothing or no one to fight. Without competitors, the level of innovation will drop. So, these pesky competitors of yours are good to have. They have a role to play in *building your brand* – strange as that may sound. We will examine more about the role that your competitors have in your brand building efforts in Chapter 16.

However, as useful as competitors are, too many of them can be detrimental. You have probably heard the saying, "Too much of a good thing can be bad for you" and competitors are like that. Too many of them can be bad for you. Competitors are like painkillers. A small dose of painkillers can help to alleviate that migraine or back pain that has been niggling you but too many can turn you into a drug addict, or kill you. Having competitors around is good as they help

---

[1]   Christensen, Clayton M, *The Innovator's Dilemma: The Revolutionary Book that Will Change the Way You Do Business*, Harper Paperbacks (2003)

to keep you focussed on your goals, they drive you to continue to innovate and to improve and they also give you credibility because as long as your company has someone to fight, your customers will perceive that you have a reason for being around.

But the problem now is that you have far too many competitors and that creates a situation of hypercompetition. Everybody is trying to get into everybody else's business. You sneeze and they run away with your customers; and you will never see those customers again. Because you are swimming with sharks on a daily basis, you need something that can protect your business from all these sharks and that something is called a strong brand.

Here is an interesting situation that we have found among many Singapore companies, and this could be something that your company is facing as well. In the last 10 years, many Singapore companies have grown. They have become bigger. They are now selling in more countries. They have more products to sell. They have seen a steady growth in their sales revenue. This is good. The only small problem is that their net profits have shrunk. In an SME 500 survey conducted by the DP Information Group, one of the biggest concerns among Singapore business owners is that their profit margins are shrinking steadily. The average net profit margin hovers around 5 per cent. To many SME bosses, this is dangerous as it means that the companies do not have a lot of money to reinvest in their businesses.

Why are these companies (and maybe yours) experiencing That Shrinking Feeling? The answer is hypercompetition. And how does hypercompetition affect the bottom line? When the market is hypercompetitive, there are bound be some companies that are desperate to grab a slice of the market and therefore willing to sell the same thing for a lower price. In the absence of any appreciable difference between the various competitors, customers will choose the cheaper alternative – and that cheaper alternative might not be you. In the face of such hypercompetition, companies will be under a lot of pressure to match their competitors in terms of pricing and that leads to an erosion of profit margins over time. This is a story that we have heard over and over again from business owners.

To make things worse, the quality gap between the best and the worst in most categories has narrowed so much that to many customers even the entry-level products or services are now good enough for their needs. That will put even more pressure on you in terms of pricing even if you think you have higher-quality products or services than your lower-cost competitors. It is a vicious cycle that affects most categories.

HOW DOES A STRONG BRAND HELP YOU?

We said earlier that you don't need a strong brand to build a successful business. This is true. If you are in the right place at the right time offering the right product or service at the right price, you can have a successful business even if you don't have a strong brand. You will enjoy a good run for a while but that will eventually end because if you have a profitable business, competitors will appear like dark clouds on the horizon in no time at all. In the past, it might have taken them a while to appear. These days, it can almost be overnight.

Whatever you can do, your competitors can copy very quickly and the scary thing is, now they can do it as well (if not better) and sell it cheaper. You can build a successful business without a strong brand but if you want that business to be sustainable, you need a strong brand. Many CEOs have told us that even strong brands cannot command a lot of premium these days because of hypercompetition. This is true. So, why do you still need to build a strong brand?

In terms of pricing, customers can be broadly grouped into three price categories:

- Premium
- Mid-Range
- Entry-Level

There are some customers who will buy premium products or services because they can afford them and they want to be seen using the premium stuff – this applies not just to luxury goods for personal use but to commercial and industrial products and services as well. There are some customers who will only buy from the mid-range suppliers because their budget only allows them to buy mid-priced products or services or they simply don't see the need to pay for the premium stuff. Finally, there are those who can or will only buy entry-level stuff.

For every price category, there are probably many companies that can meet the customers' needs. Let's say that you are a mid-range company. Your pricing is within the range that your potential customers can afford to pay. But there are probably 15 other companies in your space – most likely more – that can offer something comparable. How will your potential customers choose between these 16 suppliers?

Before you answer that question, let's turn the situation around. Let's assume you need to buy a new computer server for the office and you can afford brands like IBM, Sun Microsystems, Hewlett-Packard (HP) and Dell. Which one would you choose? They are all renowned companies. They are all reputable companies. They are all able to meet your technical specifications and service requirements. Which one would you choose? You would choose the one that you perceive to be the strongest brand. Your customers will also behave the same way. If you perceive that Sun Microsystems is the strongest brand, then you will choose Sun Microsystems regardless of how much the other three try to persuade you otherwise. On a shortlist where each competitor is equally matched on the things that are tangible, the one with the strongest brand – which is an intangible asset – wins.

FROM WORLD-CLASS BUSINESS TO WORLD-CLASS BRAND

Jacky once met a group of Silicone Valley venture capitalists who told him that in terms of innovation, many Singapore companies are actually on par with their American counterparts but they tend to lose out because their American counterparts are better at branding. We actually have a lot of world-class businesses here in Singapore as well as in other parts of Asia but many of them have yet to make the jump from being a world-class business to becoming a world-class brand.

What is a world-class brand? The definition depends a lot on who you ask. For simplicity's sake, let's use the *BusinessWeek* '100 Best Global Brands' ranking. Every year around August, *BusinessWeek* releases this ranking, which rates the brands based on their brand value. Although this is not a foolproof method of deciding what is a world-class brand and what is not, it provides a fairly good idea because in order to have a high brand value – which is an intangible asset – you will need to have a strong brand that can protect your market share and ensure that future earnings have a higher chance of materialising. The *BusinessWeek* ranking takes these factors into account when valuing the brands.

At the time of writing, the latest ranking that we have is for 2009. The table on the following page reproduces the *BusinessWeek* ranking.

Table 1: *BusinessWeek*'s '100 Best Global Brands'

Rank 2009	Rank 2008	Company	2009 Brand Value (US$ million)	2008 Brand Value (US$ million)	% Change	Country Of Ownership
1	1	Coca-Cola	68,734	66,667	3	US
2	2	IBM	60,211	59,031	2	US
3	3	Microsoft	56,647	59,007	-4	US
4	4	GE	47,777	53,086	-10	US
5	5	Nokia	34,864	35,942	-3	Finland
6	8	McDonald's	32,275	31,049	4	US
7	10	Google	31,980	25,590	25	US
8	6	Toyota	31,330	34,050	-8	**Japan**
9	7	Intel	30,636	31,261	-2	US
10	9	Disney	28,447	29,251	-3	US
11	12	Hewlett-Packard	24,096	23,509	2	US
12	11	Mercedes-Benz	23,867	25,577	-7	Germany
13	14	Gillette	22,841	22,069	4	US
14	17	Cisco Systems	22,030	21,306	3	US
15	13	BMW	21,671	23,298	-7	Germany
16	16	Louis Vuitton	21,120	21,602	-2	France
17	18	Marlboro	19,010	21,300	-11	US
18	20	Honda	17,803	19,079	-7	**Japan**
19	21	Samsung	17,518	17,689	-1	**S. Korea**
20	24	Apple	15,443	13,724	12	US
21	22	H&M	15,375	13,840	11	Sweden
22	15	American Express	14,971	21,940	-32	US
23	26	Pepsi	13,706	13,249	3	US
24	23	Oracle	13,699	13,831	-1	US
25	28	NESCAFÉ	13,317	13,055	2	Switzerland
26	29	Nike	13,179	12,672	4	US
27	31	SAP	12,106	12,228	-1	Germany
28	35	IKEA	12,004	10,913	10	Sweden
29	25	Sony	11,953	13,583	-12	**Japan**
30	33	Budweiser	11,833	11,438	3	Belgium
31	30	UPS	11,594	12,621	-8	US
32	27	HSBC	10,510	13,143	-20	Britain
33	36	Canon	10,441	10,876	-4	**Japan**
34	39	Kellogg's	10,428	9,710	7	US
35	32	Dell	10,291	11,695	-12	US
36	19	Citi	10,254	20,174	-49	US
37	37	J.P. Morgan	9,550	10,773	-11	US
38	38	Goldman Sachs	9,248	10,331	-10	US
39	40	Nintendo	9,210	8,772	5	**Japan**
40	44	Thomson Reuters	8,434	8,313	1	Canada
41	45	Gucci	8,182	8,254	-1	Italy
42	43	Philips	8,121	8,325	-2	Netherlands
43	58	Amazon	7,858	6,434	22	US
44	51	L'Oréal	7,748	7,508	3	France
45	47	Accenture	7,710	7,948	-3	US
46	46	eBay	7,350	7,991	-8	US
47	48	Siemens	7,308	7,943	-8	Germany
48	56	Heinz	7,244	6,646	9	US
49	49	Ford	7,005	7,896	-11	US
50	62	Zara	6,789	5,955	14	Spain
51	61	Wrigley	6,731	6,105	10	US
52	57	Colgate	6,550	6,437	2	US
53	55	AXA	6,525	7,001	-7	France
54	52	MTV	6,523	7,193	-9	US

55	53	Volkswagen	6,484	7,047	-8	Germany
56	59	Xerox	6,431	6,393	1	US
57	42	Morgan Stanley	6,399	8,696	-26	US
58	63	Nestlé	6,319	5,592	13	Switzerland
59	60	Chanel	6,040	6,355	-5	France
60	66	Danone	5,960	5,408	10	France
61	64	KFC	5,722	5,582	3	US
62	70	adidas	5,397	5,072	6	Germany
63	73	BlackBerry	5,138	4,802	7	Canada
64	65	Yahoo!	5,111	5,496	-7	US
65	67	Audi	5,010	5,407	-7	Germany
66	68	Caterpillar	5,004	5,288	-5	US
67	69	Avon	4,917	5,264	-7	US
68	71	Rolex	4,609	4,956	-7	Switzerland
69	72	Hyundai	4,604	4,846	-5	**S. Korea**
70	76	Hermès	4,598	4,575	1	France
71	74	Kleenex	4,404	4,636	-5	US
72	41	UBS	4,370	8,740	-50	Switzerland
73	50	Harley-Davidson	4,337	7,609	-43	US
74	75	Porsche	4,234	4,603	-8	Germany
75	78	Panasonic	4,225	4,281	-1	**Japan**
76	80	Tiffany & Co.	4,000	4,208	-5	US
77	79	Cartier	3,968	4,236	-6	France
78	77	Gap	3,922	4,357	-10	US
79	81	Pizza Hut	3,876	4,097	-5	US
80	92	Johnson & Johnson	3,847	3,582	7	US
81	82	Allianz	3,831	4,033	-5	Germany
82	83	Moët & Chandon	3,754	3,951	-5	France
83	84	BP	3,716	3,911	-5	Britain
84	89	Smirnoff	3,698	3,590	3	Britain
85	88	Duracell	3,563	3,682	-3	US
86	98	Nivea	3,557	3,401	5	Germany
87	91	Prada	3,530	3,585	-2	Italy
88	93	Ferrari	3,527	3,527	0	Italy
89	94	Armani	3,303	3,526	-6	Italy
90	85	Starbucks	3,263	3,879	-16	US
91	New	Lancôme	3,235	New	New	France
92	97	Shell	3,228	3,471	-7	Netherlands
93	New	Burger King	3,223	New	New	US
94	100	Visa	3,170	3,338	-5	US
95	New	Adobe	3,161	New	New	US
96	90	Lexus	3,158	3,588	-12	**Japan**
97	New	Puma	3,154	New	New	Germany
98	New	Burberry	3,095	New	New	Britain
99	New	Polo Ralph Lauren	3,094	New	New	US
100	New	Campbell's	3,081	New	New	US

(Source: *BusinessWeek*, 17 September 2010)

Based on the *BusinessWeek* ranking, there are nine brands from Asia and they are all from Japan and South Korea. Given that Asia is the region that is expected to grow rapidly in the next 50 years, the number of Asian brands in the Top 100 is relatively low. Where are the Singapore brands? A long way off. According to a study by International Enterprise (IE) Singapore – the Singapore government agency with the mandate to help Singapore companies expand their business overseas – the most valuable Singapore brand in 2006 was SingTel, valued at approximately S$2.7 billion.[2] The study used the same methodology employed by the *Businessweek* study. The least valuable brand on the *BusinessWeek* 100 Best Global Brands table is Campbell's, which was valued at around US$3.1 billion, or approximately S$4.4 billion.[3] Singapore has a lot of world-class businesses but not yet world-class brands that can dominate their categories in the markets they compete in.

TRANSFORMING YOUR BUSINESS INTO A BRAND

This book was originally written because we were rather unhappy with the situation in the marketplace. We kept asking ourselves, "How come we have so many well-run, highly-efficient and even world-class companies but they are not world-class brands?" In fact, if you do a brand valuation of the average Asian brand, there is a good chance that you will find that the percentage of intangible assets that makes up this total brand value is lower than that of a comparable Western brand. We also know that many company bosses in Singapore are not marketing trained. In our experience, we have found that the typical business owner falls into one of three categories in terms of background – Engineering, Finance and the Natural-Born Entrepreneur.

Now, as then, our intention is to show Singapore companies how they can transform themselves into world-class brands using the 10 rules of branding that have made many of today's successful global brands what they are. You do not require a degree in rocket science to understand these rules of branding. They are simple and straightforward. Over the years, an explosion in the number of so-called branding gurus around the world and the rise of complicated branding jargon have made it harder to understand the really important things about branding. This book aims to cut through all the complexity and jargon to get to the very heart of the matter.

Before these 10 rules of branding can be of any use to you, however, you must understand the fundamental difference between a business and a brand. A business is driven by opportunities. It will do whatever brings in revenue, regardless of the negative consequences this may have on the brand. For example, a company might start out as a department store. Then, as the property sector in that market starts to boom, the company diversifies into property development. After a few years, it might decide that given the rapidly ageing population, there is money to be made in nursing homes. So it starts to divert resources into setting

---

[2] Singapore Brand Awards 2006. Note: The year 2006 was the last time that the Singapore Brand Awards was held.

[3] All currency conversions were done at www.xe.com on 7 November 2010.

up nursing homes. Does that sound familiar to you? It should. Companies that fit this description populate the business landscape.

A brand, on the other hand, is driven by vision. It sets its mind on a specific goal and works towards achieving it. A brand does not chase every single opportunity that presents itself. A brand is willing to forgo nine out of 10 business opportunities in order to build a strong, dominant position in just one category. In other words, instead of striving to own 5 per cent of 10 markets as the typical business normally does, a brand aims to own 50 per cent (or more) of one category. That is the fundamental difference between a business and a brand. As you read this book, we would like you to bear in mind three very important things:

1. The rules of branding are like Mathematics in the sense that they are constant. One plus one always equals two. Regardless of what kind of product or service you sell, the rules of branding apply in the same way. When you are reading this book, look past the nature of business of the brands that we use as case studies. It doesn't matter if they are not from the same industry as yours. It doesn't matter if they are Business-to-Business (B2B) or Business-to-Customer (B2C). The rules of branding are the same.

2. All big successful brands started out as small struggling brands, perhaps once in even worse positions than you are in today. But these brands stuck to their guns and played by the rules of branding. Because of that, it was impossible for these brands to remain small for long. We are often asked if there are rules of branding written specifically for small companies. The answer is no. If there were rules of branding for small companies, it would mean that they were designed to keep these companies small. Why would anyone want that?

3. All successful brands – whether by design or by accident – play by the 10 rules of branding that we are going to share with you here. No exceptions. When we present the case studies of brands in this book, look past the success that they are today and what they are doing now. Instead, look at the things that they did when they were small and struggling. Look at the rules of branding that they played by to make them big, successful and sustainable global brands.

Enjoy the book.

B2B

CHAPTER
01

What Is A Brand?

BEFORE we can embark on the journey of building a strong brand, we must first define correctly what a brand is.

The journey of a thousand miles begins with the first step but if you step on a sharp nail with your very first step, that journey is going to take a long time to complete – or it may not happen at all. So it makes sense to first define what kind of an animal a brand actually is because if we are not clear on the definition of a brand, how will we know if we have actually built a strong brand?

You have read in the Introduction section of this book that a brand does not chase market opportunities, it chases a vision. Of course, brands do capitalise on market opportunities – they would be silly not to – but they don't make it the be all and end all of their reason for being. However, not all companies that chase a vision are brands or will become brands but they have set off in the right direction. Whether a company becomes a brand depends on what the vision is. BMW was still making the tiny Isetta 250 budget car after World War II when it embarked on an innovation and marketing programme to achieve its vision of becoming "The Ultimate Driving Machine". That is a great vision. A difficult vision, no doubt, but one that is worthy of chasing. Chasing that vision helped BMW to become a strong brand and the best-selling luxury car in the world today.

WHAT IS THE DEFINITION OF A BRAND?

If you ask a hundred people to define what a brand is, you will probably get a hundred different answers. Even in the best case scenario – which is unlikely to happen – you will still get at least two different answers because if we extend Newton's Third Law of Motion into the business world, then we will see that for every view that is expressed, there will be an opposite view. It happens all the time.

"What is *your* definition of a brand?"

This is one question that we like to ask participants in our branding workshops, just to see how different people define a brand. More often than not, we get a bewildering array of answers on what a brand is – even from people within the same profession or industry. To make matters worse, when you put a hundred smart, highly educated businesspeople into a room and ask them to define what a brand is, you will probably get more than a hundred different definitions. That is the way things work.

In fact, every time we gather the eight most senior people within a company and ask them to define what *their brand* is all about, we usually get seven different answers. This is an exercise that we used to conduct at the start of any branding project or even at the initial exploratory meeting with a potential client to see where the gaps were. For some strange reason, the CEO and the chief financial officer (CFO) very often come up with the same answer as to what their brand is all about but the responses from the rest of the senior management team differs greatly. We have not had time to study why the CEO and the CFO usually think alike but we are sure that this would be an interesting thesis for a PhD candidate to study. The point is, even within a close-knit team of senior management people, there are variations on how they each define a brand.

Even branding experts from around the world cannot seem to agree on a standard definition of what a brand is. We don't have the space here to print all the different definitions but from the many examples below, you can see how confusing it can potentially get because everyone seems to have a different definition of what a brand is. Unlike in accounting, law or medicine, there isn't a governing body in the area of branding or marketing that can impose a standard definition.

The closest we can probably get is the definition provided by the American Marketing Association:

"A name, term, design, symbol, or any other feature that identifies one seller's good or service as distinct from those of other sellers. The legal term for brand is trademark. A brand may identify one item, a family of items, or all items of that seller."

The American Marketing Association

This is how two of the leading English dictionaries define a brand:

> "A class of goods identified by name as the product of a single firm or manufacturer."
> *Merriam-Webster Dictionary*

> "A type of product manufactured by a company under a particular name."
> *Compact Oxford English Dictionary*

This is how some branding and marketing experts define a brand:

> "A brand is the sum of all feelings, thoughts and recognitions – positive and negative – that people in the target audience have about a company, a product or service."
> *Steve McNamara, AdCracker.com*

> "A brand is a collection of perceptions in the mind of the consumer."
> *Colin Bates, BuildingBrands.com*

> "Simply put, a brand is a promise. By identifying and authenticating a product or service, it delivers a pledge of satisfaction and quality."
> *Walter Landor, founder of Walter Landor & Associates*

> "A set of assets (or liabilities) linked to a brand's name and symbol that adds to (or subtracts from) the value provided by a product or service…"
> *David Aaker, Building Strong Brands*

> "A brand name is nothing more than a word in the mind, albeit a special kind of word."
> *Al Ries and Laura Ries, The 22 Immutable Laws of Branding*

> "A name, term, sign symbol or a combination of these, that identifies the maker or seller of the product."
> *Philip Kotler and Gary Armstrong, Principles of Marketing*

"On the most basic level, a brand is a name or some symbol or mark that is associated with a product or service and to which buyers attach psychological meaning."
Alice M. Tybout and Gregory S. Carpenter, "Creating and Managing Brands" in Kellogg on Marketing *(edited by Dawn Iacobuzzi)*

"A brand is a mindset."
Sascha Löetscher, a partner in design firm Gottschalk+Ash

"A brand is what allows people to have a conversation around a product even when the product offers nothing remarkable."
Filippo Dellosso, strategic planner for advertising agency Chiat Day

"A brand is a kind of engine that creates energy."
Pierre d'Huy, the principal of consultancy firm eXperts

"A brand is the truth, revealed over time in numerous ways."
Mike Keeler, editor of quickSilver newsletter

"The intangible sum of a product's attributes: its name, packaging, and price, its history, its reputation, and the way it's advertised."
David Ogilvy, advertising legend

WHY IS IT IMPORTANT TO DEFINE WHAT A BRAND IS?

We are sure you have heard the saying, "A problem well-defined is a problem half-solved". It is not much different when it comes to brands. You want to build a strong brand. Each of you might have a different reason for wanting to build a strong brand but the bottom line is that you want a strong brand. This may be the reason why you are reading this book.

Building a brand is a challenge. Building a brand will present you with a host of problems that need to be solved. However, in order to be successful in the quest of building a strong brand, you must first understand what a brand is. Only then will you know what to do. Only then will the ideas presented to you in this book make any sense at all. Only then will you be able to tell if you are on the right track. That is why we need to define the brand clearly, and it must be a definition that makes sense to you.

If you define what a brand is correctly, then the steps that you need to take in order to build a strong brand will be that much clearer. If you define what a brand is correctly, then you will know if you have succeeded in building a strong brand. The term "correct" here does not mean "definitive" because you might have your own strongly held opinions of what a brand is. That is all right. What we are saying is that if you can define what a brand is clearly, then you will have a better idea of how to build a strong brand based on your definition. If you define a brand simply as "the positive emotional response that people have when they see the brand", then you will have to work towards achieving a positive emotional response from your customers. If you succeed, it means that you have built a strong brand – based on your own definition.

We are certainly not saying that our definition of what a brand is should be the correct definition. We are also not saying that the other definitions given above are not accurate or nonsensical. Each of these definitions is valid in its own way but as brands are something that are targeted and marketed to customers, we would like to look at it from the customer's point of view:

- What is a brand to a customer?
- How do customers define a brand?
- What comes to mind when they see a particular brand?

SO WHAT EXACTLY IS A BRAND?

You are a customer yourself. And as a customer, do you care about all the different definitions of what a brand is? Probably not. As far as customers are concerned, they don't really care about how lawyers, academics, marketing professors and branding gurus define brands as these definitions merely complicate purchase decisions and people don't like things that complicate their lives. Instead, they look for short cuts and those short cuts come in the form of brands. Brands are things that don't exist in the real world. That is why they are often called intangible assets. A brand is something that lives only in the minds of customers.

What is a brand?
A brand is just an idea that you own in the minds of your customers.

Is that it? Could it really be that straightforward? Yes! Your mind – and that goes for your customers' minds as well – is constantly bombarded with information that it needs to deal with. The mind cannot function with disorder and confusion. It is designed to try to make sense of all the information that it is presented with. And one of the ways that our minds deal with all this information is to *categorise* it in order to make sense out of chaos. That is what our minds do when inundated with a lot of information.

We don't have Cray supercomputers nestled in our heads that can process and store mountains of data. Our minds are finite. Our minds are limited. And because of that, our minds will leak information if overloaded. We will forget things. That is why our minds need to utilise these short cuts as they allow us to quickly associate a brand with an idea so that we can make sense of the brand. That is how the brand serves as a short cut. It helps us process all the information related to the brand.

When the mind is presented with a brand, it will categorise the brand. It will slot the brand into neat little virtual pigeonholes inside the mind. Each of these pigeonholes represents an idea that is associated with the brand. That makes it easy for the mind to organise and recognise information. Sure, you can see the product represented by the brand or the brand name in the real world, but if your mind cannot associate that brand with an idea, then that particular brand ceases to exist for you. You are probably familiar with the phrase "out of sight, out of mind". In branding, the reverse is true. A brand that is out of the customer's mind will be out of the customer's sight – and that is bad news because it means nobody will purchase that particular brand.

For example, there are 14,000 paint companies in the world, according to Coatings World, the world's leading website for the paint and coatings industry. With so many companies to sort through, how does a buyer choose? Each brand comes with a lot of information that needs to be processed. Consequently, the mind organises according to the short cuts. For example, one of our clients, Asia Paint, specialises in custom-blended industrial paint. That could be the idea that customers associate with it. When a customer needs to buy industrial paint, he or she will quickly sort through all the industrial paint brands in his or her mind. When the mind comes to Asia Paint and it associates Asia Paint with the idea of "custom-blended", then the mind knows what Asia Paint is all about. If the mind comes to Asia Paint and there is no idea associated with the brand, then the brand is passed over. That is why it is important that a brand owns an idea.

> *A brand is simply an idea that*
> *exists in the minds of customers;*
> *an idea that you own.*

SUCCESSFUL BRANDS AND THEIR BRAND IDEA

Let's look at some of the brands that you are probably quite familiar with and see what these brands are all about; and the one powerful idea that each of these brands owns in the minds of its customers. After all, it is this big idea that made each of these brands famous and successful in the first place. Some of these brands might have moved on and may now be extremely diversified but it was ownership of that original idea that built the brand.

Today, FedEx is a multi-billion dollar multi-national corporation that goes by the tagline, "We Live To Deliver" but that was not always so. When FedEx first started in 1971, it faced stiff competition from an 800-pound gorilla, Emery Air (which had been around since 1946). Therefore, FedEx narrowed its focus so that it could own one powerful idea in the minds of its customers. It decided to focus only on overnight letters. In those days, it didn't deliver parcels and packages and all the other things that it delivers today. In those days, it just did overnight letters. The tagline back then said it all – "When It Absolutely, Positively Has To Be There Overnight".

As a result of its narrow focus, FedEx had a powerful brand. The brand owned the idea "overnight" and became very successful as a result. If you had been a FedEx customer back then, what would your perception of the brand have been? Probably very positive. If FedEx is so good at delivering letters overnight, it must be a great company. Therefore, it is probably very good at delivering other things. We believe that was what people thought of the brand.

As a result, FedEx grew and grew until it became the giant that it is today. Emery Air is no longer around. And all because FedEx had a brand; FedEx owned an idea in the minds of its customers. Today FedEx is no longer just an overnight brand but the brand had already been established. And it was that one powerful idea that got it there. By the way, FedEx is a B2B brand, not a B2C brand, despite what many people think. When you use FedEx, what are you most likely to use it for – work or personal? Most of the time, it's work-related. That makes FedEx a B2B brand. We just thought that we should bring this up as we have met so many people who have asked us why we don't use a B2B brand as a case study right after we have used FedEx to illustrate a concept we wanted to get across.

Starbucks is the world's most successful coffee chain. As of its 2009 financial year end, Starbucks had 16,635 stores around the world, group sales revenue of US$9.8 billion (S$12.59 billion) and a net operating income of US$894 million (S$1.15 billion), or 9.2 per cent, which is quite good for selling what is basically a commodity – coffee.[4] Granted that coffee is the second most traded commodity in the world but it is still a commodity. So much has been written about the Starbucks brand, the Starbucks experience and so on. Some have said that Starbucks is not in the coffee business serving people but instead is in the people business and just happens to be serving coffee.

Yes, Starbucks is a phenomenon. But what made Starbucks so successful? And what has allowed the brand to continue to be wildly successful after 30 years in the market? It was the powerful idea that Starbucks represented in the minds of its customers – "gourmet coffee". Today, gourmet coffee is nothing special. Gourmet coffee has become mainstream coffee. Even McDonald's is serving gourmet coffee these days – or at least it is trying to. There are many brands out there that have out-gourmet Starbucks by selling coffee that is even more exotic and more premium in pricing. But it was that one idea that made Starbucks so successful from the day it started in 1971. Starbucks equals gourmet coffee – when you are selling coffee for US$3 (S$3.90) a cup at a time when everyone else is selling coffee for US$0.90, you got to be gourmet. That was the brand idea. That was the Starbucks brand. Everything else became secondary.

What comes to mind when we mention construction equipment? You would probably have thought of the brand called Caterpillar even if you are not in the construction business or don't have the slightest interest in bulldozers, dump trucks, excavators and the like. Caterpillar is a dominant brand in this sector because it owns the idea of "construction equipment". Even in categories that are of very low interest to most people, you can still build a very strong brand if you own an idea in the minds of your customers.

---

[4] http://investor.starbucks.com

What do you take for a headache? Panadol. Why? Because it's the best? How would you know unless you are a doctor but even if you are a doctor, how sure are you that Panadol is the best? After all, Panadol contains paracetamol, the active ingredient that is also found in its competitors. So why take Panadol? Because Panadol is a strong brand that owns the idea of "pain relief" in the minds of its customers. That is the idea that you associate Panadol with. That is why you reach for a Panadol when you have a headache. And when someone you know has a headache, you automatically ask, "Do you want a Panadol?" What is the definition of a brand? The idea that you own in the minds of customers. And in Panadol's case, the brand is all about pain relief. And it is strong because of that idea ownership.

Keeping with the theme of drugs, what about Viagra? Is that a strong brand? Yes, the strongest in its class. What is the Viagra brand all about? What is the idea that Viagra owns in the minds of its customers? Performance. Yes, that's right. Viagra is not even really a drug as we tell our clients – especially those from the healthcare sector – when they object to that definition. Viagra is not a drug? Not to Viagra customers. To them, Viagra is a car – something like a Ferrari. Viagra is all about performance and that is what makes the brand so strong. It owns an idea in the minds of its customers.

Let's move on to the world of computers. Look at Dell. Say what you will about Dell but it is doing quite well, thank you very much. Against all odds, Dell managed to go from a tiny start-up in 1984 operating on a shoestring budget of US$1,000 (S$1,284) from the garage of Michael Dell's parents' home to a multi-billion dollar corporation. Why is Dell a successful brand? Dell owns a powerful idea in the minds of its customers. What is the Dell brand all about? Computers Direct. Dell is the brand that sells computers direct to its customers – regardless of whether that customer is an individual or a company. That idea made Dell strong. That idea defined Dell. That idea allowed Dell to become a Top 2 computer brand in the world.

Look at the table opposite. It lists some brands that are generally regarded as strong brands in their sectors. Let's play a word association game to see what idea comes to mind when you see the brand. Then compare your answers with ours in the next table.

Table 2A: 26 Strong Brands From A To Z

Brand	Brand Idea
Accenture	
BlackBerry	
Cisco Systems	
DeWALT	
eBay	
Ferrari	
Google	
HSBC	
Intel	
Johnson Controls	
Keppel FELS	
Li & Fung	
Marshal Systems	What Is The Idea That
Nokia	These Brands Own?
Oracle	
PSA	
Q-tips	
Rotary Engineering	
SAP	
Thermal Limitec	
Universal Studios	
VibroPower	
Windows	
Xerox	
Yarra River	
Zara	

You may not know some of the brands listed above but that is because they are B2B brands that the general public would not have heard of but within their own industry, they are renowned brands. Some of these brands have become so strong that people use the brand to describe the category. For example, many people will say, "I will Google it" to refer to an online search for information instead of saying, "OK, let me do a search on the Internet for the information on so-and-so".

Although legal experts we work with usually warn clients that if a brand is used generically, the company might lose its trademark, from a brand building point of view, it is actually good that people use your brand to describe the category. However, as with most things in life, too much of a good thing can be bad for the brand. The trick here is to try and strike a balance.

Table 2B: 26 Strong Brands And Their Brand Idea

Brand	Brand Idea
Accenture	IT consulting
BlackBerry	Mobile e-mail
CISCO Systems	Network systems
DeWALT	Power tools
eBay	Online auction
Ferrari	Exotic sports cars
Google	Search
HSBC	The world's local bank
Intel	Computer chips
Johnson Controls	Industrial controls
Keppel FELS	Oil rigs
Li & Fung	Supply chain management
Marshal Systems	Safety
Nokia	Mobile phones
Oracle	Database software
PSA	World-class port
Q-tips	Cotton buds
Rotary Engineering	Oil & gas storage
SKF	Rolling bearings
Thermal Limitec	Passive fire protection
Universal Studios	Movies
VibroPower	Custom power generators
Windows	PC operating systems
Xerox	Photocopiers
Yarra River	Wine
Zara	Just-in-time fashion

WHAT IDEA DO YOU OWN?

This is usually the most important thing that we want to know whenever we start a branding project with a new client. Unless the client is a start-up company with no track record, we will usually recommend what is known as a Perception Audit to find out what the client's various stakeholders' – from management to staff, from existing customers to potential customers, from distributors to suppliers and all the other stakeholders in between – perceptions of the client's brand is.

From the Perception Audit, you will know what idea is strongly associated with your brand and what ideas are associated with your competitors, or if your brand even owns an idea in the minds of your stakeholders. We often tell our clients that the Perception Audit can also be called The Heartbreak Audit because in 99 per cent of the Perception Audits that we have seen, there is a sizeable gap between what management perceives the brand to be and what the other stakeholders perceive the brand to be – and more often than not, we find that customers perceive the brand less well than management. There have been cases where the clients argued with us endlessly over the results of the Perception Audit because the reality didn't match their own perception of the brand.

However, the Perception Audit is the most important starting point in any branding or rebranding exercise because you need to know where your brand stands in the minds of stakeholders at this point in time before you can map out a strategy to take it to where you want the brand to go. Even the most sophisticated GPS system needs to know your starting point so that it can guide you to the final destination.

If you are fortunate enough to find that your brand actually owns a very powerful idea in the minds of your customers, that makes the branding project a lot easier because you can then take that idea that is yours and dramatise it – make it more exciting, make it larger than life – so that your brand can stand out from the crowd. If you are like the majority of companies out there and do not own a very powerful or distinct idea in the minds of your stakeholders, you can still build a strong brand but it will involve a lot more work to find a new idea, dramatise it and drive it so deep into the minds of your customers that no one can dislodge it unless you give permission to do so.

There is a simple exercise that you can do internally that will show you the kind of results that you can possibly expect from a Perception Audit. In the past, when clients objected to the cost and time commitment of a Perception Audit, we would demonstrate to them that a gap existed by asking the client to gather the eight most senior people in the company into one room. We would then give them blank cards and ask them to explain in five words or less what the brand was all about. Out of the eight most senior people in the company, we usually got seven different answers. Most of the time, the CEO and the CFO thought alike – we don't know why. But the rest of the senior management team – the CMO, the COO, the HR Director, the IT Director and so on – would have very different views. If there is a perception gap right at the top, you can bet your last dollar that as you move away from the centre of power, the gap will widen even more. These days, we rarely do this as most clients are now savvy enough to recognise that there are gaps and they come to us for assistance to find out what gaps exist, where they exist and how to close or manage these gaps.

But the first step is: Find out what idea you own or if you even own an idea at all.

WHAT IF YOU DON'T OWN AN IDEA?

This is not going to go down well with many business owners but the truth of the matter is that if you don't own an idea in the minds of your customers –

meaning that two out of three customers do not associate you with a particular idea – then you actually don't have a brand. You may have been running a profitable business but that is all it is – a business, not a brand. It is only a brand if that company of yours is able to stand for a great idea in the minds of its customers.

You can spend a lot of money on the things that many business owners do, such as ensuring that your product or service quality is at least as good as your competitors, building up an extensive distribution network, hiring the right people for the job, training your people regularly, making sure your marketing collaterals are beautifully designed, trademarking your logo and so on. All of these things are important, don't get us wrong, but at the end of the day, if your brand doesn't stand for anything in the minds of your customers, then it is not a real brand. It is a business.

And that beautifully designed and expensively trademarked logo is just that – a logo. There is actually nothing wrong with that. Some people are only interested in running a business. They don't want to build lasting brands. Jacky met a company recently that buys and sells chemicals. It is an old family business that is now run by the sons and daughters of the founders. Jacky asked one of the bosses what he wanted to do with the business and the reply was, "Well, we don't need to build a brand, okay? It is still a profitable business although our margins are razor thin – around 5 per cent. We will just run it until we retire and then the company will probably close down. After all, our kids are not interested in taking over the business so why brand?" Well, if that is your long-term plan, then yes, branding would be a waste of time, wouldn't it? Just milk the business while you can. It all depends on what your longer-term plans are for your company.

If you are still not entirely convinced that a strong brand needs to own an idea in the minds of its customers, may we suggest that you look at the brands that you buy? After all, you are also a customer. You buy things and services – some of them for personal use and some of them for business use. Look at the brands that you buy. We are sure that they can be categorised into two types. The first type will be brands that you buy because they stand for something in your mind. These are the strong brands that you wouldn't mind paying a premium for. And the second type will be brands that you buy because they are cheap. If these brands are not available, you will not break into a sweat. You will just buy the next cheap alternative. If you look at your own behaviour as a buyer and analyse your purchases, you will see that there are some products or services that you value more and these are usually brands that stand for something in your mind. For those that don't stand for anything in your mind, you usually only buy them if they are cheap.

That is how your customers behave too, more or less. If you don't stand for a strong idea in their minds, you are not a brand. And they can easily substitute you with something else. Again, that is okay as long as you are aware of the real reason people buy from you and you are willing to work very hard to maintain your cost or price advantage.

IDEA OWNERSHIP IS MUTUALLY EXCLUSIVE

Even if you are convinced that to transform your business into a brand requires you to own a great idea in the minds of your customers, the road ahead is still littered with landmines because idea ownership is mutually exclusive. Idea ownership is absolute. There are no grey areas. For example, if 3M owns the idea of "innovation", then that idea is gone. None of 3M's competitors can claim that idea. There are no shades of grey. That means Competitor A cannot claim to be "15 per cent more innovative" and Competitor B cannot claim to be "as innovative". The idea of "innovative" is gone. It is owned by 3M.

To illustrate this further, let's use a category that is easy to understand such as cars. Look at the various car brands below. Each is a strong brand but that is only because they each stand for an idea in the minds of their customers.

Mercedes-Benz owns the idea of "prestige" and, as a result, no other brand can claim the same idea even though it can make luxury cars that are as good as Mercedes-Benz or better. That is why BMW had to find its own idea, which is "performance". BMW is also a prestigious luxury car but it cannot own the idea of "prestige". That belongs to Mercedes-Benz.

Now that "prestige" and "performance" are taken up, Lexus had to find a new idea and its idea is "refinement". A Lexus is typically so refined and quiet that you feel like you are in a sensory deprivation tank. Jacky went to test drive a Lexus LS460 with a friend once and the friend remarked that the car felt very slow until he glanced down at the speedometer and saw that he was going at 120 kph – and he wasn't even on a highway yet. Audi has its own idea, which is "design", and the company has won many design awards for its simple, sleek and elegant designs.

Volvo owns the idea of "safety". You can build a safer car than Volvo but unless Volvo willingly gives up its ownership of "safety", it would be next to impossible to wrest it away from Volvo. In the year 2001, we saw that Renault was able to make cars that scored five stars in the European New Car Assessment Programme (Euro NCAP)[5] crash tests. Euro NCAP is one of the leading car safety authorities in the world. The best Volvo that we saw that year was the S80 which, at that time, scored four stars. Of course, Volvo cars are now all five stars. Although Renault produced what appeared to be safer cars at that time, it could not own the idea of "safety".

The brand idea that transformed Toyota into one of the most admired companies in the world was "reliability". For decades, you could take it for granted that a Toyota would never break down or give you any problems. Jacky used to own a Geo Prizm GSI, which was basically a rebadged 1988 Toyota Corolla GTI 5-door liftback, when he was working in the United States in the mid-1990s. The car did 220,000 kilometres in the harsh Wisconsin winter without a hiccup. Even after 220,000 kilometres, the car still felt fast and bulletproof. However, Toyota is in danger of giving up its ownership of the "reliability" idea at the time of writing due to the massive recalls over accelerator and brake problems that caused some Toyota cars to experience unintended acceleration. Somebody remarked to us during a meeting that perhaps Toyota was trying to own a new idea – "possessed". Whether Toyota can regain its former glory remains to be seen but once a company grows to such a size, changes can take a while to be implemented. What should Toyota do? Go back to the basics that made Toyota Toyota.

HOW DO YOU FIND A NEW IDEA TO OWN?

Now that we have established that idea ownership is something that is mutually exclusive and now that you know that there is a good chance that your brand might not own any great idea in the minds of customers, what do you do? How do you find a new idea to own? That is why this book is called *B2B – 10 Rules To Transform Your Business Into A Brand*. We are hoping that this book can help you to find some answers that can turn a profitable (and sometimes barely profitable) business into a strong, successful and sustainable brand. When we actually touch on the 10 rules of branding in the later chapters of this book, you should be able to see how you can find a great idea that you can tie your brand to. But before we get into those rules, there are a few other topics that we need to cover.

---

[5] www.euroncap.com

In A Nutshell

In order to build a strong brand, you must first understand what a strong brand is all about. There are many different definitions of what a brand is. We define a brand simply as an idea that exists in the minds of customers. All strong brands own a great idea in the minds of their customers. If you don't own an idea, you technically do not have a brand. You have a business. There is nothing wrong with that as long as you know the real reason why your customers buy from you and continue to work hard to ensure that the reason to buy from you remains for a long time to come. The best tool to use to find out what idea you own – or whether you own any idea at all – is a Perception Audit. In the majority of Perception Audits, there will be gaps between what each of the various stakeholder groups perceives. The Perception Audit will point out where the *perceived* strengths and weaknesses of the brand are so that you can take the appropriate actions to take advantage of the perception or put in place a programme to fix it. Idea ownership is mutually exclusive. Once an idea is owned by a competitor, you cannot claim the same idea. Idea ownership works on a first-come-first-served basis. You can't take away an idea that a competitor's brand is associated with unless that competitor becomes careless and gives it up through negligence.

B2B

CHAPTER
02

Why Do You Need To Transform Your Business Into A Brand?

MANY renowned academics and brand researchers have spent many years researching why it is important to develop a brand. We could inundate you with the details of all these studies but you could easily find such papers if you did a little search of your own. What we are more interested in are the practical aspects of brand building. Why do you really need a brand? In order to understand and answer that question, we need to give a little history lesson but don't go to sleep yet. This one is actually quite interesting.

In the book *Brand Failures*, author Matt Haig talks about how brands came about. Brands were originally developed in the late 19th century by rapidly expanding consumer products companies such as Campbell's, Heinz and Quaker Oats. There were others, of course. In the days before the Industrial Revolution, the concept of mass production was unheard of. In those days, you knew the people who actually made many of the things that you needed.

But with the advent of mass production, that personal link was severed. Instead, the products were now made in faceless factories many thousands of kilometres away. Buyers needed assurance that the products were of high quality and the makers of these products needed to provide that assurance. So they developed brands for that purpose. Each brand represented a product and each brand stood for something. And because buyers trusted these brands – and transferred the trust that they had put in their shopkeepers to the brands – the failure of mass produced products that many factory owners dreaded never happened. That is because they were successful in making the brands stand for something.

THE BRAND IS THE GUARANTEE OF PERFORMANCE

You need to build a brand because the brand acts as the guarantee of performance. That was why brands were originally created. The brand reassures customers that every time they buy your product or service, they will get the performance or benefits they expect. But that guarantee cannot be taken for granted. You have to work hard to maintain the brand so that the perceived guarantee remains intact.

The situation with brands today is a bit different compared to the late 19th century. Today, brands are in a very precarious position. Blame it on technology. Because of advancements in technology, the quality gap between the best and the worst has narrowed to such an extent that even the worst product in any category will usually still get the job done. Brands are now bought based on customers' *perception* of the quality rather than the *actual* quality. We will discuss the issue of perception in more detail later in Rule No. 1.

This has both pros and cons. The upside is that brands are now more valuable than their physical assets alone. However, it can also mean that if the perception of the brand is damaged, it can quickly lose its value and its market share. There are plenty of suitable substitutes for whatever it is that you are offering customers today.

Take Toyota for example. Has Toyota suddenly become an unsafe and unreliable car overnight? No. It might have quality glitches but that doesn't mean that the majority of Toyotas will experience sudden acceleration. Only a fraction of the tens of millions of Toyotas on the roads around the world has experienced such problems. But the perception of Toyota has been damaged. Hence, the brand is damaged. And Toyota is not the only car you can buy if you are in the market for an affordable car. There are plenty of them around.

Therefore, although the brand can act as a guarantee of performance, you need to work hard to ensure that customers continue to perceive that the brand is still a good brand to buy. Because perception is a fragile thing, it is all the more reason why you need to focus attention on building and maintaining the perception other people have of your brand.

THE BRAND IS A SHORT CUT

Because a brand is simply an idea that exists in the minds of customers, a brand can act as a short cut in the buyers' decision-making process. If you manage to make your brand stand for something in the minds of customers and potential customers, it will create a short cut that is in your favour.

Here is how it works. Assume you are in the market for an enterprise resource planning (ERP) system because your company is growing and to support this growth, you need a more sophisticated IT infrastructure. Which brand would you choose? That depends. If you are a successful, global multinational corporation, you would probably want to buy the ERP system from an ERP vendor of equal standing. You would probably veer towards SAP because SAP is synonymous with "premium ERP system". If you are a small- or medium-sized enterprise on a shoestring budget, you might choose the Microsoft Dynamics NAV system because that brand is quite well known for "affordable ERP system" (that still gets the job done).

When you build a brand, you actually hardwire the brand into the minds of your customers so that when they need something, they will use your brand as a short cut.

- Construction equipment? Caterpillar.
- Jet engines? Rolls-Royce Trent.
- Professional power tools? DeWALT.
- Prestigious car? Mercedes-Benz.
- A watch that says you have made it? Rolex.
- Diapers? Pampers.
- Tissues? Kleenex.
- Massage chairs? OSIM.
- Water treatment plants? Hyflux.
- Oil rigs? Keppel FELS.
- A great way to fly? SIA.
- MP3 player? iPod.
- Check e-mails while on the move? BlackBerry.
- Elevators? Otis.
- Tough laptops? ThinkPad.
- Stylish laptops? Apple.
- Business jets? Gulfstream.
- Turbines for electricity plants? GE.
- Semiconductors? TSMC.

The list goes on and on and on. With a brand – a strong brand – you can stay two steps ahead of the competition. Your brand should allow you to lead in the mind. If you can lead in the mind, there is a good chance that you will win in the marketplace.

THE BRAND PRE-SELLS YOUR COMPANY

If you have a brand that stands for something and you communicate this clearly and consistently, it makes the job of selling easier because your potential customers already associate your brand with certain things. All you have to do is reinforce that association through the way you communicate with these potential customers, through your actions and, of course, by consistently delivering on these expectations.

We are sure many of you participate in open tenders. And you know how frustrating this can be because you never seem to win. One client who was running a very successful project management company for the interior design of commercial buildings told us that in the early days, he submitted 86 tenders before he secured his first contract, and it was a very small project. Many of you will have experienced this in your business. It seems that no matter what you do – give more, give better specifications, give a better price – the other guy always wins. We were asked by a pest control company recently how it could overcome this problem. The problem here is that the other competitors are probably stronger brands.

If you make a pitch to a potential customer and you don't have a strong brand, this potential customer is going to say the same thing that a grumpy old man in a classic *McGraw Hill Magazines* advertisement said many years ago, "I don't know who you are. I don't know your company. I don't know your company's product. I don't know what your company stands for. I don't know your company's customers. I don't know your company's record. I don't know your company's reputation. Now, what was it that you wanted to sell me?"[6] You can substitute the word "company" with the word "brand" and there you have it. If you don't have a brand that stands for something, you don't have anyone to go ahead of you to soften the ground before you launch an attack. The brand is like an air strike. Use the air strike to soften the enemy ground and then move in with the infantry (your sales team).

THE BRAND IS A COMPASS

There are many different functions within a company and a modern company is a highly complex animal with many different departments that need to work together cohesively so that the company can move forward and in the right direction. Imagine a rowing boat with 12 people in it. The 12 must row in the same direction in order for the boat to get anywhere fast. A company is no

---

[6] www.sales-lead-insights.com/images/2010/01/McGraw-Hill-Ad.jpg

different in this respect. What gives these various departments and functions the right direction? The brand. Really? Surely it can't be that simple? But it can.

Let's say you are Harley-Davidson. What is the Harley-Davidson brand all about? What is the Harley-Davidson brand idea? Rebellious. The way a Harley-Davidson looks, feels and sounds. The type of free-spirited, open road, outlaw image that a Harley-Davidson bike evokes. All of that can be summed up in one word – rebellious. That is the brand. That is the brand idea.

How does the brand give the many different departments in Harley-Davidson a clear direction? Imagine you are a designer at Harley-Davidson. You don't need a lengthy lecture to tell you how a Harley-Davidson should look. All you have to ask yourself is this, "If I design the fuel tank to look like this, is it consistent with the Harley-Davidson brand idea of 'rebellious'?" If yes, then you would do it. If no, then you would find a new direction. The same applies to every single department. The brand idea is the simplest way to provide direction to each of these departments.

When it comes to innovation and marketing, the brand also provides the right direction. Much has been said, written and published about innovation and marketing since these two disciplines were invented but Peter Drucker, the father of modern management, said it best when he wrote in 1953, "The business enterprise has two – and only two – basic functions: marketing and innovation. Marketing and innovation produce results; all the rest are costs."

We tend to agree with Peter Drucker because if you look at the essence of what a company does, everything leads back to innovation and marketing. If you don't innovate, you will become outdated very quickly and you will allow competitors to overtake you. And innovation covers all aspects and functions within an organisation. Innovation is not only about inventions or technology or research and development work. You can innovate your administration processes so that they become more efficient. You can innovate your accounting processes so that they are more accurate. Innovation covers everything that your company does. You need to innovate to stay abreast of the competition.

You also need marketing because if you don't take care of your marketing, even your most innovative products and services will fail. If you don't take care of the marketing, you will not be able to communicate your differentiating idea properly. That will eventually lead to the failure of your brand. It might not happen overnight but failure will come.

However, you need the brand to ensure that your innovation and marketing programmes are headed in the right direction. Many companies will tell you that innovation and marketing are important but we have also noticed that many of these companies are all over the place in terms of their innovation and marketing programmes, precisely because they don't have a strong brand to guide them. The example of Milwaukee Electric Tool Corp. below will give you an idea of how a strong brand can actually give direction to your innovation and marketing programmes.

Milwaukee Electric Tool Corp. is an American company that makes all kinds of professional power tools. What does the Milwaukee brand stand for? Ergonomic design. That makes it easy for the entire company to do the right thing and run in the right direction. From the CEO to the intern, all that anyone needs to do is ask, "Is this consistent with the Milwaukee Electric Tool's brand idea of ergonomic design?" Yes, it can be that simple. Managing and growing a company is not an easy thing. You need all the help you can get. Let the brand do some of the heavy lifting work for you.

THE BRAND ATTRACTS HUMAN CAPITAL

People want to buy the best brands that they can afford. That's human nature. And it is also human nature to want to work for the best brands that their qualifications and experience can afford them. You don't need in-depth research to tell you this fact. Many SMEs have told us that because they cannot afford to pay as well as the MNCs, they just have to settle for second-rate or even third-rate talent.

However, a research project that Wilson undertook while he was doing his MBA at the University of Strathclyde in Glasgow showed some surprising results. He studied how small companies in Scotland competed – successfully – for talent with the big boys. He and his team came to the conclusion that the brand played a big part. Pay matters but that is not the only thing that matters. People are attracted not to a big pay cheque alone but to strong brands. The size of the company and the salary that it offers does not automatically mean it hires people more easily. The strength of the brand is what matters. We have seen this in Singapore companies as well.

In the mind, the size of the company does not correspond to its brand strength. Alienware is a very small computer company by the standards of HP, Dell, Acer and even Lenovo. But Alienware is a powerful brand among people who want computers with serious speed – gamers, for instance. Alienware is a small company but a strong brand. So, is it hard for Alienware to hire people? No. People want to work for Alienware. It is a strong brand that knows what it wants, and what it wants is for its employees to design and build computers as if they were designing and building for their own use. Do any of the big computer companies have such a clear brand direction? We think not.

We have also seen this in many SMEs in Singapore. Some of our SME clients have managed to attract some of the leading brains in their industry to join them because they have a brand that stands for something that is important for this top talent. If you are not able to hire people, take a look at your brand. What does the brand stand for? Is the brand attractive to potential employees? If not, what needs to be done?

THE BRAND CAN BE SOLD FOR MORE MONEY

In accounting, there is an item called intangible assets, or goodwill. What this means is how much more a potential buyer of your company is willing to pay because you have a strong brand. If you want to sell your company and the buyer is just willing to pay for the net tangible assets of the company, then you will definitely get a lot less than if you have a strong brand. Take a look at the table below. This is from BrandFinance250, an annual report on the 250 most valuable brands in the world. This particular report was published in 2007.

Table 3: The Top 10 Brands In The World In Terms Of Enterprise Value

Brand	Enterprise Value (US$ million)	Value Contributed By Brand (per cent)	Brand Value (US$ million)
Nike	21,151	84	17,818
Prada	5,159	77	3,984
Acer	3,181	71	2,255
Avon	14,074	68	9,627
Bvlgari	3,378	68	2,284
Chanel	16,183	66	10,737
Estée Lauder	8,688	61	5,309
Quiksilver	2,534	60	1,518
Calvin Klein	3,094	58	1,806
adidas	9,408	56	5,260

(Source: http://brandfinance.dda.co.uk/Uploads/pdfs/BF250%20FINAL.pdf)

There are two values being indicated in the table above – the Enterprise Value, which shows how much the entire company is worth, and the Brand Value, which shows how much the brand alone is worth. In this table, we can see the Top 10 brands in the world in terms of the value that brand contributes to the overall company value. Nike is at the top of the list, with 84 per cent of the company's value being contributed by the Nike brand. If Nike had not built the brand, then it would only be worth a fraction of the US$21.1 billion (S$27.1 billion) that it is now worth.

You will also notice that all the brands in this table are B2C brands. You can see this as B2C companies have more valuable brands and they are savvier in terms of brand building. What we see, however, is that there is a lot more room for B2B companies to grow in terms of brand value. In terms of total company value, the highest-ranked brand in the list is Microsoft which ranked No. 2 with an Enterprise Value of US$248 billion (S$318.6 billion) but the value contributed by the Microsoft brand is only 15 per cent. IBM is No. 5 with US$149.4 billion (S$191.9 billion) in Enterprise Value and a brand value contribution of 23 per cent. There is definitely room for B2B companies to grow their brand values – especially the B2B companies in Singapore.

So, if you want your company to be worth more, you need to build a brand. Intangible assets can increase in value much faster than tangible assets. After all, the value of the intangible assets – and the brand is an intangible asset – is based on perception. As long as people perceive that the brand is worth $X, then that is how much it is worth. But you also have to bear in mind that perception can cut both ways. If the perception of the brand is damaged, then the value can plummet rapidly. So what is the ideal value in terms of percentage? There is no hard and fast rule although one-third would seem like a good balance.

Besides being worth more money when it comes to the time to sell, a strong brand also performs better financially. In 2008, StrategiCom and DMG Research conducted a joint study to see if there was an association between a company's perceived brand strength and its financial performance. There have been many such studies in the West using Western brands. All have found that companies with a high brand strength index outperform companies with a lower index. In fact, strong brands tend to outperform the stock market in most cases. However, there did not seem to be comparable studies in Asia. That is why StrategiCom and DMG Research decided to team up to do a study on Singapore companies listed on the Singapore Exchange. What we found was very interesting. There is, indeed, an association between brands that are perceived to be strong and their financial performance. Financial performance in this case was defined as share price expectation.

THE BRAND GIVES THE ENEMY PAUSE

If you build a strong brand, it makes it easier for you to erect barriers of entry for potential competitors. In this day and age of hypercompetition, everybody is trying to get into your business. Unless you are operating in a market whereby you are protected from competition by the law, there isn't a lot that you can do to stop competitors from playing in your backyard and messing it up. Your best protection is a strong brand.

A strong brand provides the best type of entry barrier – the psychological type. Once you have scored a psychological win, the rest is a lot easier. Once you have beaten them in the mind, you have won. And when a strong brand copies its challengers because the challengers came up with some great ideas, it is seen as protecting its turf. When a weaker brand copies the stronger brand, it is seen as a copycat and a wannabe. We have come across many cases of relatively unknown Singapore companies coming up with highly innovative products. Within half a year, the leading brands would come out with their own versions of these innovative products and theirs would become the bigger-selling items. Life is not fair if you do not have a strong brand.

If you are up against a stronger brand, how do you react? You think twice, don't you? But why should you always be on the receiving end? It's time to turn the tables on your bigger competitors with a stronger brand. And yes, it can be done. How many of the top brands today were born big? None. They all started as tiny tots and built a strong brand through various means. You can and should do the same.

In A Nutshell

There are many reasons why having a brand – a strong brand – is a good thing. You will be able to find many research studies that came to the conclusion that a strong brand gives its owners many benefits. The Top 7 reasons why you need to transform that business of yours into a strong brand are:

1. The brand serves as a guarantee of performance so that potential customers have more confidence in buying from you even if you launch a new product or service that is as yet untested.

2. The brand acts as a short cut for the buyers. If you have a strong brand, it basically bypasses a lot of the roadblocks that a typical company has to go through. Why do people buy IBM? It's a strong brand and "Nobody gets fired for buying IBM" so it's safe to buy.

3. The brand pre-sells your company. If your brand is strong, then by the time you get to a potential customer's door, half the selling job is already done. You just need to do the other half. The brand gets you halfway up the mountain.

4. The brand provides direction for every department and every person in your company. Strong brands can move more cohesively because everyone in the organisation uses the brand as a compass.

5. The brand helps you to hire people. You can't grow if you can't get the right people into the company. The brand helps to attract the right people.

6. The brand is worth more money than the company alone. If you have a strong brand, it adds value to your balance sheet.

7. The brand is also a great entry barrier for would-be competitors. If you become the 800-pound gorilla in your category, the other guy will think twice about picking a fight with you.

B2B

CHAPTER 03

What Are Branding, Marketing And Sales?

IF you ask a hundred people what branding is, you will probably get a hundred different answers. Many of these people will either give you very textbook kinds of answers or very grandiose and complex definitions of what branding is all about.

Some people say that branding is part of marketing. Some people say that marketing is a subset of branding. Some people say that branding is all about advertising. We certainly have come across many companies who have called us up to say that they want to do branding but when we met them, we found out that all they actually wanted was advertising. And yet there are some people who think that branding is all about the logo and to rebrand a company means to redesign the logo.

With so many different definitions of what branding is, it is bound to get confusing, that's for sure. So what actually is branding? And how is branding different from marketing or advertising or sales? Which definition should you use? Well, you are of course free to decide for yourself which definition of branding you want to adopt. But before you do, please allow us to explain to you what branding is all about – from our point of view. This is something that we get asked about a lot by clients.

SO WHAT EXACTLY IS BRANDING?

In order to understand the concept of branding better, it is necessary to know about the origins of branding. It would seem that branding only burst onto the market in the 21st century but it is not that new a concept. We often ask our clients and participants in our branding workshops to guess how old branding is and no one so far has even got close. We will give you a clue. It is not a 21st-century concept, that's for sure. It is not a 20th-century concept. It is not even a 19th-century concept.

Branding actually dates back more than 4,000 years.[7] In those days, cattle owners found it very difficult to tell each others' cows apart and, as a result,

---

[7] www.barbwiremuseum.com/cattlebrandhistory.htm

when a cow was stolen, there was no way of identifying which cattle owner really owned the cow. So they needed a way to differentiate each others' cows to prevent theft and disputes over which cow belonged to whom. Since they didn't have identification chips that could be implanted under the cows' skin back then, they invented branding. The concept was simple. A branding iron with a unique design – usually sporting the owner's insignia or initials – was heated by fire until red hot, then used to burn the unique identifying mark onto the cows' rumps. Once a cow is branded, it becomes a lot easier to differentiate one from the other. Even slaves were branded in those days, usually on the chest.

Over the course of the last 4,000 years, the human race has made many advancements but people still can't tell one cow from another cow so branding is still used for the purpose of differentiating cows. Of course, the branding iron used today is a little bit more sophisticated. It is now electric powered.

What we have established here is that branding originated with cows 4,000 years ago. Branding was invented as a means of differentiating cows. So, branding is all about *differentiation*. Today, branding is still used to differentiate cows but the cows now come in many different forms – the original cows (the ones that moo), companies, products, services, non-profit organisations, countries and even people.

The art and science of branding has evolved tremendously over the last 4,000 years as well. Branding is now widely used in relation to commercial as well as consumer products and services. Numerous books and articles have been written on branding. An entire branding industry has sprouted up around the world to help companies brand themselves. Many different schools of thought on branding have also emerged. The end result is a certain degree of confusion on the part of companies regarding what branding really is.

Although branding has evolved tremendously over the last 4,000 years in terms of sophistication and scope of application, the *function* of branding is still the same – it is still about differentiation. Branding is not about logo design even though it did begin with a logo, but that logo was there for the purpose of differentiation. Branding is not about advertising. Branding is not about marketing. Branding is not about sales. Branding was, is and will always be about differentiation.

When you say you want to undertake a branding project, what you are really saying is, "I want to find a way to differentiate my cows from my competitors' cows." Your cows refer to the products or services that you sell. And they need to be differentiated from your competitors' cows, not so much to protect against theft but to create preference for your products or services. You have to remember that the market is crowded with way too many competitors selling more or less the same type of cows today. For every category or market or customer, there are way too many competitors that can meet the needs of this category or market or customer. The market is hypercompetitive. The market is too crowded with competitors that can do what you do, sell what you sell and offer the same benefits, functions and price that you offer.

SO BRANDING IS ONLY ABOUT DIFFERENTIATION?

The short answer is yes. Don't get us wrong. To build a brand is not easy. You need to do the right thing and you need to do things right. And there are many things that you need to get right over a period of time in order to build a strong brand. But branding is basically differentiation. The process of branding – while not easy – is simply the process of differentiating your brand from all the competing brands in the market that are vying for the same customers' attention and wallets.

There will be a lot of people out there who will try to convince you that branding is an extremely complex thing that requires a degree in rocket science to fully comprehend. Don't listen to them. People are always trying to make things more complicated than they need to be. Why do you think the world is in so much trouble today? Remember the subprime crisis? Remember the Lehman Brothers debacle? Remember the whole financial crisis of 2008? Yes, we agree that these were partly due to greed but another contributing factor was the fact that people just want to make things very complicated.

We are usually very wary of so-called experts who try to make branding into something that is complicated and difficult to understand. In all the things that we do, we try to simplify things for our clients because we never mistake complication for sophistication. Neither should you. Jack Trout, one of the greatest branding gurus in the world and the man who invented the concept of positioning way back in 1969, wrote in his book *The Power Of Simplicity: A Management Guide to Cutting Through the Nonsense and Doing Things Right* that you should never trust a consultant that you cannot understand. We think that is fantastic advice. Jack Trout is one of those rare consultants who "gives it to you straight" and we like his style.

A lot of people confuse complexity with sophistication. They are not the same thing. People are afraid to keep things simple because they are under the impression that simplicity will be viewed as stupidity. No one wants to be labelled a Simple Simon because that implies you are a village idiot. But if you want to build strong brands, simplicity is the way to go.

Simplicity doesn't mean that your products or services are not sophisticated or that they are low-tech. Some of the most powerful brands in the world are built around complicated technologies but they have never been presented as complex. On the contrary, they are such strong brands because they have been built around simple ideas!

The BlackBerry is a highly sophisticated portable e-mail computer. But it is a simple product in the sense that it only does one thing – send/receive e-mails. Sure, the latest 8700 model also does other things like make/receive phone calls but the powerful idea behind the BlackBerry is a simple one, which makes the job of marketing it very easy. What is a BlackBerry? It's a portable e-mail computer. Eureka! That idea, and the brand attached to that idea, is lodged firmly in the mind.

The Nintendo Game Boy is a high-tech gaming device. But it is also simple enough to be positioned strongly in the mind. What's a Nintendo? It's a portable game console. Nintendo didn't try to make the Game Boy a complicated multifunctional product like the PlayStation Portable. What's a PSP? It's a portable game console that also does all kinds of other things – DVD player, MP3 player and may even be able to run complicated NASA programmes if given the chance.

Despite all the hype, PSP is nowhere near Nintendo in terms of market share. Nintendo has a 55 per cent share of the portable gaming console category.[8] Sure, competition will erode Nintendo's market share eventually. After all, it is hard for a leading brand to maintain a market share of over 50 per cent in the long run. But Nintendo will probably still be the leading brand because it operates on the principle of simplicity. By the way, Nintendo made more profit between 1996 and 2005 than the entire Sony empire combined. Nintendo: US$5.9 billion (S$7.6 billion). Sony: US$4.8 billion (S$6.2 billion).[9] Think about it.

The iPod is a sophisticated device. It is the leading MP3 player in the world. But despite all the technology that went into the iPod, it is a simple device. It plays MP3 music files. It doesn't try to double up as a flight controller for a

---

[8] www.forbes.com/2009/01/28/wii-playstation-xbox-personal-finance-investing-ideas_0128_videogames.html

[9] www.hoovers.com

space shuttle, which is what a lot of consumer electronics gadgets seem to be aiming for. An iPod is a simple idea with a simple design and a simple interface. And it rules the MP3 category.

But a simple idea is hard to find. A simple idea is probably the hardest thing in the world to come up with because in order to arrive at that simple idea that can be expressed simply, a lot of hard thinking needs to be done first. Simplicity is the result of lots of deep thinking. Only after you have thought through everything can you distil it into something simple.

Study the history of successful brands and you will always find that they have been built on the principle of simplicity.

Boeing makes really complex aeroplanes but it is built on a simple idea: Jumbo jets.

BMW makes very complex cars with more computing power than the early mainframes but it is built on a very simple idea: The Ultimate Driving Machine. With that simple idea in mind, BMW could concentrate its engineering talent on making cars that drive like nothing else on the road.

Cray makes the most complex computers in the world but it is built on a simple idea: Supercomputers. Computers that are really, really fast.

Sharp's Aquos TV is so complex that only a handful of companies have the expertise to make the screen, but Sharp is built on a simple idea: LCD TVs.

Southwest Airlines runs an airline, which is one of the hardest things to do, but Southwest is built on a simple idea. Low-cost point-to-point air travel. The idea is to provide the lowest-cost air travel to customers. With that simple idea in mind, Southwest could concentrate its resources on achieving that well-defined goal. It operates only Boeing 737 jets to minimise training and maintenance costs. It doesn't have reserved seating. It flies fixed routes. It doesn't serve food. It doesn't have any hubs. And it has been profitable for most of the years since its inception while many other American airlines have been struggling just to break even in recent years.

So, if you want to build a powerful brand, remember to keep things simple. The more complicated you make things, the harder it is to build a brand. And simply put, branding is what you do to differentiate yourself. There are many ways to differentiate yourself but not all of them are relevant to customers, desirable as well as defensible against competition. We will discuss more about the 13 differentiation strategies in Rule No. 5 of branding.

WHAT IS MARKETING?

If branding is what you do to differentiate your brand, then marketing is what you do to communicate your differentiating idea to your customers using the various communications channels that are available. There are basically two types of communications channels – static and dynamic.

The static channel refers to a non-people channel. The static channel is a lot easier to manage as it does not involve people in the equation. Below are some examples of the components that you can find and use in the static communications channel:

- Advertising
- Public relations
- Events
- Roadshows
- Logos
- Websites
- Brochures
- Flyers
- E-mails
- Videos
- Packaging
- Uniforms
- Vehicles
- Signage
- Corporate presentations

The list can go on and on. You need to ensure that your differentiating idea – the thing that makes you different from all the rest – is properly dramatised and communicated through your static communications channel. This channel is designed to bring your differentiating idea alive so that your brand can become firmly lodged in the minds of your customers.

The other communications channel is the dynamic channel. It is called the dynamic channel because it involves people and, as a result, it is very difficult to achieve consistency in terms of communications as people are hard to manage and control. You need to be aware that the dynamic channel can do a lot of damage to your brand if you don't manage it properly.

The people that make up your dynamic communications channel include – but are not limited to – the following:

- Management
- Employees
- Former employees
- Investors
- Media
- Customers
- Suppliers
- Distributors
- Principals
- Partners
- Others

The dynamic channel requires a lot of hard work to align to your brand. Basically, your goal is for everyone in your dynamic communications channel to say the right thing and to say the same thing. You want them all to sing the same song and dance the same dance. It is not easy – even for the big brands – because people have minds of their own and they are not always very cooperative. But you need to try nevertheless – starting with your own management and employees.

What we typically do for our clients once the brand strategy is settled on is develop an Integrated Marketing Communications platform. This platform includes a critical component called Internal Brand Alignment whereby we conduct workshops to try and align everyone in the organisation to the brand strategy and to the communications messages. Our clients like to call these the brainwashing workshops.

And we can tell you that this is exceedingly hard to do. Even under the best of circumstances, we estimate that two out of three people will not want to cooperate. That is why it is important for the company's management to continue this internal alignment after the consultants are done with the workshops. It needs to be an ongoing effort. Rome was not built in a day and, likewise, proper internal brand alignment is not achieved with a few training workshops. It is important to continue this effort because if you cannot align the brand internally, what are the chances that you will be able to communicate the brand to the outside world with a strong and cohesive voice?

THE WALL, THE NAIL AND THE HAMMER

If you keep this picture in mind, you will probably find it easier to relate branding and marketing. We have defined a brand as simply an idea – a strong and positive idea – that your brand owns or is associated with in the minds of your customers. So, to build a strong brand, you need to get that idea into the minds of your customers. Now, imagine that the mind is like a wall that you need to penetrate.

Branding is like the nail. Branding gives you the idea that differentiates you from all the other competitors out there. The sharper your nail, the easier it will be to penetrate the wall. The job of your branding exercise is to find a nail that is sharper than the nails used by all of your competitors. You need a sharper nail because your competitors are also trying to penetrate the same wall as you. So find a sharper nail by finding a better differentiating idea. A better differentiating idea does not necessarily mean a better product or service as we have determined earlier.

Marketing is like the hammer. Marketing refers to the activities that you do to communicate your differentiating idea. The bigger your hammer, the easier it will be to drive that nail into the wall. A good hammer needs to be made from the right mix of materials. It needs to be properly designed. It needs to be properly balanced. It needs to be properly manufactured. And it needs to suit the user.

Likewise, a proper marketing programme needs to be properly thought out. You need to think about the proper mix of components that you are going to use within both the static and dynamic channels. You need to design the marketing programme properly. Which words and which graphics will you use to communicate? You need it to be balanced. That means you need to make sure that the money you spend is spent in the right areas. It needs to be properly executed. If you run your marketing programme in a slipshod manner, it doesn't matter how great your differentiating idea is – the brand will fail. And finally, you need to make sure that the marketing programme is suitable for the customers or audience that you want to target.

The wall is the minds of your customers.
The nail is branding.
The hammer is marketing.

Keep the above in mind and you won't get confused about the difference between branding and marketing.

AND WHAT ABOUT SALES?

If branding is differentiation and marketing is communications, what then is sales? In our definition, sales is basically what you do to close the deal; to turn a prospect into a customer. Once you have differentiated your brand properly and communicated it consistently, you will start to get onto the radar of potential customers. We are speaking from our own experience as well the experience of our clients.

Once you are on the radar of these potential customers, they will consider you the next time they need to buy something that you happen to sell. If you are a B2C company with a shop, they will walk in and check out whatever it is that you are selling and ask your salespeople some questions. If you are a B2B company, they may call you for a meeting to find out more about your company or they may invite you to submit a quotation or proposal for the products or services that they need from you.

Having a strong brand that is properly communicated helps to open doors for your company. What you do once you step through that door will determine whether you convert that prospect into a customer or you walk away empty-handed. That is the sales process. If you are a B2B company, this is where you talk to your potential customers to understand their needs more and then see if you can put together the combination of products or services that can meet their needs. Each customer's requirement is different in a B2B purchase so you will need to customise, that's for sure.

As part of the sales process, you will also negotiate the price and the discounts with your customers. This goes back and forth until both parties come to a price for the package that is acceptable to both the buyer and the seller. If such an agreement cannot be reached, then there is no sale. If both parties can agree, then the sale can be concluded. It does not mean that if you have a strong brand, you will automatically win. Even strong brands need to get their pricing strategy and cost-benefit ratio to a point that is acceptable to customers.

As we mentioned earlier in this section, having a strong brand opens the door for you. It gets you onto the shortlist. Wilson led a very interesting study in 2007 called the 'B2B Branding Study For Globalization'. The study was commissioned by the Singapore Business Federation and funded by IE Singapore. StrategiCom was appointed to carry out this study to discover the factors that are important for companies when they shortlist suppliers and when they appoint suppliers. This was the first time that such a study was conducted in Singapore.

The first phase of the study involved 100 companies with a turnover of S$30 million or more and investigated the factors that were important to them when shortlisting potential suppliers from Singapore. We found that during the shortlisting phase, the five most important factors in order of importance were:

1. The potential supplier's track record
2. The potential supplier's knowledge of its products/services
3. The potential supplier's reputation
4. The potential supplier's financial strength
5. The potential supplier's leadership position in its industry

All the five items listed above have to do with how strong a brand is. All these five items can be used to differentiate one brand from another. What we can conclude from this is that in the shortlisting stage, having a strong brand will help you to get shortlisted. Companies normally select only a handful of suppliers for consideration out of the total pool of potential suppliers and in most categories, the total number of suppliers can be very high but only four or five will be shortlisted typically.

The second phase of the project involved 300 companies with an annual turnover of S$30 million or more. In this phase, the companies had already shortlisted the suppliers. We wanted to find out which factors were the most important in determining who they ultimately awarded the deal to. This is where the findings were very different from those of the first phase. What the study revealed is that in the final selection stage, the three most important factors were:

1. Service quality, which is defined mainly as the contact person's accessibility, responsiveness and efficiency
2. Pricing, which is defined as having a price that is competitive in relation to the other suppliers being considered
3. Delivery quality, which is defined as the buyer's belief that the supplier is able to adhere to the agreed upon delivery timeline

The No. 1 factor is actually service quality. Since service quality here is defined by the buyers as the contact person's accessibility, responsiveness and efficiency, it is something that is related to the selling process. If your potential customer perceives that your salespeople are easily accessible, responsive to customer enquiries and efficient, then you will have a better chance of closing the deal. This is something that you need to take into account when selecting your salespeople as well as in their training and evaluation.

In A Nutshell

In order to develop a strong brand, you also need to understand what branding is all about. There are many definitions of what branding is. When we came up with our definition of branding, we actually went back to its origins. Branding was originally invented to differentiate cows 4,000 years ago. Based on these origins, we define branding as the process of differentiation. Branding is still used to differentiate cows today but the cows now also come in the form of companies, products and services. Marketing is a closely related concept but it is not the same thing. Marketing is what you do to communicate your differentiating idea through the static and dynamic communications channels that are available to you. Sales refers to the process of closing the deal through the process of understanding the customers' needs, proposing a solution comprising either a combination of products or services or both that can meet these needs and pricing it correctly. A strong brand can charge a premium but it cannot be too high compared to its closest competitors. If you think of the minds of your customers as a wall that your brand must penetrate, then branding is the nail (the process of finding the idea that differentiates you), marketing is the hammer (the activities that you do to communicate the brand idea) and sales is the paint that is applied to the wall once the nail is in. This is the simplest way that we can define branding, marketing and sales.

B2B

CHAPTER
04

Anything Can Be Branded

WHICH is a more difficult process – to produce petrol or to produce bottled water? We think you will agree that the former is much more difficult, not to mention far more dangerous. You have to carry out extensive geological surveys to find the oil. You have to build ultra sophisticated oil rigs that can drill deep enough into the earth to get to the oil and these days, oil companies have to go further out to sea to search for oil. Even if you drill for oil on land, it is still a very complex job. After you extract the crude oil, you have to send it to a refinery to be processed into petrol. And then you need an extensive distribution network to transport the petrol to the petrol stations to sell to customers.

Now compare that to making bottled water. It's still not an easy process. You need to have a sophisticated plant to filter the water and then add whatever minerals you want into the water. You also need an extensive distribution channel. But it is not as difficult as the process of producing petrol. For bottled water companies like Evian, the process is even easier. According to Evian, it lets the Alps do all the filtering and fortifying with natural minerals. All it has to do is pump the water from the ground and bottle it for sale. All very natural and most of the work has already been done by Mother Nature.

At the time of writing, we went out to buy a 500 ml bottle of Evian to see how much it cost. It cost S$1.60, which means it is S$3.20 per litre. Then we went to our regular Esso petrol station to fill up our tanks. We used the most premium Esso Synergy 8000 98 octane petrol. The cost? S$1.92 per litre. Why is a litre of Evian more expensive than a litre of premium 98 octane petrol from one of the most established oil companies in the world? We asked many people that question and we got many different answers such as competition, government regulations and so on. These are most certainly valid answers but all those things alone cannot explain the price differential between a litre of Evian and a litre of Esso Synergy 8000.

And how do you explain the price differential between Evian and other brands of mineral water? The answer lies in the brand. Evian is positioned as a premium brand and more importantly, it is perceived as a premium brand. Hence, Evian can charge such a high price and get away with it.

YOU CAN EVEN BRAND A COMMODITY LIKE WATER

If you look at the product that is represented by Evian, it is nothing more than a commodity. Water is a commodity. As 80 per cent of the world is covered with water, it is probably the most common commodity in the world. But why is Evian able to charge luxury goods prices for what is essentially a commodity? To find out why, we will have to look a little more closely at this very fascinating brand.

If you visit Evian's website, you will see that the company communicates the differentiating idea of the Evian brand very consistently. It has even made a video to show the process of how the water is purified through natural processes. Evian tells the world that Evian water is different from any other brand of bottled drinking water because every drop of Evian water starts as a drop of rain or snow high up in the peaks of the French Alps. The water droplets then travel slowly through a vast network of mineral aquifers deep within the mountains, untouched by any human, and the naturally filtered water eventually emerges at the spring of Évian-les-Bains. The process takes 15 years to complete.

Evian goes on to elaborate its differentiating idea by telling its customers that the path travelled by the water is protected by thick geological layers built up by glaciers 30,000 years ago. This area is untouched by humans and has a perfectly sound microbiological composition. Evian also further reassures its customers by communicating that it takes samples of the water at 20 different points between the protected catchment area and the bottling plant at the spring where the water eventually ends its 15-year journey.

When is water not water? When the water takes 15 years to travel from the peaks of the French Alps through a vast layer of mineral aquifers that is protected by a thick geological structure. When the water is Evian water. Evian found its differentiating idea. Evian dramatised it. Evian communicated it very clearly. This is how you can turn a commodity like water into a branded product that costs more than petrol.

ARE YOU SURE THAT ANYTHING CAN BE BRANDED?

Some clients have argued with us that there are things that simply cannot be branded. One of the examples they mentioned is sand. Sand cannot be branded because it is just sand. The problem is not that sand cannot be branded. The problem is that nobody has bothered to brand sand. Furthermore, sand is in such short supply because of the demands of the construction sector in many rapidly developing as well as developed countries that if you owned sand, you would be able to find buyers easily. But if you want to brand your sand, you can. You can do what Evian did with water.

You have to bear in mind that branding is a process that takes place in the minds of your customers. The battlefield of branding is not in the real world. It is not in the marketplace. The battlefield of branding is in the mind. Whether you win or lose depends on how well you fight your branding battles in the mind. Because a brand is just an idea that exists in the minds of your customers, branding is a battle that is naturally fought in the mind. In order for you to successfully brand anything – including the most boring and most commoditised of commodities – you need to look beyond that product or service. Don't just look at what coffee beans or sand or cement are literally but look at what idea these products can own in the minds of customers.

The fact that no other company in your industry has attempted to brand its products or services or companies should not act as a deterrent. Whenever we sign up a client whose competitors have not bothered to develop a strong brand, we bring out the champagne (which is consumed mostly by Jacky as Wilson is allergic to alcohol) because it is a fantastic opportunity. It means that this client has a first-mover advantage and could be the first one to establish the brand in the minds of customers and other key external stakeholders.

We recently signed up a company that specialises in making small and complex parts for mobile phones and medical devices through a hybrid injection moulding technology. The client asked us for examples of companies in their industry – and there are many – that could be considered a strong brand. We could not find a single one and that got the client worried. The chairman asked us, "If nobody in our industry has managed to create a strong brand, isn't it dangerous for us to try? After all, we don't have any precedents to learn from." We told the client that it is actually a great position to be in because it would give the company the opportunity to become the first branded company in their industry. While it is true that the client does not have any industry case studies to learn from, it also means that the client has the opportunity to be a trailblazer and, on top of that, has a clean sheet of paper to work with.

It is like the story of the two shoe salesmen who were sent by their respective companies to a foreign country to develop a new market for shoes. Neither had been to the country before. It was very far from their homeland and the journey there was long and hard. When the first salesman got there, he surveyed the market and, within an hour, called headquarters and said, "Guys, I am coming home on the next flight. There is no market for us here because nobody wears shoes. They either run around barefooted or they wear sandals. They don't need shoes. See you when I get home."

The second shoe salesman also surveyed the market. Within an hour of getting there, he also placed a call to headquarters and told them, "Hey guys, send me 10 containers' worth of shoes. I don't care what kind of shoes. Just send me shoes. Men's shoes. Women's shoes. Kids' shoes. Sports shoes. Walking shoes. Boots. Anything that you can get from the warehouse. Just do it fast. This is going to be a huge market for us! The folks in this country don't have shoes! All they have are sandals. We can be the No. 1 brand for shoes here. Back home we are nobody because there are over 200 shoe companies there. Over here, we will be the only one. We will be king. So drop everything you are doing and get me my shoes fast! Over and out."

Anything can be branded if you want to build a brand out of it. Look at your company. Look past the products that you sell or the services that you provide. Look past what you are now. Instead, look at what kind of brand you can become. Look at what idea you can try to own in the minds of your customers. Look at what you can do to become the leading brand in the minds of your customers. If you can lead in the mind, you can lead in the marketplace. Wilson tells customers at the start of every branding project, "The process of branding is to create a differentiated brand. With a differentiated brand that is properly communicated at all customer touch-points, you will be able to build mind share. Once you have built mind share, you can build market share."

BRANDING IS LIKE MATHEMATICS

Besides the fact that anything can be branded, there is also one thing about the branding process that you will find very interesting. Branding is actually a lot like Mathematics. Now we know that some of you out there will be like Jacky who is quite hopeless at the subject but don't let it be a cause for concern. Branding is like Mathematics but we are not referring to the kind of ultra-complicated Mathematics that is required of nuclear physicists but rather basic Mathematics.

What we mean is that the principles of branding are like the principles of Mathematics. In Mathematics, there are rules that you need to follow. One plus one equals two. Regardless of which country you are in, 1 + 1 will always equal 2. Those are the rules of Mathematics. And they apply equally to everything. Branding is the same in the sense that there are rules of branding as well and these rules are the same regardless of which continent you are operating in or whether you operate in every country in the world. The rules of branding also apply equally regardless of which industry you are in, regardless of whether you are a B2B or B2C company and regardless of whether you are a small, medium or big company.

We have also mentioned briefly in the Introduction to this book that there are no separate rules of branding for small companies to follow. The rules of branding are very egalitarian and very fair. Many smaller companies have asked us why there aren't any rules of branding specifically for small companies because obviously the resources that are available to a small company are very different from those of a big company. When you ask such a question, you are actually missing the point.

While we agree that there are a lot of things that big companies do that small companies cannot even dream of attempting, these big companies also started out as small companies operating in a dingy garage (Dell is one such company) or a living room (eBay is such a company). You should be looking at the principles of branding applied by these small companies to make them become big and successful corporations. These rules are the same rules that apply to all the big successful brands that you see today – regardless of whether they are Western or Asian brands and regardless of which industry these brands are from. These same rules of branding will help you go from small to medium to big.

In terms of branding rules, 1 + 1 = 2. It doesn't matter if you are big or small. The rules are the same. If you want to become a successful businessman and there is a successful businessman whom you admire and would like to emulate, what do you do? Do you try to do everything that this businessman is now doing after he has become successful? If you do, you would probably make yourself bankrupt because obviously you cannot live the same kind of high-end lifestyle that this businessman is now living. You have to study what this businessman did *before* he became successful. He probably experienced many failures along the way. Learn from his mistakes. He probably had to do a lot of work that was unglamorous and hard. Do the same thing.

The bottom line is you've got to study the successful brands before they became successful and apply the same rules of branding that have helped them go from the initial zero to the eventual hero. That is how you build brands.

WHEN IS BRANDING NOT NEEDED?

Although you can brand anything and everything, there are situations where you do not want to build a brand. One of our clients told us that there are basically two types of companies in the world – the type that lives on innovation and the type that lives on efficiency. If you are a company that lives on innovation – such as Intel, Gillette, IBM, Nintendo, Boeing, BlackBerry – you will need to develop a strong brand to wrap around your innovation. If you are a company that lives on efficiency – such as IKEA, Southwest Airlines, Walmart, Dell – you will need to find a way to keep your costs as low as possible for as long as possible. It depends on what kind of company you are or what kind of company you aspire to be.

If you are an innovation company, then you need to brand your innovations so that you can get the maximum mileage out of the innovative products, services, processes or business models that you have created. In 2010, StrategiCom conducted a national study called 'Branding Innovation: A Study Of Singapore SMEs' on 100 small- and medium-sized companies to find out what they do in terms of innovation and what they do in terms of branding their innovations. The study was carried out by Wilson and two other of our colleagues – Mervin Teo (one of our consultants) and Lerisca Lensun (one of our research analysts).

The results of the study were presented at the Singapore Brand Conference 2010 and widely published in the Singapore media. We will share with you some of the more salient findings of the study because we believe they will be of use to you:

1. Ninety-one per cent of SMEs in Singapore have a contemporary understanding of what innovation is, which is defined as "the introduction of a new thing or method; the first attempt to carry out a new idea; and a corporate culture that drives value creation".
2. For companies with no R&D, they can still create innovation when they use at least three of the following four tools: (a) increasing incentives for managers and employees to engage in innovation activities, (b) establishing cross-functional teams to work on innovation projects,

(c) studying customers, suppliers and even competitors to help drive innovation and (d) partnering with external parties to undertake joint innovation projects.

3. Only 21 per cent of SMEs undertake at least three of the activities listed above.

4. The innovation successes enjoyed by this 21 per cent of companies that undertake innovation activities include (a) the development of new products or services that they did not have before, (b) improvements in efficiency, (c) improvements in quality and (d) the creation of a new business model that allowed the company to be more competitive.

5. Ninety-one per cent of companies with innovation successes chose to brand their innovation through various means such as (a) public relations campaigns, (b) marketing activities, (c) corporate branding programmes, (d) working with independent branding consultants, (e) design activities and (f) trademark registrations.

If you are an innovation type company, branding is very important because a proper branding programme allows you to differentiate yourself in the minds of your customers. It also allows you to establish your brand firmly in the minds of your customers before your competitors can get there. If you don't brand your innovations, competitors can – and most certainly will – copy what you have done and then try to claim that innovation as their own. If you have not established your brand firmly in the minds of your customers as the brand that is behind this innovation, then you will allow your competitors to overtake you.

IBM wasn't the first company into the market with the mainframe computer. Apparently, it was UNIVAC. But IBM branded its mainframe better so despite being highly innovative, UNIVAC failed to make an impact in the computer market.

What if you are an efficiency type of company? An efficiency type company competes on its ability to provide customers with the most low-cost solutions. The only way for such a company to continue to generate business is if it can maintain a cost advantage over its competitors. So if you are such a company, you need to run efficiency improvement programmes that can help you to drive costs down. You may even need to undertake some innovation programmes that can help to improve your efficiency. StrategiCom's 'Branding Innovation: A

Study Of Singapore SMEs' showed that efficiency improvements is one of the outcomes for Singapore SMEs that make use of the innovation tools that are available to them.

If you are an efficiency company, then branding is not needed. You just have to make sure that you are cheaper than your competitors. However, in recent years, we have noticed companies have generally become so efficient that of all the companies that are operating within any category, there will be at least four to five companies that can match each other in terms of cost. If you are a business owner, you might have noticed this happening in your industry too. No matter how efficient you become, there always seems to be a handful of competitors that can match your price or even better.

In business, the price of your products or services is never a factor unless there is perceived parity. This means that nobody will haggle over your price if they perceive that your brand is worth it. Look at Mercedes-Benz. Would anyone wanting to buy a Mercedes-Benz complain that the price is too high and then go and buy a Volkswagen instead? Would you? Probably not. You will find ways and means to get your hands on one. Price is not a consideration because there is no perceived product parity. Most would-be Mercedes-Benz buyers already perceive Mercedes-Benz to be superior.

But the reverse is also true. You should pay close attention to this paragraph if you are an efficiency type company. If there is price parity between all the different players in a category, then what happens? How does the buyer choose? How would you choose if you had five suppliers who could meet your technical specifications for something that you needed to buy for your company or factory or client project that you are managing? And on top of that, all of them fell within your price range? You would choose the one that you perceive to have the strongest brand.

This is something that efficiency companies have to watch out for. If you are an efficiency company, you don't need branding unless your key competitors can match or better you in terms of cost efficiency. If you can't pull away from the pack on cost, then you will have to pull away based on your brand. It's funny, isn't it? What goes around usually comes around again. For an innovation company, price is not a consideration unless customers perceive their competitors to be equally strong brands. For an efficiency company, brand is not a consideration unless customers see that its competitors are equally cheap.

THE COMMODITIES CONTINUUM II

There are other situations where you don't need – or perhaps don't want – to brand. It depends where you fall on what we call The Commodities Continuum. In the book *Killer Differentiators*, we talked about this rather interesting scale, which can be used to determine what kind of company you currently are and help you make the decision as to whether you need to undertake a branding project or not. Basically, The Commodities Continuum is a scale.

The left hand side of the scale represents highly commoditised products or services that are bought mainly on price. These products and services are undifferentiated and buyers have very little loyalty to the suppliers. They buy from whoever can give the lowest prices. The right hand side of the scale represents products or services that are highly branded. These products or services enjoy a high degree of differentiation, even if the differentiation is only in the brand and nothing else. These products and services can usually be sold at a premium and they engender more customer loyalty.

What we would like to do here is introduce a revised model of The Commodities Continuum that is more comprehensive. The diagram below illustrates The Commodities Continuum II model. It is basically the same thing except we have now broken it down into four segments, ranging from Pure Commodities to Strong Brands.

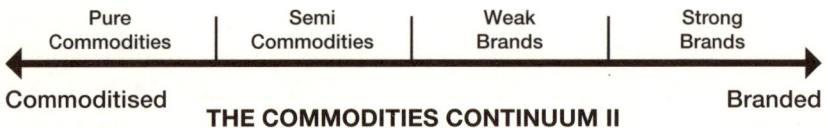

Pure Commodities	Semi Commodities	Weak Brands	Strong Brands

Commoditised   **THE COMMODITIES CONTINUUM II**   **Branded**

Pure Commodities

If your products and services fall into the Pure Commodities quarter of The Commodities Continuum II, there is no need for branding. Pure Commodities are defined as commodities that are sold as they are, such as coffee beans, tea leaves, crude oil, wheat, lead, gold, platinum, cement, sand and so on. These are the things that are traded on commodities exchanges around the world. These things are extremely price sensitive and are bought and sold based on price.

Having said that, you can still brand these commodities if you really want to provided you are willing to commit the time, money and resources to do it.

The other thing that you can consider is not the branding of the commodities but the company selling the commodities. One of our clients is Intraco Limited, a successful trading company that is listed on the Singapore Exchange. Intraco trades in commodities. When we were working on the branding project of Intraco, someone asked the then CEO, Mr Teng Theng Dar, "Mr Teng, coffee is coffee is coffee. So why should anyone buy from Intraco?" That was the question that gave impetus to the project. Mr Teng's instructions to us was, "Coffee is coffee is coffee unless it is coffee sold by Intraco. How do we do this?"

So, we set out to differentiate not the coffee beans sold by Intraco but Intraco itself because Intraco doesn't own any of the farms that produce the coffee beans. Any attempts to differentiate the coffee beans would have been mission impossible. However, we were able to make use of Intraco's heritage, reputation and country of origin to form part of its differentiation strategy. If you are a company like Intraco, maybe you can't brand what you sell but you can still brand the company so buying a commodity from you is not the same as buying a commodity from your competitors.

Semi Commodities

There are many products in the world that have brands but they exhibit all the characteristics of commodities. And they are not necessarily low-tech products. Some of the most technologically advanced products in the world are Semi Commodities. Desktop computers are very much like commodities although all of them have brands. We used to ask companies what computers they bought. In most of these companies, we noticed that different brands were being used. When we asked if they would buy a Dell or an Acer if an HP computer was not available, most said they would as long as the specifications were the same. There really wasn't a lot of brand loyalty as far as we could see.

Thumb drives are also high-tech products that are highly commoditised. Most companies don't really care much for the brand on the thumb drive as long as the price is affordable for the capacity they are looking for. It doesn't end here. There are many other technologically advanced products – for consumer, commercial as well as industrial use – that are Semi Commodities.

What do you do if your products or services fall into the Semi Commodities quarter? There are two things that you can do. One, do nothing. Keep the status quo. If you do nothing, you better make sure that you are prepared to battle it out based on price because if you fall into this category of products or services and you do nothing, then market forces and competitive pressures will gradually force you into the Pure Commodities quarter. That's the way it works.

The second thing that you can do is differentiate your products or services more effectively against your competitors so that you can move to the right hand side of The Commodities Continuum II. It will not be easy but since you already have a brand to represent the products or services that you sell, you might as well try and develop that brand into something that can own a powerful idea in the minds of your customers instead of letting it languish among the other similar products or services in the Semi Commodities quarter.

Weak Brands

As you move further to the right, you will see Weak Brands. These products and services have brands and these brands do stand for something in the minds of their customers and they have some level of customer loyalty that has been built up over the years. However, these brands are still not properly differentiated. That is why they are Weak Brands. And although these brands do stand for something in the minds of their customers, what they stand for is not very clear or not very strong or not very cohesive.

A strong brand owns a powerful and clear idea in the minds of its customers. For example, if you say Caterpillar, people will think of construction equipment. That's a strong brand. What about Komatsu? It also makes construction equipment and very high-quality ones. But the idea of construction equipment is owned by Caterpillar. So we would say Caterpillar is the stronger brand. If you say 3M, the idea of innovation probably comes to mind. 3M owns the idea of innovation. If you say Apple, people will probably think of cool gadgets. That is a strong brand. Harley-Davidson? Rebellious. That is a strong brand. Oracle? Database software. Again, a strong brand. Hyflux? Water treatment. That is a strong brand. Accenture? IT consulting. That is also a strong brand as a result.

The problem with Weak Brands is that if you do a Perception Audit on their customers, you will not get at least two-thirds of their customers to associate the brand in question with a particular idea. The benchmark that we use is two-thirds. If you have two out of three people saying that your brand stands for one thing, then that is the idea that your brand owns. In most situations where companies have Weak Brands, you will find something along the lines of 20 per cent of customers saying this, 25 per cent saying that, 15 per cent saying another thing and the rest saying something else. So the brand does stand for something but it is fragmented.

What do you do with a weak brand? The first thing that you need to do is find out what kind of brand you have and where it falls along The Commodities Continuum II. Many companies don't know for sure where they fall along this scale. You need to be sure so that you know what steps to take next. If you have a weak brand, you need to make a strategic decision. One, do nothing except try to milk your brand for as long as you can before competition forces it to the commoditised end of the scale. Two, try to differentiate the brand more effectively so that it can gradually move to the right side of the scale. The decision is always yours.

Strong Brands

If you are fortunate enough to fall into the Strong Brands category – meaning you are highly differentiated and own a great idea in the minds of your customers – then there is only one thing that you can do and that is maintain the brand as best as you know how. This means you need to know what differentiates you and you need to constantly remind your staff, customers, distributors, suppliers and all the other external stakeholders of your differentiating idea. You have to work hard to ensure that your differentiating idea is not in danger of being stolen by competitors because you neglect it. You have to make sure that your differentiating idea is communicated clearly and consistently at all customer touch-points using both static and dynamic communications channels.

In A Nutshell

You can brand anything, including commodities. Branding is about differentiation and since branding happens in the mind, you can differentiate your brand in the mind by making it stand for a unique idea that is not associated with your competitors. Branding is also like Mathematics in the sense that the rules of branding apply equally to any company – regardless of whether it is a B2B or B2C company, a product or service company or operating locally or internationally. Branding is not needed if you are an efficiency type of company that competes based on your ability to provide more cost-effective products or services compared to your competitors. If that is the case, you just need to run efficiency improvement programmes and make sure that you are able to keep your costs down. Branding is also not needed if you are selling Pure Commodities. You can if you want to but you must be prepared to invest the time, money and effort. The alternative is to brand your company and not the commodities so that buying commodities from you is not the same as buying commodities from your competitors. There are products and services that have brands but they are classified as Semi Commodities because they are bought mainly on price. Some of the most high-tech products in the world are Semi Commodities. If you fall into the Weak Brands category, then you can either run a branding programme to push your brand to the right of The Commodities Continuum II or leave it alone. For companies that fall into the Strong Brands sector, brand maintenance is necessary to keep them there.

B2B

CHAPTER
05

Not Everything
Can Be Rebranded

REBRANDING is commonly used jargon in the business community as well as in

the branding industry. More and more companies are talking about rebranding exercises. You will hear CEOs talking excitedly about the rebranding exercise that they are undertaking which will usher in a new era for the company whereby the brand will be stretched into new market categories. We love that kind of talk from CEOs. It's good for the economy. You will also hear of branding consultants talking excitedly about the rebranding exercise that they have completed on behalf of a client. They will proudly showcase the brand and rightfully so. We also love that kind of talk because we believe that if more people took pride in their work, the world would be a better place – not just the business community but the whole world.

But there are big problems. At the risk of sounding like know-it-alls, we are going to say that most rebranding exercises are doomed to fail because most people – that includes CEOs and branding consultants – fail to understand the basic definition of rebranding. Between the two of us, we talk to several hundred companies a year. The number is large enough for us to see a certain pattern emerging and thus allows us to form a fairly solid conclusion that most people do not understand what a rebranding exercise is all about.

The following example is very common. We meet a company CEO and he tells us that he is going to do so-and-so with the company. He also tells us that in preparation for the company's new strategic direction, he has recently completed a rebranding exercise that involved changing the company's logo from a 16-pointed star to a nine-pointed star. By now we are experienced enough not to fall out of whatever chairs we are sitting in when CEOs tell us such things. Not all CEOs are like that. We have met many visionary CEOs who get it. There are many CEOs who understand that rebranding the company does not just mean *revamping the logo*. They may not share or know our definition of rebranding but they do know that rebranding goes a lot deeper than changing the logo to something new.

While we completely agree that a rebranding exercise will usually involve some cosmetic changes to the company, that is not all that it is about. The cosmetic changes must be the end result of a new strategy. The cosmetic changes should also bring that strategy to life, dramatise it and communicate it clearly to the world. This is what we look out for like hawks when we look at any rebranding exercise. The cosmetic changes must be driven by a solid strategy. It should not be done just for the sake of change. It should not be done just for the sake of having something different to show the world.

There are many different definitions of what rebranding is. Again, you can find these definitions easily with a little bit of research. And you will also find that if you go around your company and hand out little white cards to your colleagues and ask them to write down what their definition of rebranding is, you will get a plethora of different answers. With so many different ways of looking at rebranding, how do you know what rebranding really is? Remember, a problem that is well defined is a problem that is half solved. Likewise, a rebranding exercise that is well defined will be a rebranding exercise that is already 50 per cent successful. We would like to propose the definition of rebranding that we use at StrategiCom for your consideration.

THE DEFINITION OF REBRANDING

When we were asked by our clients to define what a brand is, we looked at all the various definitions of brand and then we asked our clients, "Which is the most important stakeholder group to your company?" Our clients tell us that people are important. You need people who believe in the company's products or services enough so that the company has customers. You also need people who believe in the company enough to want to work in the company to deliver the kind of products and services that customers expect from the company.

So, the most important thing is people. Therefore, in order to define what a brand is, we need to look at what a brand means to the people who matter to our clients. What is a brand? The brand is simply an idea. The brand is simply whatever idea the stakeholders of the company associate with the brand.

The definition of brand: An idea that exists in the minds of your stakeholders.

When we were asked by clients to define what branding is all about, we again looked at all the various definitions of branding and asked ourselves, "Where did branding come from? How did it come about? Why was it invented in the first place?" That was how we discovered that branding was actually created 4,000 years ago in response to the need of cattle owners to differentiate their cows.

The definition of branding: Branding is all about differentiating your cows from all your competitors' cows. And your cows are represented today by your company (the Corporate Brand), your products (the Product Brand) or your services (the Service Brand).

If branding is all about differentiation, is rebranding then about the process of redifferentiation? Well, no. It is not that straightforward. Branding is about differentiating your brand so that it can penetrate the minds of customers and own a piece of real estate there which is represented by the idea that is strongly associated with your brand. In order to rebrand your company, you will need to *remove* the existing idea that your brand owns in the minds of your customers. And after you have removed the existing idea, you need to plant a new idea in the minds of your customers.

THE PROCESS OF REBRANDING

A successful rebranding exercise is a three-step surgical procedure. After you have read the three steps, you will probably know why we have likened a rebranding exercise to surgery.

Step 1: Diagnose

In the first step of the rebranding exercise, you will need to find that one idea that your brand owns in the minds of the people who matter to the brand. Again, this can be accomplished with a Perception Audit.

Step 2: Remove

In the second step, you need to remove the idea that you own from the minds of your customers. This is basically you telling your customers, "Look, Mr Customer. We know from the Perception Audit that you so kindly participated in that you perceive our brand to stand for [the brand idea] but we want to tell you that from now on, our brand no longer stands for [the brand idea]."

- That is like Mercedes-Benz telling its customers that it no longer stands for prestige.
- That is like Xerox telling its customers that it no longer stands for photocopiers.
- That is like Intel telling its customers that it no longer stands for computer chips.
- That is like Dell telling its customers that it no longer stands for computers direct.
- That is like Amazon.com telling its customers that it no longer stands for books online.
- That is like eBay telling its customers that it no longer stands for online auction.
- That is like Keppel FELS telling its customers that it no longer stands for oil rigs.
- That is like Hyflux telling its customers that it no longer stands for water treatment.
- That is like OSIM telling its customers that it no longer stands for massage chairs.
- That is like Milwaukee Electric Tool Corp. telling its customers that it no longer stands for ergonomic power tools.
- That is like Harley-Davidson telling its customers that it no longer stands for rebellious.
- That is like Lady Gaga telling her fans that she no longer stands for outrageous outfits.

Step 2 of the rebranding exercise seems like a walk in the park, right? How difficult can that be? We can tell you that it will be ridiculously difficult. Trying to remove an idea that is strongly associated with your brand from the minds of your customers is like trying to pull a leech off your skin once it has attached itself. Come to think of it, pulling that leech off your skin might be an easier thing to do than trying to erase the idea that you own from the minds of your customers.

But that is not such a bad thing, is it? After all, if you own a great and unique idea in the minds of your customers, why would you want to remove it? Why would you want to rebrand? Keep the brand as it is! Do everything that you can to make sure that you continue to own that idea. Do everything that you can to keep that idea from falling into the hands of another competitor. It is so difficult to own an idea in the mind and that is why we are amazed that so many companies try to throw away what they own.

The problem with many companies is that they often forget what made them a strong brand in the first place. With success comes pride. With pride comes the misguided attempt to stretch the brand into areas that it has no right to be in. A brand is simply an idea that exists in the mind. Xerox equals photocopiers. That is why when Xerox tried to move into computers, it failed. Kodak equals photographic film. That is why when it tried to move into digital cameras, it didn't do that well. It has not failed yet but would you buy a Kodak digital camera? Most people would probably go for Nikon, Canon, Sony or Casio. Swatch stands for colourful watches. That is why when Swatch wanted to build a car in a joint venture with Mercedes-Benz, we predicted that it would fail. The brand never took off. In fact, we won't even consider a Swatch watch a real Swatch watch if it is not colourful and funky.

If you want your rebranding exercise to be successful, you have to carry out the second step successfully. If you can't do this, there is no way that the rebranding exercise will be successful no matter how beautiful and striking your new logo looks, no matter how eloquent and frequent your new brand messages are, no matter how much time and money you pump into the rebranding exercise.

The stronger your brand, the harder it is for you to successfully complete the second step. A strong brand is one that is strongly tied to an idea in the mind. Therefore, it will be much harder to remove the idea because customers don't like to change. They like the things that they know. You know that Volvo is a safe car. So, Volvo equals safe. If we show you a Japanese brand that achieves the same levels of occupant protection as a Volvo in crash tests, what would you do? You would still think Volvo is the default safe car. You don't like change. Neither do your customers. If Volvo comes to you and tells you that it is now a high performance car, what would you think? You would think, "Hang on. The high performance car in this category is BMW. Volvo is a safe car." What if Volvos come with more performance than the equivalent BMWs? You would still think of Volvo as the safe car. You don't like change. Neither do your customers.

That is what makes the second step so difficult but if you fail to execute the second step, your rebranding exercise will be an exercise in futility.

Step 3: Replace

To complete the rebranding exercise, you will need to replace the old idea with a new one. This is important. If you leave a void, competitors will rush in to fill it. If you leave a void, you will also give your competitors the opportunity to manipulate your brand. If you leave a void, your brand will be buffeted from pillar to post by the storm of competitors who would like nothing better than to see you fail.

The problem with the third step is that even if you are able to remove your existing idea, what are you going to replace it with? If there is a great idea in the marketplace, chances are your competitors have tried to claim it already. In any category, there are probably no more than seven ideas that are relevant, desirable and defensible. And in the crowded marketplace that we have today, what are the chances that these seven ideas are not already taken?

Psychologists have shown that the human mind will find it hard to remember more than seven bits of information at any one time. It is no coincidence that phone numbers started out with no more than seven digits. What this means is that the typical customer probably won't remember more than seven brands. And if there are already seven competitors that have claimed the seven slots in the mind through their ownership of one of the seven ideas, then life becomes almost impossible for you. Let's go back to the Volvo example. If Volvo doesn't want to be safe, what can it be? Mercedes-Benz owns prestige. BMW owns performance. Lexus owns refinement. Alfa Romeo owns sexy. Jaguar owns gentleman's express. Toyota reliable – at least until its unintended acceleration saga. All the great ideas are taken. Even though Volvo has been bought over by Chinese carmaker Geely, it can't own the idea "Chinese", that's for sure.

Now do you see why the title of this chapter is "Not Everything Can Be Rebranded"? The stronger the brand, the harder it is to rebrand even if the company no longer likes its brand idea or if the brand idea has become obsolete. Polaroid used to own the idea of "instant photography". That category eventually went the way of the dodo. It became extinct. So, Polaroid desperately needed to rebrand itself because the idea that it owned had become outdated. But that proved impossible because Polaroid is too strong a brand. It helps if you are a weak brand. That makes rebranding easier. But if you are a weak brand – meaning that you don't stand for an idea in the minds of your customers – you don't even need a rebranding exercise. You need a *branding* exercise. You need to find a differentiating idea.

If it is almost impossible to remove an idea that is very strongly associated with a brand and next to impossible to replace the existing idea with a new idea since all the great ideas will have been taken by competitors, then there is no point in rebranding, is there? That's not what we are saying. We are saying that it would be very hard but it is still possible. The 10 rules of branding that we will be talking about in the later chapters of this book are designed to help you find a way to create a strong brand. There are also a few tips in the rest of this chapter that will give you some ideas.

WHY DO COMPANIES REBRAND?

There are many reasons why companies attempt a rebranding exercise. The list here is quite comprehensive but it is by no means exhaustive. These are the main reasons why companies undertake a rebranding exercise but like we said, there could be other factors that lead companies to consider rebranding exercises.

1. Mergers

This is one of the most common reasons why companies feel the need to undertake a rebranding exercise. When one company merges with another, there is a need to decide what to call the merged company. The easiest – not to mention the laziest, most unimaginative and probably the most destructive – method is to combine the two companies' names into one.

In this case, if one company is called Ding and the other company is called Dong, then the merged company will be called Ding Dong. What's wrong with that? Merging the two companies in this manner destroys the brand equity that each one has. Let's say that Ding is famous for "over-engineering" its products and Dong is famous for its products' "stunning designs", what would Ding Dong stand for? Over-engineered products with stunning designs? We wish it were that simple but it is not. Just because you merge two companies that are each famous for different things, it doesn't mean that the merged entity automatically owns the two different ideas. Ding is known for over-engineering and gradually over time it can acquire other capabilities, such as stunning designs, but just because Ding and Dong merged doesn't automatically confer the idea of "stunning design" on Ding.

Companies that merge very often say that it is a merger of equals. In the book *Winning*, Jack Welch, the master of many mergers and acquisitions during his tenure as GE's CEO, wrote that there is no such thing as a merger of equals. We agree. It is too idealistic and it will not work. Just imagine if a company has two CEOs – both with equal authority. That is a recipe for disaster. The buck must stop with one person. One person needs to take ultimate responsibility for the company's success or failure. That person can delegate authority, of course. And that person can surround himself with as many talented advisors and assistants as he needs, but the buck must stop with him. Same thing with a merger. One company must lead. Otherwise, you will have a behemoth that doesn't know its head from its tail, and that behemoth will soon become paralysed.

So, how should the merged entity be rebranded? If you ask us, we will recommend that the merged entity should carry a new brand. Wouldn't that destroy the brand equity of both the individual brands? If Ding and Dong merged and became a new entity called Hoo, for example, then the brand ideas owned by Ding and Dong would be destroyed as Hoo is an unknown entity, right? Hoo doesn't stand for anything. Yes, that argument is correct but because Hoo doesn't stand for anything, you can make it stand for whatever you want.

The alternative is to allow Ding and Dong to operate separately but both are fully owned subsidiaries of Hoo. This requires some clever Brand Architecture work but would help to preserve the identities of both Ding and Dong while still allowing them to be part of the same group. Whatever it is, calling the merged entity Ding Dong is not a good idea.

Even worse is the scenario of the merged entity merging again with other entities and the merged name becoming long and unwieldy. Let's say Ding Dong merges with two other companies called Immortal Charm and Korny. Ding Dong Immortal Charm Korny sounds too long and it's too confusing. So what is the expeditious way out? Shorten it to DDICK. Brilliant. What on earth is DDICK? These are fictitious examples, of course, but you can see the scenario above being played out all over the world whenever a merger occurs.

2. Acquisitions

Acquisitions is another reason why companies rebrand but the rebranding exercise is normally done on the company being acquired. Many companies will just affix the acquiring company's name in front of the acquired company's name. This is also the easy and unimaginative way out.

So if Moe Engineering acquires Sugar Offshore & Marine, Sugar Offshore & Marine will become Moe Sugar. If Moe Engineering acquires Fatt Choi Bunkering, then the acquired company will become Moe Fatt Choi Bunkering. If Moe Engineering acquires Honey Oil Rigs, Honey Oil Rigs becomes Moe Honey

Oil Rigs. This is still not as bad because there is at least some consistency. At least there is a dominant brand in that equation.

3. Scandals

Scandals – especially financial scandals where the company involved is found guilty of fraud or the public perceives that the company in question is in the wrong – can also be the trigger for a rebranding exercise. Usually, these companies are trying to repair a damaged brand image. It might not always be successful depending on how serious the damage is. If the damage is of the magnitude of an Enron or a Lehman Brothers, then there is probably not much that a rebranding exercise can do.

Anyway, the best strategy to adopt in such situations is actually a three-step approach:

1. Apologise for the mistake.
2. Do everything in your power to right the wrong.
3. Lie low for a while because as time passes by, there will be other scandals for people to sink their teeth into and they will forget about your infraction.

4. Dying Industry

If your industry is becoming obsolete because of technological changes, and this happens all the time, you will need to rebrand. This means that you will have to find something new to tie the brand to. However, you also have to bear in mind the possibility that your rebranding exercise will involve killing the brand and launching a new one. You can keep the company but you might need to launch a new brand.

When analogue mobile phones became obsolete, Nokia had to launch a new range of digital mobile phones. It didn't need to change the brand because Nokia still stood for mobile phones. If the mobile phone category becomes obsolete, then Nokia might have to launch a new brand to tap into whatever new thing that comes along.

When the category called word processors became obsolete and computers became the new thing, Wang died along with it because the Wang brand could not cross over to computers. If Wang had moved quickly into computers with a new brand, then the company might have had a better chance of surviving.

5. Trademark Conflicts

As companies grow, they expand into new international markets. The chances of running into another company that has the same name are very high. Sometimes, these companies are in the same industry. Sometimes, they are operating in different industries. Whatever the case may be, you can be sure there is potential conflict. Even a company that is not in the same industry as you might object to you using the same brand name in its market because of the potential confusion. We read somewhere that the Porsche 911 – one of the most iconic sports cars of all time and arguably the most successful and longest-lived – was originally going to be called the 901 but it was renamed the 911 because Peugeot claimed that using model names made up of three numbers with a zero in the middle was its right.

Marconi of the UK was originally called General Electric but it is not related in any way to the American General Electric. General Electric of the UK is a specialist in communications equipment for military applications – especially submarines. It had to change its name to Marconi because of the potential conflict with General Electric of the USA, which is the larger and better known entity.

6. Initial Public Offering

An initial public offering (IPO) usually triggers some frenzied rebranding activities within a company. We like to watch in amusement as these companies scamper to rebrand themselves six months or a year before the IPO. That is probably not the best approach. A brand takes time to build. Rebranding also takes time. You can't just slap everything together and expect the IPO to be a roaring success – not in these straightened times. During the dot.com boom, you could do a bit of window dressing and still have a successful IPO. Hopefully, those days will never return because they do more harm than good.

We usually advise clients who tell us that they are planning for an IPO to start planning at least three years ahead, not just from a branding point of view but also from a financial point of view. You have to build up your books over time. You need to work hard at making sure that you show good growth and good returns which will then help to build up a healthy balance sheet. At the same time, you should also work on building the brand so that it has better mind share. A strong brand coupled with a strong balance sheet will give you a better change of a successful IPO. Rome wasn't built in a day. Neither are successful IPOs built in six months.

7. Line Extension

When companies want to grow, there are two things that they can do assuming that their home markets have become quite saturated. They can either take the same products or services and move into new markets overseas. Or they can stay in the same market and sell other products and services. The latter is also a viable option for expansion if the home market is a very big one like the United States, China or India. Even a country like Malaysia is big enough to support a company's growth through the addition of new products or services.

The only problem is that companies are often lazy or overconfident. They think that just because their brand is successful in one thing, they can sell anything under that brand. That is dangerous thinking. That is the kind of thinking that leads companies to sell products and services that are unrelated to the core business under the same brand. That is fine if you don't have strong competitors in your market but in this day and age, there is always a competitor or twenty who will be waiting to pick a fight with you. If you rebrand the company for the purpose of line extension, our advice is to think again.

REBRANDING MAY REQUIRE A NAME CHANGE

If you have a brand that is strongly associated with an idea and you no longer want that idea or if that idea is starting to become obsolete, then you will need to change the name of the brand. A brand is an idea. That idea is represented by the name of your brand. That is the name that customers see. That is the name that is linked to that idea in their minds. If that name is too strongly tied to one particular idea, then it will be next to impossible to separate the name from the idea. That is why in order to successfully rebrand, a company needs you to do three things.

The first thing that you need to do is to define what the new brand is. What is the new idea that you want to insert into the minds of your customers? That new idea needs to be unique and it needs to be available for you to own – at least in your major markets of operation. That idea could be owned by a competitor but perhaps not in all markets. If that is the case, that idea is available for you to own in some of the markets. If that idea is still not claimed by another in the markets that you want to operate in, then you can own it. But you definitely need to define what that new idea is because without an idea to attach to the brand, there will be no brand or there will be a weak brand.

The second thing that you need to do is to attach that new idea to a new name because the old name stands for something else. Many companies hang on to an obsolete name because of sentimental reasons or because of unrealistic expectations or because they simply don't know what to do. A new idea needs a new name. That may be a scary thing for the majority of companies out there, but it is sometimes necessary.

The third thing that you need to do is to communicate the new name and the new idea clearly and consistently at all customer touch-points using as many of the components within your static and dynamic channels as possible. You need to move fast and you need to hit the market hard so that you can get the new name and the new idea into the customers' minds before competitors mess things up for you. If you are too slow, then customers may lose interest and move on to the next available brand. You know people have very short attention spans these days.

Remember that changing the name alone is not enough. We have come across some companies that are very trigger-happy when it comes to changing names. It doesn't matter how often you change your name. If you change your name but you don't define the new idea that you want to associate with the new name, then it is not a rebranding exercise. If customers cannot associate the new name with an idea, then the name is just a name. It doesn't cross the chasm that lies between a name and a brand.

REBRANDING NEEDS A GREAT STORY

You need to create a great story around the rebranding exercise because people love stories and the better the story, the more they will remember the brand. Great brands are great story tellers as well. The story needs to be dramatic and convincing. Basically, you are trying to answer some of the key questions that all your stakeholders will have. Why are you rebranding? Is it because the company is in trouble? People panic easily so you have to reassure them with the story. People are also sceptical so you need to convince them that the rebranding is a legitimate and needed exercise. What can I expect from you now that you have rebranded? The story must have somewhere to go. People also like odysseys. They like to know that there is a future. They like to know where the brand is going next. What it is going to do next and how. And your brand story needs to take them to the future. It is not all fairy tales. People are not stupid and presumably that is the reason why they buy from you. As such, the story needs to be grounded in facts but romanticised.

Package everything together nicely. Sell the story internally so that your people – the brand ambassadors – know the story and how to tell it to the outside world. After that, you need to sell the story to the media and to your customers. They need to be convinced. This is both an art and a science. A branding project can help you refine this story but you have to tell it. We always tell CEOs who are not comfortable telling the brand story as often as needed (and then some) to the world that they better find a new CEO because if even the CEO won't tell the story, who will? After that, keep telling the story consistently until you are so sick of it and then tell it some more – this time with feeling. That is what it takes to create a brand story that will help build your rebranding.

REBRANDING TAKES TIME

Oak trees don't grow overnight and in order for the rebranding project to sink its roots into the minds of your customers, you need to move fast, as we mentioned in the preceding section, but rebranding is not the 100 metres sprint. It is more akin to a marathon. It takes time. You need patience. You need stamina. And you need to have a strong heart to see it to the finish line. How long does it take? There is no hard and fast answer. It takes as long as it takes. But you need to keep at it for at least three years, and along the way you need to track the progress that the rebranding exercise is making by conducting periodic Brand Tracking – for our clients, it is usually done at six-month intervals. The purpose of this is to see how stakeholders are perceiving the new brand. If the perception is not moving in the direction that you want, then you have to diagnose what the problem is and fix it. In our experience, the root cause is usually in the communications of the new brand. The problem usually arises because companies don't communicate enough, don't communicate clearly, don't communicate enthusiastically (yes, enthusiasm plays a part as well) or don't train their people to say and do the right thing to promote the brand.

The bottom line is rebranding is hard work.

Think carefully before you jump into a rebranding exercise – knowing that rebranding is not just about revamping your entire corporate identity and advertisements and other communications material. Rebranding goes deeper than just a cosmetic makeover.

In A Nutshell

A brand is an idea that exists in the mind. The stronger the association between the brand and the idea, the stronger the brand. A strong brand is very hard to rebrand because rebranding involves divorcing the brand from the idea and then replacing the old idea with a new one. It is a very tall order. When you have a brand that stands for a unique and powerful idea in the minds of customers, it is better to just leave things alone. It is better to just try to maintain that idea so that you continue to own it. However, if you need to rebrand, for whatever reason, then you need to define the new idea that you want your brand to stand for, find a new name to represent that idea because the old name stands for the old idea, and then you need to communicate it clearly, consistently and often. Packaging everything into a great and memorable story will help the rebranding process. People are not interested in you, your company, your products or your services. But they like a good story. If they like the story, they will remember the new brand. If they like the story and believe it, the new brand has already got into the mind. Rebranding also takes time. It requires patience. Once you have decided to rebrand, stick with it for as long as it takes. For those of you who must have a timeline, then at least three years, but along the way you need to monitor the progress of the brand and then be ready to rectify problems as they crop up because there will be problems. Nothing that is worth doing is ever easy but everything that is worth doing is worth doing right and worth doing big.

B2B

CHAPTER
06

"But We Are Not Selling Coca-Cola," Says The CEO

SOMETIME in 2005, Wilson was invited by the marketing director of a B2B branding company to make a presentation to the company's senior management on the nuts and bolts of a typical branding project because the marketing director thought it was time for the company to review its brand strategy. Five minutes into the presentation, the CEO stopped Wilson and said, "Excuse me, Mr Chew. We are not selling Coca-Cola, you know? Why are you talking to us about branding?" This was the first time that either one of us was asked this question but it certainly wasn't the last.

Back in those days, many CEOs of B2B companies would ask us this question. They were simply not convinced that a B2B company needed to undertake a branding project. Their contention was that since B2B companies are very different in nature to B2C companies, branding was not important to B2B companies and would not make any difference. Today, the situation has changed. More and more B2B companies are realising that branding is actually *more important* to them than to a B2C company.

What happened in the last half a dozen years to bring about this change? Before we answer that question, we want to first look at why many B2B companies in the past did not think that branding was important. Come to think of it, many of these companies probably fell off their chairs laughing after we left the boardroom.

So, it was a tough sell back then. It still is a tough sell today but B2B companies are more receptive these days. There are still B2B companies that don't believe in branding, have a very warped idea of what branding is or, even worse, think that they are unique and therefore don't have any competitors. The last part is just wishful thinking. Try telling your customers that they should buy from you because you don't have any competitors and they will name you a list of competitors that you have. To you, these may not be classified as competitors but as long as your customers see them as alternatives, then they are competitors. That is the way of the business world.

Even if you have no competitors now because you have just invented a new process or a new technology or a new product, rest assured that within the space of a year – and usually less – there will be a host of competitors. You will be amazed how fast competitors can reverse engineer whatever you have without infringing on your patents and you will be further amazed at how cheaply they can do it. You have to keep running to stay where you are. If you look at how quickly even complicated new technologies can be copied, you will know that you are in trouble. We are sure you watch TV. After Panasonic launched its plasma TV, it was quickly copied by everyone else. After Sharp launched its LCD TV, it was copied in no time by everyone else. After Samsung launched the world's first LED TV, LG followed very closely. Before you know it, every competitor will be offering an LED TV.

WHY SOME CEOS THINK BRANDING IS NOT IMPORTANT FOR B2B COMPANIES

For every action, there is an equal and opposite reaction, according to Newton. And every coin has a flip side. Likewise for B2B branding. Some think it is important. We obviously do or we wouldn't have dedicated StrategiCom to the art and science of B2B branding strategy.

But we also realise that what we say will be perceived as biased because we have a vested interest. Therefore, we will let you make up your own mind. We will present you with the arguments against B2B branding and let you decide. These are the arguments that have been put forth by many CEOs of B2B companies. We have spent many hours in boardrooms listening to objection after objection from CEOs who simply cannot believe that branding has any value for a B2B company.

Objection #1
B2B Buyers Are Rational Creatures Who Are Not Affected By Intangibles Like Brands

Some CEOs of B2B companies – as well as many of the executives who work in such companies – have told us that a B2B purchase is a very rational one that is driven by cold, hard objectivity that is devoid of emotions, unlike a B2C purchase. Basically, they are saying that the heart takes a back seat and the head rules.

These CEOs have argued that what matters in a B2B purchase are things such as whether the supplier is able to meet their technical specifications, whether the quality of the products is excellent, whether the performance is top-notch and so on and so forth. To them, the whole decision-making process is as clinical as a German factory.

Unfortunately, the decision makers are not a bunch of robots or a computer program. They are human beings like you. They have emotions. They have prejudices. They have preferences. They can be influenced by brands. For example, if you are a construction company, wouldn't you want the world to see that you are using a top construction equipment brand like Caterpillar? If you are a tunnelling company, wouldn't you want the world to see you using a top tunnelling machine brand like Herrenknecht? If you are a hydropower company, wouldn't you want the world to see you using a top electric turbine brand like General Electric? Whether you can afford these brands is another thing but you would if you could, wouldn't you?

If your customers are not influenced by brands, then how come every time you compete with a top brand for a customer, you seem to lose more often than you win even though *objectively speaking*, you are better and cheaper? Food for thought?

Objection #2

B2B Purchases Are All About Relationships

This is another objection that B2B companies have against branding. They claim that a B2B purchase is all about the relationship between the individual sales representative and the buyer. What these companies are saying is that if the B2B brand means anything, it is the meaning that is created by the sales representative.

Jacky just met a company that is providing testing services for petrochemical companies in the South East Asian region. The CEO told him that branding doesn't matter. All that matters is his relationship with the buyers. If the relationship is strong, then there is a deal. If the relationship is weak, there is no deal.

While we do not deny that a strong relationship with your customers is always a good thing, doesn't the brand have anything to do with the purchase decision? If you are of the opinion that branding plays no role in a B2B company and relationships are all that matter, have you stopped to consider why this is so? Maybe these companies have resorted to relationships to sell because they have never bothered to build a strong brand.

It's like the insurance sector. The CEO of one insurance company once told Jacky, "Insurance is not something that is bought. It is something that is sold." What he meant is that nobody wants to buy insurance unless you sell it to him or her. If you don't have a strong brand, you better have a strong relationship but that only works if the rest of your competitors are equally weak in terms of their branding. What if one or two of your competitors have much stronger brands?

Let's reverse the picture. Let's take you as an example. You have to implement a new ERP system for your company. You have a very good relationship with a local IT company that tells you it can do a customised ERP system for you from scratch. This IT company is not known for ERP. Microsoft Dynamics NAV is a strong brand in low-cost ERP systems for the SME sector. Are you willing to bet your company's operations on an unknown IT company no matter how good your relationship is when there is a reasonably priced but strong ERP brand available?

Objection #3
Price Is The Only Thing That Matters In A B2B Purchase
As the 'B2B Branding Study For Globalisation' showed in 2007, price is not a consideration during the shortlisting process. It is a consideration when it comes to awarding the contract to the shortlisted vendors but if you don't have a strong brand, you wouldn't be shortlisted in the first place. Again, perhaps you can look at how you buy for your own company. Does price matter? Of course it does. You don't have a bottomless pit of money but you can always find a handful of suppliers who are equally matched – on paper at least – in terms of price, performance, quality, etc. So, how do you choose from these suppliers? The one with the strongest brand, perhaps? Price matters in a B2B purchase but it is not the only thing that matters. If you have participated in tenders, you will know that the lowest price doesn't always win. Very often, you will find that the tender was finally awarded to a competitor that is between 15 per cent and 25 per cent more expensive than you although what you offer is more or less the same. Ever wondered why? Perhaps the other guy has a brand that inspires more confidence in the customers?

Objection #4

B2B Products Or Services Are Largely Invisible So Branding Won't Help

Many CEOs have argued with us over this in the past. Some companies still do. They all claim that since a B2B product or service is never seen by the end customer, the brand doesn't matter at all. Branding won't help an invisible product or service. Ever heard of Intel? Unless you have been living in a cave for the past three decades, you will have heard of Intel for sure. The next question might make you pause. Do you know what a computer chip looks like? Many of us have no idea. So, why do we still check to see if there is an Intel chip in a computer before we buy it?

Objection #5

Our Customers Know A Superior Product When They See One

Many B2B companies work under the assumption that their customers have perfect knowledge. Well, just because you are very knowledgeable and objective in your field doesn't mean that your customers are too. Many B2B companies seem to forget that their customers are very often – not always but very often – not as knowledgeable as them.

If you work under the assumption of perfect knowledge on your customers' part, it is a very dangerous thing to do because your customers don't know everything. Very often, the person who is making the purchase decisions is not even trained in your field. That makes it difficult to sell because you have to spend a lot of time and effort educating and persuading your customers. But the upside is that these customers – because of their lack of perfect knowledge – will gravitate towards stronger brands just to be on the safe side.

Objection #6

B2B Products Are Not Aspirational

Many B2C products are aspirational. They are symbolic in nature. A Rolex watch says you are wealthy. A Hugo Boss suit says that you have impeccable taste. A BMW says that you are a driven and successful executive. An iPhone says you are cool and young. A Birkin handbag says that you are one of the elite few who know what a Birkin is and important enough to be able to get one. A Harley-Davidson says that you are carefree and someone who beats his own path.

B2B products do not promise to make you cool or sexy or anything like that. They are not aspirational in nature. They are utilitarian. B2B products are not status symbols. No company will aspire to own a B2B product. Yes, B2B products or services are utilitarian in nature. They perform a function but the best ones can be status symbols as well. If you are a building owner, wouldn't the installation of Otis elevators and escalators be something to aspire to because they tell the world that you use the world's top brand of elevators and escalators? If you are a logistics company and you use Crown electric forklifts and reach trucks in your warehouses, wouldn't that make you proud to show off your warehouses to potential customers? If you are a systems integration company, wouldn't it confer more status – and credibility – on your brand if you buy Cisco networking products?

The answers to the above questions could be yes, no or maybe. But that doesn't mean that a B2B product or service cannot be aspirational.

Objection #7
B2B Companies Don't Sell To Millions So Branding Is Not Needed

It is true that the pool of customers that a B2B company has is definitely less than the potential customers that a B2C company has because there are definitely more people in the world than there are companies. A B2C brand like Coca-Cola can sell to billions of people around the world whereas a B2B brand typically has customers numbering in the thousands. Most of our B2B clients have fewer than one thousand potential customers worldwide. One of our clients is so specialised that they told us there are fewer than 50 companies in the world that can use their service.

So, many B2B companies in the past have argued that since they don't sell to millions of customers, branding is not important. But the thing is, you don't have to sell to millions of customers to need branding. Even if you only have 50 companies that could potentially be customers, you will still need a strong brand because you will always have competitors. These competitors can and eventually will copy everything that you can offer. If they can match everything that you do and you cannot counter that with a stronger brand, then life is going to be hard. Everything being equal – and over time, it tends to be – the stronger brand wins.

Objection #8
B2B Products Or Services Are Too Complex To Be Branded

We absolutely love this one which is why we have left it till last. We don't know why there are people who think that complex products or services cannot be branded. They absolutely can. In fact, the more complex your products or services, the more you need to brand because a strong brand simplifies the decision-making process.

Accenture delivers extremely complex IT solutions to its clients. Accenture is a highly branded IT company. You may not understand fully what Accenture does but you would trust your IT needs with Accenture.

Accuray makes a highly complex machine called a stereotactic radiosurgery device, which it has branded as Cyberknife. This is basically a giant gamma ray gun that is guided by a sophisticated computer that allows surgeons to zap cancer cells with sub-millimetre accuracy. Cyberknife is a great brand and that is why so many surgeons and tens of thousands of patients have used it.

The brand is simply an idea that exists in the minds of your customers. The brand simplifies a complex product or service, distilling it into a simple, powerful and easy-to-understand idea. The more complex and difficult to understand a product or service is, the more you need to brand it so that the brand helps to simplify the decision-making process. That may sound like a contradiction but imagine this. If you are selling a complex product or service and you have key competitors selling something that is equally complex, how will you sell it? If you can associate this complex product or service with a simple idea, you will make it easy for customers to understand you better and that will give you the upper hand.

That was what IBM did. Instead of calling its super complex and gigantic machine an electronic numerical integrator and computer, it called it a mainframe computer. The machines makes thousands of complex calculations a minute (in those days, that was pretty fast) so it is a computer and it is gigantic (weighs 60,000 kilogrammes or thereabouts) so it is a mainframe computer. Easy to understand. Well-branded, IBM. When Cray launched its ultra-fast and ultra-complex computer that is faster than anything that the world has ever seen, Cray simply called it a supercomputer. Easy to understand. Again, well-branded, Cray.

WHAT ARE THE DIFFERENCES BETWEEN B2B AND B2C COMPANIES?

Understanding the differences between a B2B and a B2C company will help you to understand the branding and marketing requirements of these two types of companies. The principles of branding are still the same. Branding principles are like Mathematics, remember? One plus one equals two. Below are the seven key differences that exist between a B2B company and a B2C company.

Difference #1
Inverse Relationship Between Market Size And Purchase Value

The market size in terms of the number of customers for a B2B company is much smaller compared to a B2C company. There are definitely more consumers than there are companies in the world. We would be in serious trouble otherwise. The consumer market is measured in the millions whereas the B2B market is measured in the thousands – at most.

However, the purchase value of a B2C product or service is relatively small compared to a B2B product or service. Even expensive consumer products like luxury goods are rarely more expensive than B2B products. One power generator from our client VibroPower could cost anywhere from S$200,000 to over S$1,000,000 depending on power and size. One oil rig built by our client SembCorp Marine could range from S$150,000,000 to over S$500,000,000. But the number of customers that VibroPower and SembCorp Marine could potentially serve is definitely smaller than that of say, Apple.

Some marketers measure the lifetime value of a customer. If you take this into account, then the gap between the sales value of a B2B and a B2C widens even further. It is hard to sell to a B2B customer but once that customer is secured, research and our clients' experience suggest that this customer is very unlikely to switch suppliers unless the seller violates the buyer's trust.

Once a B2B deal is secured, very likely, the buyer will come back and repurchase because it is less hassle. If you have bought a crane from Komatsu and you are happy with the crane and the service level, you would go back to Komatsu and buy more cranes if you needed more in the future. A B2C customer, however, is easier to lose because the complexity and cost of switching is lower.

Difference #2
The Buying Process In B2B Is Much Longer

The decision-making process in a B2C purchase is nowhere near as lengthy as that of a B2B purchase. In a B2B market, the buying process is longer because the company has to consider many variables and also because the process involves more people. There are between four and 10 decision makers and influencers that are involved in the B2B buying process. Therefore, it is not unusual for the buying process to take at least six months to two years depending on the complexity of the buyer's requirements.

Difference #3
The Selling Process

In a B2C environment, companies can sell a product or service using two basic channels: (a) a retail outlet and (b) direct sales – mail order via catalogues or e-commerce website. In a B2B environment, the sales channels are more elaborate even though there are fewer total customers to sell to. A B2B company is characterised by well-paid salespeople with in-depth product knowledge – that's not an option as the products are complex and that's why you see many engineers eventually taking up the role of salespeople. Besides that, a B2B company also has distributors, business partners and independent agents who engage in selling as well as the fulfilment of the orders. It is a much more complex web.

Difference #4
The Cost Of Sales

Because of the way a B2B sales channel is structured, the cost of selling is actually quite high even though B2B companies don't usually advertise. That is why most B2B companies have lower margins compared to B2C companies. The cost of sales for a B2B company would typically go into sales commissions; training the sales team, distributors and partners; exhibiting in trade shows where B2B buyers congregate and sales lead generation. For a B2C company, the cost of sales is typically made up of components such as advertising, promotions, public relations activities, discounts and bundling deals.

Difference #5
The Communications Channels

As B2B companies have a smaller pool of potential customers, they typically don't use mass communications techniques such as TV commercials, radio commercials, billboards or print advertisements in newspapers. They will use targeted media instead such as trade or industry journals, seminars, industry networking events, technical forums and trade or industry associations. You may argue that some big B2B companies like GE, IBM and Intel advertise aggressively. That may be true but you need to bear in mind that these companies are advertising to maintain the brand. The brand is already built. They are just advertising to keep the brand in the minds of customers. And even then, the advertising budget for these B2B giants is nothing like that of B2C giants such as Coca-Cola, Gillette and Nike.

Difference #6
Lead Generation Versus Sales Generation
B2B marketing campaigns are typically designed to generate a lead which will then be passed on to a member of the sales team or a distributor to follow up. It is very unlikely for a B2B marketing campaign to generate a direct sale unlike in B2C marketing.

A B2C marketing campaign is usually more immediate and designed to create the urge to rush out and buy something. Unfortunately, most B2C companies do a bad job these days when advertising their brands because they place creativity above strategy. Some of these campaigns simply don't make sense. For example, we saw an advertising campaign from Buick – a brand of car owned by General Motors – that featured Tiger Woods as a spokesperson. That was long before Tiger Woods' marital troubles. Hang on a second. A Buick is a car that is driven mostly by middle-aged, middle-class folk in America. You really believe that people will believe that somebody like Tiger Woods would drive a Buick?

Well, that's just an interesting distraction. We now need to move on to the biggest difference between a B2B and a B2C brand. We have dedicated the next section to cover this topic.

DIFFERENCE #7: THE RISK FACTOR IN A B2B PURCHASE

Buying a B2B product carries a lot more risk because it usually involves more money and it is usually other people's money. Let's say that you bought the wrong brand of shampoo for your children. What is the worst that can happen? They might throw a tantrum and refuse to wash their hair but you will still have your title of "daddy" or "mummy" for a few more decades to come. But if you make a mistake when purchasing supply chain management software for your company or if you buy the wrong heat seal packaging machine for your production line, it could affect the company's operations, cause your company to lose millions of dollars and ultimately cost you your job. That is why, when you buy a highly risky B2B product like supply chain management software, you will tend to buy from a strong brand.

Does IBM make better products than its competitors? Not necessarily. But IBM has a far stronger brand. So strong that it inspired this saying in the business world, "Nobody ever got fired for buying IBM." When Jacky was working in the United States right after his graduation, he often heard purchasing managers saying, "Jacky, when in doubt, always buy Big Blue (IBM's nickname). You can't go wrong with good old Big Blue."

When Jacky pointed out that IBM products actually cost more than its competitors' (sometimes a lot more) and were not necessarily better, he was told it didn't matter because nobody ever got fired for buying IBM. That is the true measure of the power of a brand. People buy your brand even though it is more expensive. For a lot of people, paying more for IBM is justifiable because IBM is a strong brand. Wouldn't you like to be in that position rather than having to compete on price all the time?

Buying a mainframe computer – as with any B2B purchase – involves a lot of risks and that is why buyers tend to stick with the stronger (meaning more differentiated) brands to guard against the risks. There are basically five major risks that are associated with B2B products or services. We discuss them below.

1. Technical Risk

Will the product perform as it is supposed to? Many B2B products or services are technical in nature. And buyers are very concerned about the technical risks involved. If the product doesn't perform, then the buyer's business could be severely affected. So what do buyers do? They buy from leading brands that have built up strong reputations in that particular category.

Many B2B companies are very secure in the knowledge that their products or services are technically superior compared to those of their competitors. We have consulted for many companies that can actually claim (and prove) that they have a better product or service than the two leading brands in their categories but they are still nowhere near the leading brands in terms of market share. At the end of the day, they find themselves losing out to their competitors. Why is that so?

B2B companies often make the mistake of assuming perfect knowledge on the part of their target customers. They think that because their products and services are better, people will automatically buy from them. But customers don't have perfect knowledge! They can't possibly know more about your product or service than you. That is why their decisions will still be influenced by the brand.

2. Financial Risk

Is it good value for money? B2B buyers are not just concerned about the cost of their purchase. They are concerned about the value that they are getting. A product or service that is the cheapest is not necessarily the best value for money because it may not be able to perform certain functions, it may become obsolete fast, it may not be scalable or it may have a lot of compatibility issues.

We have a client that has managed to develop a powerful three-direction sensor gate that can read radio frequency identification device (RFID)-tagged merchandise with almost 100 per cent accuracy. You have probably seen such sensor gates located at store entrances and exits to detect unpaid merchandise being taken out of the store.

This company's sensor gate is superior compared to its competitors from Germany, South Korea and Japan. And it is priced lower than its competitors' sensors. Sounds like a winning formula, right? Wrong. This company only managed to sell a handful of these powerful and cheap sensor gates. Why? Because this company's potential clients do not perceive it as a strong brand. As a result, they would rather buy from the more well-known brands despite the higher cost and lower accuracy. Strong brands mitigate the financial risks faced by a buyer.

3. Delivery Risk

Can the company deliver on time? This is a major concern for B2B buyers. We are sure you have had this experience before. Maybe you hired a cheap-and-good but not-so-reputable printing company to print an important brochure for a new product launch and the printer couldn't deliver the entire order on time. That would have disrupted your product launch and maybe caused a heart attack or two. We are willing to bet that you will use a more reputable printer next time.

Delivery risk is a very real concern for companies. The most direct example would be courier services. If you have an important document to send overseas and it has to be there by a certain time, which courier would you use? The cheap-and-good but not-so-well-known courier or FedEx? Our guess is that you would use FedEx or one of the other reputable brands like DHL or UPS. Maybe the lesser-known brand can still deliver as well as the more established brands but B2B buyers are often not willing to take that risk – especially for big and important jobs. That is why they will buy from a strong brand to reduce the risk of non-delivery of the product or service.

4. Service Risk

Will the company be around long enough to provide after-sales service? If you buy a server from Sun Microsystems, you can be quite sure that the company will be around long enough to service the machines that you have purchased but the same cannot be said for a less-established server brand.

Most B2B products require servicing in order to function properly. And some of these products are so specialised that only the company that made them have the necessary tools and expertise to service them. How many times have you heard about companies throwing away a product they have bought simply because their supplier couldn't provide reliable after-sales service or because the company they bought from has closed down? Probably more often than you should. If you have a strong brand, it reduces the perceived service risk and, as a result, buyers may be more willing to buy from you.

5. Professional Risk

How will this purchase affect how my peers view me? This is a very important consideration for many B2B buyers. Let's say you are an architect and you need computer-aided design (CAD) software. If you buy a brand that other architects have a low opinion of, it will affect your reputation as an architect. And when word gets out that you are using "sub-standard" software, it might affect your business.

If you are a professional, you probably want other people to see you as a professional. And part of projecting this image is to use tools or brands that will enhance the image that you are an expert in what you do. For example, if you claim to be a professional video production house, you probably want your clients to see you using professional video editing systems like AVID instead of something that is more mass market.

The above are very real concerns for the typical B2B buyer. So what do customers do to protect themselves? They buy from companies with strong brand reputations. Strong brands act as a guarantee of performance for buyers. If you are not sure which brand of photocopier to buy, you will probably default to Xerox. Is it the best? Toshiba or Minolta might be just as good if not better but Xerox is a stronger brand, so you will seriously consider it.

If you are looking to buy accounting software and you are not sure what to buy, you will probably go with the brand that other companies buy. It might be ACCPAC. It might be MYOB. But you would buy a known brand.

If you want your books audited for a potential investor, do you go with a small certified public accounting (CPA) firm or one of the Big Four? One of the Big Four, probably. They may not necessarily be better but they have better brands. It gives you and your potential investor that extra ounce of confidence. That is why branding is critical for a B2B company.

ACCORDING TO JOHN

John A Quelch is the Lincoln Filene Professor of Business Administration at Harvard Business School. In an article titled 'B2B Branding: Does It Work?' written by Professor Quelch on 28 November 2007 for the *Harvard Business Review*, he mentioned that many CEOs of B2B companies view marketing as the domain of B2C brands.[10]

According to Professor Quelch, CEOs of B2B companies should pay attention to brand building because of the following reasons:

Firstly, B2B marketers will have to address thousands of small businesses as well as enterprise customers. They will not be able to do so economically by using the traditional direct sales force since they can't possibly hire that many people.

Secondly, if left unattended, individual managers will have a tendency to carry out their own ad hoc marketing programmes. The result will be a hotchpotch of corporate logos, taglines and packaging that will confuse customers and send out the message that the company is a highly disorganised one.

Thirdly, B2B marketers are starting to realise that if they develop brand awareness among their customers' customers, they will be able to capture a larger share of channel margins and build loyalty that can protect them against lower-priced competitors in the longer run.

---

[10] http://hbswk.hbs.edu/item/5819.html

Professor Quelch also asked readers to consider these examples:

1. Intel is probably the ultimate ingredient brand since it makes no sales to end consumers. Despite that, Intel was able to build consumer demand pull for its chips, which required every PC manufacturer to incorporate these chips into their products and use the "Intel Inside" logo on their advertisements. Other ingredient brands include GORE-TEX, Teflon and even the Boeing 787 Dreamliner (as a differentiating ingredient for early adopter airlines).

2. GE and Microsoft are hybrid brands with some direct-to-consumer sales that have helped build the reputations of what are primarily B2B firms. But although these enterprises are selling primarily to businesses, they want to be in touch with end consumers as well. According to Professor Quelch, that is a source of competitive advantage in driving their innovation agendas.

3. Accenture is an IT consulting company that sells nothing to consumers. But its "Performance Delivered" campaign, backed by its spokesperson, golf legend Tiger Woods, has created a positive awareness of the brand among hundreds of thousands of people who may be working for the enterprises to which Accenture consults (or is seeking to consult). Furthermore, we also cannot underestimate the motivational value of inviting top customers, prospects and employees to golf events involving the legendary Tiger Woods. Of course, Tiger Woods has recently fallen out of favour but Professor Quelch believed that when the Tiger was still in vogue, his presence helped Accenture in its brand building.

4. Would Dupont's shareholder value be the same today if the company had not undertaken the efforts to make consumers become aware of Nylon? Did Lycra and Stainmaster and linked these innovations to the Dupont name? Probably not.

IS B2B BRANDING A FINANCIAL BURDEN TO SHAREHOLDERS?

Some B2B companies have objected to branding because they are of the opinion that branding is not maximising shareholder value. They would rather focus on acquisitions, cost cutting, expanding the distribution network, etc. All of these are great to have but they don't necessarily add more value to a company than branding. Do you know how many mergers and acquisitions fail? Around 70 per cent. But that doesn't answer the question of whether B2B branding is a financial burden to shareholders. Let's examine the evidence.

We would like to quote an article called 'B2B Branding: A Financial Burden To Shareholders' written by Lars Ohnemus and published by the *Harvard Business Review* on 15 March 2009. The article mentioned that based on an examination of almost 1,700 companies listed either on the US or European stock exchange, B2B companies that have a balanced corporate branding strategy generally yield up to 7 per cent higher returns to shareholders. The study concluded that it is important for key executives of companies, and that includes members of the board, to have a systematic method to assess and monitor the strategic branding position of their company and how well their branding investments are performing against competitors. The study also revealed that shareholders should insist on having systematic performance feedback from the corporation on all key items in the balance sheet – and that includes branding. The study found that only a handful of the companies in the study have an optimal balance between branding and their financial performance.

There you have it. Branding is actually important for B2B companies because it adds value to shareholders – not financial burden.

MEASURING THE ROI IN B2B BRANDING

Whether you are a public listed company or not, you need to measure the return on investment (ROI) for your branding project. How do you do that? The ultimate aim of developing a strong B2B brand is so that you can generate maximum shareholder value. But how do you know you are on the right track? How do you know that you will have a higher than 50/50 chance of maximising shareholder value? In short, how do you know that your branding programme is working?

The answer is you first measure how well your brand is performing in the only arena that matters – in the minds of your customers. You need to take a "before" and "after" picture of the brand. The before picture is taken through the Perception Audit, which is designed to measure the perception of key stakeholders regarding your brand vis-à-vis your competitors. Then you develop and implement your branding strategy. Once the strategy has been developed, approved by your board of directors and implemented, you will need to take an after picture at regular intervals – the usual interval is every six months for two to three years depending on your budget. The after picture is done through an exercise known as Brand Tracking.

From the Brand Tracking, you will know if perception of the brand has improved. If yes, continue to do what you have been doing. If no, you need to find out what has gone wrong and rectify it. We spent a lot of time developing and refining a brand strategy for one particular client. After the strategy was implemented, perception didn't improve. That got us wondering if our strategy was the right one. We attempted to ascertain – from the client's customers – why perception had not improved.

It turned out that our client's customers perceived a lot of inconsistency between what management said and the actions and words of the salespeople. We dug further to find out why this was so and the root cause was that new members of staff were not being trained properly. So, we made certain recommendations to fix that problem. You need to find the root cause of the problem and fix it quickly so that perception can improve.

In A Nutshell

In the past, many CEOs of B2B companies that we met did not think that branding had any relevance for a B2B company. This thinking has changed dramatically over the last six years as CEOs discovered that in a hypercompetitive business world where competitors can – and will – copy everything they do, often at a lower cost. In a hypercompetitive world where everyone is a match – more or less – for everyone else, the brand provides the ultimate competitive advantage.

But it is worth examining why B2B CEOs used to object to branding (and some still do). The eight key objections are:

1. B2B buyers are rational creatures who are not affected by intangibles like brands.
2. B2B purchases are all about relationships.
3. Price is the only thing that matters in a B2B purchase.
4. B2B products or services are largely invisible so branding won't help.
5. Our customers know a superior product when they see one.
6. B2B products are not aspirational.

7. B2B companies don't sell to millions so branding is not needed.
8. B2B products or services are too complex to be branded.

The biggest difference between a B2B and B2C brand is *risk*. Buying a B2B product or service involves a lot of risks such as technical risk, financial risk, delivery risk, service risk and professional risk. Because there is a lot of risk involved, B2B buyers tend to gravitate towards stronger brands.

According to renowned Harvard Business School Professor John Quelch, branding is important for any B2B company because:

1. B2B companies cannot economically address thousands of potential customers using the traditional direct sales force.
2. If left unattended, individual managers will each do their own ad hoc marketing, which will result in a lot of customer confusion.
3. B2B companies are realising that developing a strong brand can help them capture a larger share of channel margins as well as build loyalty.

A balanced corporate branding programme has also been found to help companies generate up to 7 per cent better returns on investments. However, companies need to keep track of the brand through a Brand Tracking exercise that measures improvements in customers' perception of the brand. This is important because if perceptions don't improve, the brand will not be strong and, as a result, it will not perform well.

B2B

Other Branding Myths That Can Kill Your Company

THEprevious chapter was dedicated to debunking the myth that branding is only for B2C products or services. If CEOs of B2B companies continue to hold on to the belief that branding is not important just because they are not selling to the masses like Coca-Cola or Nike, then many B2B companies will be stuck in the commodities trap – forced to compete on price alone and yet still not able to make much headway against competitors with stronger brands. This is an observation that we have noted from our extensive dealings with B2B companies over the years.

Now that we have dealt with the myth that branding is only for B2C companies, products and services, there are other common myths of branding that apply to both B2B and B2C companies that we would like to deal with in this chapter. What we discuss in this chapter is also based on dealings that we have had over the years with B2B companies from a multitude of industries.

Branding Myth #1
The Return On Investment For Branding Cannot Be Measured
This is something that many CFOs have told us after they have sat through one of our branding presentations. Jacky often had CFOs walk up to him after his presentation and say something along the lines of, "I enjoyed your presentation and what you have presented is interesting and makes sense but I don't think I can justify embarking on a branding project because there is simply no way for me to measure the returns on investment. As the group's CFO and a CPA, I have to be able to measure the returns on every dollar spent. If you can't measure it, how do you know that it's working?"

This is a valid argument and something that we totally agree with. We can understand these CFOs' scepticism. When Jacky was programme manager for branding at IE Singapore, he worked with many local and international brand consulting firms. He asked every one of them how they measured the ROI on a branding project and got a wide range of answers. None of them satisfied the requirements of the CFOs of the many internationalising companies that IE Singapore served at that time.

One afternoon in 2004, when Wilson went to IE Singapore for a meeting, Jacky ran into him and asked him this question, "Wilson, you have a Master's of Science degree in International Finance and Strategy, right? So, tell me, how would you measure the ROI on a branding project from a financial point of view?"

Wilson's answer was simply this, "My friend, you cannot. The problem with most people is that they try to find a direct correlation between a dollar spent on branding and the return, in terms of sales, on that dollar spent. If you do that, you will only run into one brick wall after another. You can measure the ROI on branding but you must know what you are measuring."

Jacky asked, "And what should I be measuring?"

Wilson said, "You need to take a before and after picture of the brand. The before picture is done through a Perception Audit. This measures the state of the brand in the minds of customers. How do customers perceive the brand? Good, bad or ugly? With this, you at least have a starting point for the branding project. You now know where you are. Next, you run the branding project to try to improve the perception of the brand or to change it. Then, you take an after picture. This is done through a Brand Tracking exercise. It measures how customers perceive the brand after the branding project has been implemented. The improvement in the perception is your ROI on the branding dollar spent."

To this, Jacky said, "That makes sense. If perception improves, the brand is stronger. If the brand is stronger, then potential customers will be more likely to buy from this brand or, at least, give it some serious consideration. Over time, this should lead to growth. So, if we measure the perception, we can get a good idea of how it will affect the company's financial performance in time to come. Okay, this is something that we can use to convince CFOs. Nice work, man."

The above conversation formed the basis for StrategiCom's *Consilium* brand strategy model, which is used in most of the branding projects that we undertake for clients. That model formed the missing link in the measurement of branding ROI. Ultimately, you want your investment in branding to yield better sales and financial returns, among other things, but if you are measuring the ROI on branding, you need to be measuring the improvement in your brand's perception with the only people who matter – your stakeholders.

And perception is something that is very quantifiable. You measure it and you can find a correlation between the implementation of your branding strategy and the improvement in your brand perception. If perception of your brand improves, you will have a better chance of improving your market share, sales performance, etc. That is how you measure if your branding dollar has been well spent.

And even if the perception of your brand has not improved, the Brand Tracking exercise will help you uncover what has gone wrong during the implementation of the strategy. We had one client that got us very worried because despite everything that it had done, perception of the brand remained flat. The client asked us to find out why and from the Brand Tracking exercise, it was discovered that the company's HR department could not cope with the training of new employees because of the heavy workload. In just one year, this client had expanded its headcount substantially and most of the new employees were customer facing. The lack of training and indoctrination into the corporate culture affected the way they communicated with the client's customers and, as a result, perception of the brand did not improve. We recommended the setting up of an Organisational Development department to take care of this function, and over time that helped the client to gradually improve the perception of its brand.

Branding Myth #2
Branding Is Only For Big Companies
So many companies that we met in the past told us that they believed that branding was very important but they were currently too small for branding so would undergo a branding exercise when they got big. If that is how you think, then we have bad news for you. Branding is not the *reward* for success. It is the *reason* why the successful – and big – global brands that you see today became successful in the first place.

If you think that branding is only for big companies, then you subscribe to the idea that branding is the reward for success. It is not. The first type is the brand building activity. This is when you develop a powerful branding strategy and implement it consistently over a period of time to build the brand. After the brand is built, you need to undertake a different type of branding activity – the brand maintenance activity.

Which activity you undertake depends on where you are right now. Brands that have already been well-established such as Intel, Nike, Honeywell, Apple,

Cisco, Starbucks, BlackBerry, Singapore Airlines, IBM and Mercedes-Benz need to undertake brand maintenance activities to keep the brand in the customers' mind. When you look at the branding efforts of these big companies, remember that it is for brand maintenance. These behemoths actually started out a long time ago as tiny tots. Yes, they were once small potatoes too. But they put in the time, the effort and the resources to build their brands in the early days. And that is the reason they became big.

If you are reading this book, you are probably an SME trying to grow into an MNC. If you wait until you are a big brand before you take your branding strategy seriously, you will be waiting for an eternity and the day will never come. The market you are operating in today is not really a market anymore. It is a killing field in which you have many competitors who are hungry and armed to the teeth – ever ready to cut your throat and steal your customers. And whatever you can do, they can too. They will copy all your great ideas and innovations, and they will do it better and cheaper. The only thing that they can't copy is your brand. If you don't pay attention to your branding strategy to gain a competitive advantage, how are you going to grow in the face of all the roadblocks that your competitors are going to erect before you? For every move you make, there will be an equal and opposite countermove. You push, they push back. So, nobody makes any headway. There is no way you can pull away from the pack if you still hold on to the idea that branding is the reward for success and not the reason for it.

Branding Myth #3
Branding Is The Job Of The Marketing Department
Many people equate branding with marketing and vice versa. As we have discussed earlier in this book, they are related but are not exactly the same. But because of this misconception, for many companies, the branding function automatically falls onto the laps of the marketing department.

Some of the companies that we have met are even weirder. They put their accountants in charge of branding. We often ask these companies why they put the accountant in charge of branding and the answer that we get is usually, "Since branding involves money, the person in charge should be the accountant." No offence to accountants or marketers around the world but the chief branding officer of any company should not be anyone other than the CEO. Shouldn't the CEO be relieved of some duties such as branding since he/

she is already so busy with a thousand and one things? Unfortunately, this is one role that the CEO cannot delegate.

Why is that so?

The answer lies in the fact that the gap between the best and the worst product or service in any given category has closed so much that even if you buy a cheap entry-level product, it will still usually get the job done. In some cases, the cheap entry-level product gets it done even better. Some years back, Jacky bought an expensive state-of-the-art DVD player that looked like something made from the exoskeleton of *The Terminator*. Jacky's brother bought a cheap DVD player that cost one-tenth the price of the high-end DVD player. The cheap DVD player had no problem playing all kinds of DVDs whereas the expensive one refused to play certain DVDs.

Since the quality gap between the best and the worst has closed tremendously in recent years due to technological breakthroughs, what is left to differentiate your product or service? The brand. This also means that branding is a critical function within the company. For such a critical function, if the CEO doesn't drive it, who will? For such a critical function, if the CEO doesn't take charge of it personally, then the company is in trouble. And if the CEO doesn't get his/her hands dirty so to speak, it sends out the message to the rest of the company that the issue of branding is probably not very important and, therefore, no one will pay any attention to it.

We will not take on a branding project if the CEO tells us that he/she will not be actively involved in the process. The CEO needs to drive the project. If he/she doesn't, the project becomes a white elephant that wastes the company's time, effort and resources. Branding is – and always should be – the job of the CEO. Look at some of the brands that you might admire. You will see that for each of these brands, the CEO is very hands-on in the brand building and brand maintenance activities. And you will very often find that when the CEO takes his/her eyes off the brand, the company runs into trouble eventually. Simple observation will tell you that this is true.

Branding Myth #4
My Products Or Services Are Better, So There Is No Need For Branding

Someone once said that in order to catch more mice, you have to build a better mousetrap. We agree with that statement but unfortunately, over time, many people have misunderstood what a better mousetrap means. In the past, when mousetraps were slow and unreliable, the definition of a better mousetrap meant that you had to solve the *quality* problems. These days, however, we imagine that mousetraps are extremely effective and reliable in terms of engineering so the definition of a better mousetrap needs to change. If you want to build a better mousetrap today, you have to make your mousetrap more *attractive* to the mouse. In other words, you need to "brand" your mousetrap.

The same thing applies to products and services. You may think that your product or service is better than the competition's in terms of all the quantifiable performance measures but just because you claim that yours is better doesn't mean that it will attract the mice or, in your case, the customers. In this day and age where the quality gap has narrowed to such an extent that it makes very little difference, being better will not get you very far because of three reasons.

Reason number one is that the customers don't really know – in most cases – what is better. You are assuming that your customers are as knowledgeable as you but most customers cannot have the kind of expertise or knowledge that you have in your field. So, how would they know which is better? Even if you show them test results that prove that you are better, those test results might not be meaningful or useful to them. We have seen this phenomenon first hand. When CEOs are presented with the option of buying computers powered by an Intel chip or an AMD chip, most will say, "Just buy the one with Intel inside but make sure we get a good price." Even when they are presented with benchmarking tests that show that the AMD chip actually performs 20 per cent better, they will still default to Intel. Many years ago, before Jacky joined StrategiCom, he worked for a subsidiary of a very well-established public listed company. In order to save costs, Jacky tried to get his former boss to switch to AMD-powered computers. Together with the vice president of IT, Jacky made a pitch – using test result after test result – to try to convince the president of the company. Jacky thought they had made a watertight case for the AMD machines. The president ended up approving only Intel-powered computers. When Jacky asked him why, the president said, "*Aiyah*! Intel is better, *lah*." The president of this company was actually not wrong. Intel was better as far as the president was concerned because he perceived Intel to be the better *brand*. Branding matters after all.

Reason number two is that nobody is going to believe you when you say that you are better because you are a biased party. You have a vested interest. Of course, you will say that you are better than your competitors. Either that or you will say that you are not as good but you are a lot cheaper. If you don't have a strong brand compared to your competitors, even if you can prove that you are better, customers might not believe you. In the previous chapter, we talked about the risks involved in buying a B2B product or service. There is also risk involved in buying a B2C product or service although to a lesser extent. Whenever there is risk involved, what would you do as a buyer? Default to the strong brands. If you behave that way, wouldn't it be reasonable to expect that your customers will too?

Reason number three is that your competitors can copy what you do and eventually match you in terms of quality and performance, and if your competitors have stronger brands, then the market will see that they are defending their market. The market is more forgiving – or blind – when you have a strong brand. If a weaker brand copies a stronger brand, then the weaker brand is labelled a copycat.

This is something that happened to an innovative Singapore company that specialises in the engineering and manufacturing of polycarbonate lenses for spectacles. It came up with a new type of lens that is thinner, lighter and clearer than what the top two players in the world could manage. We were told by the company that within four months, the top brands copied its product and came out with their own versions – without violating its patents. And when this Singapore company tried to convince its potential customers that it had invented this type of lens and the other players had copied the product, it was met with a lot of scepticism. This company learnt a big lesson that day: Even if you are better, you might still lose if you don't have a better brand.

Branding Myth #5
I Am Selling Cheap, So There Is No Need For Branding

We often tell our clients that there are two ways to get business – differentiate your brand or sell cheap. If you are not differentiated, meaning that your customers cannot perceive any useful difference between you and the other brands out there, then they will just buy from whoever is cheaper. The same thing applies to you when you are the buyer. You either buy from strong – meaning highly differentiated – brands or you buy from the cheapest supplier.

If you are selling cheap, there is no need for branding so this myth is not a myth, right? Yes, as long as everything remains *ceteris paribus* – a term often used in economics that means "everything else being equal". The problem for many companies that sell cheap is that there are so many competitors that can also sell cheap. The race to the bottom of the price chain is never-ending. You can never be the cheapest player because there will always be someone out there who can match you for price no matter how low you go.

Your customers will usually have a shortlist of suppliers that they want to buy from – typically four to five based on our clients' experience. From this shortlist, if they can't perceive any difference between the various players, they will buy from the cheapest one. The reverse is also true. Your customers will usually have a price range, or a budget. If they can shortlist suppliers who can meet their price requirements and specifications, then how will they choose? They will buy from the strongest brand among all these cheap suppliers. Ironic, isn't it? But it makes perfect sense. Think about it for a moment. If there is no difference between the brands, you buy from the cheapest. If there is no difference between the prices, you buy from the strongest brand. It's as simple as that.

The bad news is that although you can find buyers if you sell anything cheap enough, you will still need to brand your cheap product or service because there will always be competitors that can match you for price. However, if you have a *structural cost advantage* – a cost advantage that comes about naturally because of the way you do business – that allows you to be the cheapest player in the market, then you don't have to worry about branding. Dell has a structural cost advantage. Dell sells direct. HP doesn't. So, Dell has a cost advantage that it can use to generate big volumes. We will discuss this in more detail when we come to Rule No. 5 of branding.

Branding Myth #6

If It Works For The Leading Brands, It Must Work For Me

This is actually a very dangerous myth. Many companies have this follow-the-leader mentality, or as psychologists call it – the herd mentality. There is absolutely nothing wrong in wanting to emulate successful companies – nothing at all – but the problem is deciding what to emulate. And this is where many companies fall flat on their faces because they are too lazy to think. They will look at the leading brands in the market and copy them blindly. Their thinking is, "If it works so well for the big brands, then it must be a good thing. Therefore, I will do the same." It doesn't work that way.

There are a lot of things that the leading brands can do that you can't. You can copy their strategy but it will not work for you because of a couple of reasons. One, you are not the originator of the strategy. Therefore, you will not be given due consideration by customers. A brand is simply an idea that you own in the minds of customers and the mind only has room for one brand per idea. If Milwaukee Electric Tool Corp. was the originator of the idea of "ergonomic power tools" and it is successful in owning that idea, you can copy Milwaukee's idea but you can't own it. So, you can produce your own line of ergonomic power tools but you will not overtake Milwaukee.

Two, there are so many competitors out there that can do the same thing. They, too, can copy the leader. So, in the end, it's stalemate. Nobody gains because everybody is the same. Some CEOs have asked us, "But what choice do we have? If we don't follow, we will be left behind." This is true but also bear in mind that copying the leader will only help you maintain your position, not improve it. If you are happy with that, then there is nothing wrong with this approach but most companies want to improve, not stand still, unless you are already the No. 1.

Today, Samsung is one of the most highly-regarded consumer electronics companies. But Jacky still remembers that when he was studying in the United States back in the early nineties, Samsung was a brand that nobody wanted because it was seen as a cheap and inferior copy of leading Japanese brands. In those days, Samsung adopted a follow-the-leader strategy. It was a fast follower but that didn't help much. Then, Samsung decided to invest in design, innovation and brand building. It decided that it was done with copying the leading brands of the day such as Sony. When that happened, Samsung's fortunes started to turn around. Today, Samsung is the leader in many categories of consumer electronics products such as LED TV. Samsung pioneered this category, and the clarity and sharpness of these LED TVs are simply astounding. The Japanese players were left in the dust. Not content, Samsung went on to launch 3D LED TVs that further solidified its position as the leader in LED TVs.

When Samsung copied the leaders, it didn't get anywhere. When it decided to do its own thing, it got somewhere and became a big brand. Sure, not many of you can afford to spend billions of dollars in R&D the way Samsung did but there are still ways around this problem. We will discuss this in more detail under Rule No. 4 of branding.

Branding Myth #7

Brand Strategy Must Be Localised Because Each Market Is Different

This is again something that is very perplexing. Many CEOs tell us that they need to adopt a different branding strategy for each market because every single one is different and they have to pander to local market conditions. Yes, you do need to take into account local market conditions – it would be suicidal not to – but you don't change your brand strategy. You change your tactics. The brand strategy should remain the same. This is something that smaller companies can and should learn from the global brands. The successful global brands don't change their brand strategy every time they enter a new market. They maintain the brand strategy but change their tactics.

For example. Starbucks has over 9,000 outlets around the world. Starbucks didn't change its strategy for every single market. Starbucks is still the "gourmet coffee brand" regardless of which market it enters. Coca-Cola is The Real Thing regardless of which market it enters. If you change your strategy for every market, you are going to run into so many problems. You are going to have to develop a new strategy for every single market. That is all right if you have five markets. What if you want to enter 50 different markets? On top of that, if you have a different strategy for every market, you are going to end up with an extremely confused brand. That's fine if you feel that your life is way too easy and you need something more challenging to make it worth getting out of bed every day.

What you should do is keep the brand strategy the same but the way in which you execute the strategy in every market can be different. Barilla is "Italy's No. 1 Pasta". That strategy remains the same regardless of which country Barilla ventures into. All that changes is maybe how Barilla runs its marketing campaigns in each market. That is what you should do. Look at GE. It wants to be No. 1 or No. 2 in every market that it ventures into. That doesn't change. What changes is how GE carries out this strategy in every market. Remember: The strategy remains the same but you can add local flavour to how you execute this strategy.

Mercedes-Benz is positioned as the prestigious brand. That means it is expensive. If the local distributor of Mercedes-Benz in a certain market tells Mercedes-Benz that the market for mid-priced cars far outstrips the market for premium cars and Mercedes-Benz should lower its prices to compete, what do you think Mercedes-Benz should do? We would ignore that market and seek another market. Don't you think it is ridiculous for Mercedes-Benz to keep changing its brand positioning according to the market? It is. So, don't do the same thing to your brand. You will end up with a mess and then you will have to pay consultants like us a lot of money to come in and help you clean it up. Not that we mind but we would rather come in and help you get to the next level of growth than dig you out of a hole that you have dug your brand into because you believe in this localisation myth.

Branding Myth #8
Brand Strategy Must Be Changed Regularly To Keep It Fresh
There are two types of people who believe strongly in changing the brand strategy regularly. The first type is brand consultants who want their clients to keep "refreshing their brand" so that there will be a constant flow of work for them. Jacky met many such brand consultants during his three-year stint as programme manager for branding at IE Singapore. It is only logical when you think about it. If a brand consultant develops a brand strategy that can last the client a lifetime, where is the repeat business potential? We don't subscribe to this because we are of the opinion that if we develop a lasting brand strategy that helps clients to grow, they will come back and engage us to do other things – and over the last four years, we have seen this happen over and over again.

The second type of people who believe in changing the brand strategy regularly are company bosses who fail to get the strategy right in the first place. Again, think about it. If your strategy is the right one, why do you need to keep changing or refreshing (the term that many people like to use) it?

We have observed that many SMEs don't spend enough time on their brand strategy. Some company bosses have even told us, "What is strategy? It is useless. We need to focus on sales. Build up distribution networks. Motivate the distributors. Keep them happy and they will keep selling." Again, we must say that there is nothing wrong at all with building up distribution networks and all that but that is a *push strategy*. You have to keep pushing your products down the distribution pipe. If you have a strong brand, you will add a *pull strategy* to the mix.

Having a good brand strategy is like having a good exhaust system for your car. In order for the engine to produce power, it needs to take in a mixture of air and atomised fuel. This mixture is burnt to generate power. The burnt mixture then needs to be expelled from the engine through the exhaust system. If you have a poorly designed exhaust system, the waste gas cannot get out of the engine fast enough and that will result in the fresh air fuel mixture not being able to get in quickly. If you want your products to move quickly through the distribution pipe, you need a push and pull strategy. You need a well-designed exhaust system and once you get the exhaust system right, you don't keep changing it. The way to do it is to spend enough time getting the design of the exhaust system right before you fit it into the car.

The same goes for your brand strategy. Don't leave it till the very last minute. Don't be lazy. Give yourself enough time to get it done right. Some companies come to us and tell us that they have one month to get the entire branding exercise done because they are launching a new product at a major exhibition. That means we need to create a new brand name and a new branding strategy within one month. The normal process takes four months. We tell these companies that the fees for undertaking such an exercise will be the same regardless of whether it is done in one month or four months so why not take four months to get it done properly. They say they can't wait because they have booked space at the exhibition and have already announced that they will be launching a new product. Well, for one such client, we actually managed to get the project done in one month but the team worked almost 24/7. Still, the client was happy with the end result. We also thought that we had done a pretty good job but that's not the point. The point is if you leave it till the last minute, you are taking a huge risk regardless of how good your consultants are.

Branding Myth #9
I Have No Competitors, Therefore I Don't Need Branding
As brand strategy consultants, one of the first questions that we need to ask a potential client is, "Who are your competitors?" The reason being if we don't understand the competitive landscape, we won't be able to do a very good job at developing the brand strategy. Every now and then, we come across company bosses who keep insisting that they have no competitors. After they make that statement, we will continue the conversation and talk about other things but we keep coming back to the issue of competitors. After a couple of times, these company bosses will usually get quite agitated with us and tell us, "No, no, no! You don't understand. Let me explain to you again one more time, okay? We are really quite a unique company because we are [so and so and so]. Therefore, we don't have competitors. We are unique, you see?"

There is no such thing as having no competition unless you operate in a monopolistic market whereby the government has passed a law that states you are the only company allowed to sell a certain product or service. Other than that, you will always have competitors. Even if you have invented something that is truly new and groundbreaking, you will still have competitors. When Xerox launched the world's first automatic plain paper photocopier, it was unique. Xerox could have said that it had no competitors but competition still existed in the form of thermal photocopiers and eventual copycats. When Caterpillar launched the world's first bulldozer that ran on tracks instead of wheels, it could claim that it had no competitors and therefore did not need branding. But competitors eventually arrived and if Caterpillar had not already built the brand by then, it would have had a hard time. When UNIVAC launched the world's first mainframe computer, it had no competitors. No need to focus on brand building, right? Then what happened? IBM arrived and ran away with the market. Sure, IBM arrived late but it won because UNIVAC hadn't focussed on the brand.

You cannot operate under the assumption that you have no competitors even if you have invented something so new that the world has not seen anything like it. Even if you have no competitors in the beginning, before you manage to celebrate the first anniversary of your invention, you will have a host of me-too competitors snapping at your heels. If you didn't use whatever lead time you had to build the brand up in the minds of your customers and potential customers, you will need a miracle to stay alive in the face of all the hungry pretenders to your crown.

Branding Myth #10

My Customers Know Who I Am, So There Is No Need For Branding

This is another common myth – especially among B2B company bosses. The reason being that B2B companies do not have as many potential customers as B2C companies. If you are a B2B company, you sell a product or service to another company.

A typical B2B client that we serve usually has less than 2,000 potential customers worldwide, some have fewer than 50. If your potential market size is 2,000, it is actually quite easy to target these customers and once you have secured a customer, it is likely that you will get to know this customer quite well because you don't have that many customers to serve. A B2C company like

Apple will have hundreds of millions of customers so there is no way it can get to know each one well. Therefore, it is logical to argue that a B2B company with a limited number of customers doesn't need branding because its customers would already know them very well.

Yes, your customers may know you but what do they know you for? One of the first things that Wilson does upon the commencement of any branding project is to run a one-day brand management workshop for the client's senior management and the first question that he asks is, "Why do customers buy from you?" All the senior management then offer very detailed explanations as to why customers buy from them. We then ask the customers the same question and compare the answers.

About 99 per cent of the time, there is a gap between what senior management says and what its customers say. Sometimes, this gap is very dangerous. For example, if you think that customers buy from you because your service level is the best in the industry but your customers actually buy from you because of the reputation of the third-party products you carry, then this is a dangerous gap. What if you lose your distribution rights for some of these products? If it is true that customers buy from you because of your service level, then it doesn't matter which principals you represent. If customers buy from you because of the products that you carry, then the story is very different. Your customers may know you but what do they know you for? Finding out how customers perceive your brand is part of a branding exercise.

And even if you are already a strong and famous brand, you will still need to undertake brand maintenance activities. A brand is like any other asset that you own. It needs to be maintained in order to continue to function well. Companies that hold on to the belief that branding is not important because their customers already know them will wake up one day to find that some clever competitors have figured out a way to steal their customers away. Don't let that happen to you.

Branding Myth #11

Brand Strategy Should Be Done From The Inside Out

This is again something that is not true. It is also something that raises plenty of vehement objections from business owners and CEOs every time we say it. "What do you mean that the brand strategy isn't done from the inside out? This is my brand that you are talking about. I own the brand. I have control of my brand. The strategy is controlled by me."

Unfortunately, that is not true because of two reasons.

Firstly, you don't really *own* the brand. You do, from the legal point of view, but since a brand is simply an idea that exists in the minds of customers, the ownership of the brand lies with the customers. They control the brand. In this day and age of hypercompetition, the power has shifted from the company to the customer. What you do or can do is determined by how your brand is perceived by your customers. For example, if customers perceive Toyota as reliable but boring transportation, then there is no use in Toyota advertising its cars aggressively as "sexy" but many Toyota TV commercials have attempted to do that. It is not going to work because real ownership of the brand lies with the customers and not Toyota. So, Toyota's brand strategy has to take into account external factors. It cannot be 100 per cent inside out.

Secondly, you have to take into account another external factor – the position of your competitors and how they are perceived by potential customers. For example, Volvo may want to position its brand as high performance but Volvo is perceived by most people as a safe car, not a high performance car. To make things worse, the high performance position is owned by BMW.

Even though you should take charge of your brand strategy, you should also remember that you don't have the power to do just about anything that you want with the brand because of the two reasons above.

Branding Myth #12

The Brand Can Be Stretched To Cover Different Products Or Services

This perception is extremely dangerous but is very common among companies. So many companies want to park just about anything under their brand. Jacky once met a public listed company whose CEO was trying to develop a proprietary brand to sell consumer electronics products, home appliances and even toothpaste! And he was wondering why the company's share price was not doing as well as his key competitors'. A brand is an idea. One idea. Not two. Not ten. Not a hundred. When you stretch your brand into areas that are unrelated, you will damage the brand. This is so important that we will discuss it in detail when we talk about Rule No. 4 of branding.

In A Nutshell

These are the 12 myths of branding that could derail your company.

Myth	Truth
#1 – The Return On Investment For Branding Cannot Be Measured	Yes, it can but you need to measure the improvement in perception of the brand. Perception is the ROI.
#2 – Branding Is Only For Big Companies	Branding is the reason why the big brands became successful. It is not the reward for success. The big brands were once small but they became big because they got their brand strategy right.
#3 – Branding Is The Job Of The Marketing Department	It is the job of *everyone* in the company but the CEO must lead. The CEO must play the role of Brand Champion. Otherwise, no one will think that branding is important.
#4 – My Products Or Services Are Better, So There Is No Need For Branding	You can have a better product or service but you will still fail if your competitors have a better brand.
#5 – I Am Selling Cheap, So There Is No Need For Branding	That is true as long as you are the cheapest. If there are competitors out there who can match you for price, the customers will buy from the *strongest* brand among the cheap players.
#6 – If It Works For The Leading Brands, It Must Work For Me	The leading brands can copy the challenger brands but not vice versa. If you copy the leading brands, you are labelled a copycat.
#7 – Brand Strategy Must Be Localised Because Each Market Is Different	If you do that, you will end up with a thoroughly confused and messy brand. In this respect, copy the leading brands. They don't change their strategy but they change the way they market the brand idea.
#8 – Brand Strategy Must Be Changed Regularly To Keep It Fresh	Again, if you do this, you will end up with a messy and confused brand. Changing strategy regularly shows that you haven't got it right.
#9 – I Have No Competitors, Therefore I Don't Need Branding	There will always be competitors. Even if you have invented something new, competitors will show up soon enough. You have to build a strong brand before the competitors come knocking.
#10 – My Customers Know Who I Am, So There Is No Need For Branding	Yes, they may know you but maybe not for the same reason that you think.
#11 – Brand Strategy Should Be Done From The Inside Out	Brand strategy cannot be done in a vacuum because the brand is an idea that exists in the minds of customers so customers have some control over the brand. You also need to take into account your competitors' strategies.
#12 – The Brand Can Be Stretched To Cover Different Products Or Services	A brand is an idea that exists in the mind. One idea. Not two. Not ten. Not a hundred. It cannot be stretched.

B2B

Rule No. 1 –
Perception Is Reality

THERE are a lot of similarities between business and war. In war, you have a battlefield. In business, the battlefield is known by companies as the marketplace. In war, you have enemies to fight. In business, the enemies are known as competitors. In war, you have a target to conquer. In business, the target is represented by the customers. In war, you have generals, lieutenants and soldiers. In business, you have CEOs, marketing directors and salespeople. In war, you have intelligence units. In business, you have market research teams. In war, you have battle plans. In business, you have marketing plans. In war, you have weapons – fighter jets, missiles, tanks, guns, bombs, battleships, etc. In business, you have weapons – advertising, public relations, promotions, search engine optimisation, exhibitions, direct sales, etc.

According to Sun Tzu – the great Chinese military strategist – "All warfare is based on deception. Hence, when able to attack, we must seem unable; when using our forces, we must seem inactive; when we are near, we must make the enemy believe we are far away; when far away, we must make him believe we are near."[11]

If military warfare is based on deception, then business warfare is based on perception. Perception is reality. This is the first rule of branding. In the battle of the brands, the one that is able to create the best perception wins. But before we talk about perception, we need to first define the battlefield of branding.

THE BATTLEFIELD OF BRANDING IS IN THE MIND

At the start of this chapter, we mentioned that most companies see the battlefield as the marketplace. That is not true. When brands win, they gain market share. They win new customers. They make more money. Their share price goes up. All of these happen in the marketplace so why is the battlefield of branding not in the marketplace? This is because what happens in the marketplace is not

---

[11] http://thinkexist.com/quotation/all_war_is_deception/149682.html

the victory that has been won but the *results* of the victory that happened in the real battlefield – the minds of your customers.

Sun Tzu once said, "Victorious warriors win first and then go to war, while defeated warriors go to war first and then seek to win."[12] We find this to be so relevant to brand building. What Sun Tzu is talking about is the art and science of developing a winning strategy before you even launch an attack. We find that far too many companies don't have a winning strategy before they launch an attack. Even those who have a strategy very often find it too tiresome to spend the necessary time and thinking to refine that strategy before going to market with it. Company bosses are by nature impatient for success. They are usually men and women of action. They are like Spartans. They are warriors of the business world. They charge. But charging without a plan to ensure victory is like putting tactics before strategy and, once again, Sun Tzu has this to say, "Tactics without strategy is the noise before defeat."[13]

So, what do you need to do to ensure victory? The first step is to understand that the battlefield of branding is in the minds of your customers. If you win in the mind, then you will win in the marketplace. A brand is something that is intangible. The brand doesn't exist in the marketplace. It exists in the minds of your customers. The brand is just an idea that is associated with your brand in the minds of customers. That idea is shaped by the perceptions that customers have of your brand.

THE MIND IS FILLED WITH SPECIAL PIGEONHOLES

To win any battle, you must know the battlefield. The battlefield of military warfare is usually filled with landmines but the battlefield of branding – the mind – is filled with pigeonholes. In order to conquer this battlefield, you need to slot your brand into one of these pigeonholes and each brand can only occupy one pigeonhole. A brand is simply an idea in the minds of customers. One brand can only be associated with one idea, hence one pigeonhole per brand. The mind hates chaos. It likes things to be organised and neat so that it can access information easily. The mind is like a computer. In a computer, information is stored according to a system for easy access. The mind does the same.

The mind needs to make some order of the barrage of information it receives every day in order to function properly. Even the most disorderly person has a mind that needs to categorise things for easy reference. Otherwise, there will be

---

[12] www.brainyquote.com/quotes/authors/s/sun_tzu_3.html
[13] www.brainyquote.com/quotes/authors/s/sun_tzu_2.html

utter confusion and chaos. Because of this need to categorise, your mind will automatically create pigeonholes for everything that it comes in contact with.

The pigeonhole marked "Safe Cars" is occupied by Volvo.
The pigeonhole marked "Reliable Cars" is occupied by Toyota.
The pigeonhole marked "Driving Machines" is occupied by BMW.
The pigeonhole marked "Prestigious Cars" is occupied by Mercedes-Benz.
The pigeonhole marked "Sexy Car" is occupied by Alfa Romeo.
The pigeonhole marked "Sporty Mass-Market Car" is occupied by Mazda.

This goes on and on. Once a pigeonhole is occupied by a brand, it is very difficult to displace it. That is how your mind works. That is how your mind categorises things for easy reference. Once a perception is formed in the mind, it is very hard to change. When was the last time you changed your mind about a brand? Even if you are a fickle-minded person, chances are you have never changed your mind about Volvo. It is the safe car.

This is also the reason why our job as branding consultants is so difficult because once a client's mind is made up, it is extremely difficult for us to get him or her to change it. We may have evidence to show that a particular strategy has the best chance of succeeding but if the client has already made up his or her mind to use another strategy, there is usually very little that we can do to change that mind.

That is why it is very important for a brand to form the right perception in the minds of its prospective customers from day one. In today's brutally competitive marketplace, you don't get a second chance. If your brand fails to make a deep, positive and lasting first impression, you will only increase its chances of failure.

PERCEPTION IS REALITY

In the mind, all that matters is perception, not reality. Now, we would like you to read the sentence below very quickly. What does it say?

M Y B R A N D I S N O W H E R E

Some of you will read this sentence as "My Brand Is No Where".
Some of you will read this sentence as "My Brand Is Now Here".

Whatever you perceive this sentence to be, that is what it is. Your perception of this sentence is what makes it real to you. It doesn't matter what we, the writers of this sentence, intended it to be. All that matters is how you read it, how you perceive it. Perception is reality. And perception can work for you or against you.

The same principle that applies to how you read the above sentence also applies in the battle of brands. Whatever people perceive your brand to be, that is what it is. You can say all you want about what your brand is and what it isn't. It doesn't really matter. The success of your brand depends almost entirely on how it is perceived by other people, not by how superior it is. What is more important than creating a superior product is creating the perception that you have a superior product because in this day and age, technical superiority is fleeting. Within months, your competitors can tear apart your product and produce something as good or even better.

We know some of you are probably shaking your heads in disbelief. How can an objectively superior product be perceived as inferior, and vice versa? Let us prove it to you. Let's play a word association game. We will name a category and you name the first brand that pops into your mind. Let's compare the results afterwards.

1. Soft drinks
2. Massage chairs
3. Instant coffee
4. Computer chips
5. Credit cards
6. Computer software
7. MP3 players
8. Premium watch
9. Airline
10. Portable e-mail

You probably answered in the following manner:

1. Coca-Cola
2. OSIM
3. NESCAFÉ

4. Intel
5. VISA
6. Microsoft
7. iPod
8. Rolex
9. Singapore Airlines
10. BlackBerry

Why? Do these brands really make the best products in their categories? Not necessarily but people perceive them to be the best brands. That is why these brands come to mind when their categories are mentioned.

Branding is a battle that is won or lost in the mind of the customer, not in the real world. It is, therefore, a battle of perceptions, not products. In the branding war, perception is all that matters. Whatever the customer perceives, that is the truth as far as the customer is concerned. It doesn't matter if it really is the truth or not. All that matters is what the customer perceives to be the truth. Many of the companies that we have dealt with can produce test data that prove that they have a superior product compared to their competitors. But despite that, they were unable to increase their market share. The reason for that is very simple. These companies are not perceived to be category leaders but their main competitors are.

We are not saying that quality is not important. It is. Your quality must be at least as good as your major competitors' or you won't even be considered by potential customers. But quality alone is not enough to build a brand as many companies have discovered to their dismay. Quality is just the price of entry. To win, you need to engender better perceptions of your products and services.

PERCEPTION MAY NOT BE THE REAL THING BUT IT'S WHAT THE MIND KNOWS

This is something that many company bosses cannot get their minds around – especially B2B company bosses who are used to quantifiable measures of quality, performance, durability, etc. Sometimes, when we show them that customers do not perceive them to be very good at customer service for example, they will jump up and tell us that they spend a lot of money on customer service and they do their best to take care of customers. That may be true but what you need to remember is that when your customers perceive you to be good at something or bad at something, that may not be the *truth* but as long as that is what they perceive you to be, then that is what you are.

For example, if you are a competitor to Nippon Paint and you can produce paint that is as innovative and as good – or even better – what does that mean? It means nothing unless you can create the perception that you are better. The fact that you are perceived to be inferior does not mean that you are. And the fact that you are perceived to be superior also does not mean that you are superior. But that is how it works in branding. You operate the same way as well, right? You have certain perceptions of the brands that you buy – both for work and for personal use. It doesn't matter what anyone says, you believe in your own judgement. You believe in your own perception.

The mind doesn't like to make too many changes. Once the mind is made up – "Brand X good. Brand Y bad. Brand Z ugly." – it doesn't want to change. That can be your biggest strength or your biggest stumbling block. It all depends on what people perceive your brand to be. But even if you manage to create a strong, positive perception of your brand, you will still need to work hard to maintain that perception.

As you will see from some of the surprising examples below, perception can be a very powerful ally or a powerful foe when you are trying to build and maintain a brand. This depends largely on which side of the perception fence you are on.

REALITY IN SOFT DRINKS

Blind taste tests conducted in the United States have shown that more people think Pepsi tastes better than Coca-Cola. When Jacky was studying in the United States in the early nineties, he used to watch TV commercials for Pepsi that advertised this fact. In fact, out of the 800,000 or so people who took The Pepsi Challenge blind taste test, 480,000, or 60 per cent, said that Pepsi tasted better than Coca-Cola.[14]

And yet, more people continue to buy Coca-Cola than Pepsi. According to the 24 March 2010 issue of *Beverage Digest*, Coke continues to dominate the carbonated soft drinks market in the United States despite Pepsi's challenge. Take a look at the table on the following page.

---

[14] *Beverage Digest*, 4 March 2005

Table 4: Top 10 Carbonated Soft Drinks Brands For 2009 In The USA

Rank	Brand	2009 Market Share (%)	2008 Market Share (%)	Cases Sold In 2009 (millions)	% Change In Cases Sold
1	Coca-Cola	17.0	17.3	1,598.0	-4.0
2	Pepsi-Cola	9.9	10.3	936.4	-5.5
3	Diet Coke	9.9	10.0	936.3	-2.5
4	Mountain Dew	6.7	6.8	630.1	-3.5
5	Dr Pepper	6.1	6.1	575.9	-1.7
6	Diet Pepsi	5.6	5.7	525.5	-4.5
7	Sprite	5.5	5.6	515.2	-4.0
8	Diet Mountain Dew	1.9	1.8	177.2	+4.5
9	Fanta	1.8	1.8	168.8	-4.0
10	Diet Dr Pepper	1.8	1.6	165.2	+4.8

(Source: *Beverage Digest*, 24 March 2010)

In 2009, Coke had a 17 per cent market share with Pepsi-Cola in second place with 9.9 per cent. Coke still commands a huge lead over Pepsi-Cola despite being rated as not as good tasting as Pepsi-Cola. We are sure a lot of the people who rated Pepsi as better tasting than Coca-Cola in those blind taste tests still bought Coca-Cola when they went to the supermarket subsequently.

Don't you find this illogical? Pepsi is better tasting after all! It is clearly a superior product and Pepsi proudly advertised the results of these blind taste tests. But it didn't change a thing. Coca-Cola is still the leading brand in the cola category because many people still perceive Coca-Cola as the superior brand. They say Pepsi tastes better but when they are actually faced with a purchase decision, they buy Coke because in their mind, Coke is the best. Perception is reality in the soft drinks market and this is borne out in Coca-Cola's sales figures.

REALITY IN MICROPROCESSORS

Jacky used to run the marketing communications department for an education software company. The IT guys were very fond of showing him benchmarking tests that proved AMD microprocessors were faster than Intel's. And Jacky believed them because at that time, he had an AMD-powered computer at home that definitely ran faster than the brand new Pentium-powered computers from a leading brand (which shall remain nameless) that were used in the office, despite the fact that the AMD chip was rated 0.8 GHz slower than the Pentium chip.

Did all that matter? Not to a lot of people because they perceive Intel to be the best computer chip. Jacky used to tell his former CEO to buy AMD-powered computers because they were faster and cheaper. The CEO was shown the test results. After much consideration, the CEO decided to buy Intel machines.

Naturally, Jacky was more than a little puzzled and questioned the CEO as to his decision. The CEO said he somehow had more confidence in the Intel brand and he regarded Intel as a more solid purchase. Jacky argued that the test results clearly showed that AMD was faster but this made no difference to the CEO. In that CEO's mind, Intel was the best and that was the end of the argument. Perception is reality in the microprocessor market and that must be helping Intel maintain its market share of around 86 per cent.

Sure, there are some people who will buy the fastest chip regardless of who makes it. But it would seem that there are more people who would buy from the brand that they perceive to be best and that would be Intel.

REALITY IN PHOTOCOPIERS

Why do people continue to buy Xerox photocopiers? Because they are the best? Or because they are perceived to be the best? If we were to give you photocopies made by Xerox, Canon, Minolta, Toshiba and Ricoh machines and then asked you to rank those copies in order of quality, how sure are you that the Xerox copy would come out tops?

You would probably have a lot of difficulty telling the copies apart. We know this because we have tried this before and the copy that was rated the sharpest was actually made by a Toshiba machine. The Xerox copy came in third.

But when the subject of photocopiers is raised, the first brand that invariably comes to mind is Xerox. This is because people perceive Xerox to be the leading photocopier brand. Xerox is photocopier and vice versa. We don't know what other people perceive Toshiba to be but in our minds, it is either a washing machine or a laptop computer. In another person's mind, it could be a refrigerator. Or an air-conditioner. It could be any number of things. We are sure the Toshiba photocopier salespeople will tell you that there is no difference between one brand and another in terms of quality so you might as well buy Toshiba but there is a difference and that difference exists in your mind.

REALITY IN COFFEE

Why is Starbucks still the No. 1 coffee chain in the world? Does it serve better coffee than its competitors? To find out, the *Straits Times* sent *Life!* reporter and former barista Sujin Thomas to conduct a taste test of the various premium coffee brands' single shot espresso. The test was conducted in Singapore.

This is what Sujin discovered:[15]

Brand	Price	Aroma	Body	Acidity
Starbucks	S$3.00	Mild and discernible only at close sniff	Watery, lacking volume	Fairly sour aftertaste
Spinelli	S$2.90	So strong it's a wake-up call	Full and round	The barest hint of sourness
Coffee Club	S$3.00	Zaps you but is not overpowering	Fairly rounded but with a weak feel	Mildly sourish aftertaste
The Coffee Bean & Tea Leaf	S$3.20	Faint	Thin, tastes very diluted	A sharp jolt of it
The Coffee Connoisseur	S$3.90	Strong and inviting	Full and heavy feel that lingers on the tongue	Just a hint of it

From the taste test, you can see that Starbucks does not serve the best coffee. In fact, Spinelli trounced it convincingly in all the three attributes of aroma, body and acidity. Does it matter? Did the publication of these test results cause a cataclysmic downward shift in Starbucks' fortune?

More than five years have passed since that article came out. From our observation, it hasn't affected Starbucks noticeably. People still perceive Starbucks as the leading brand and therefore they continue to frequent it. Most Starbucks outlets here in Singapore are doing a roaring trade.

This doesn't seem fair on the other guys who actually have better coffee, does it? But that is the first rule of the branding game. Branding is not a battle of who has the better product but who can create the perception that it has the better product. Perception is still reality in the premium coffee market.

WHY CAN'T THE BETTER PRODUCT WIN THE BRANDING WAR?

In the next chapter, we will examine how these leading brands managed to create and maintain the perception of leadership in the minds of their customers but first, we will look at why the better product strategy doesn't work in branding.

We have met a lot of executives at functions and seminars who must have thought that we were prime candidates for the mental hospital when we said that the better-product strategy their companies are so hell-bent on using

---

[15] *Straits Times*, 23 January 2005

does not work. But being polite people, they tried their best not to laugh. What we are saying here goes against conventional wisdom. How can the better product not win? How can you have the best product in the market and not be the leading brand? The idea that if you build a better mousetrap, you will sell more mousetraps than the other mousetrap makers has been so ingrained in companies that it is actually stopping them from building powerful brands.

A brand is nothing more than an idea that you own in the mind and that idea is shaped by perceptions.

If you want to buy a safe car, what is the brand that comes to mind? Volvo. Why? Because that is what the Volvo brand stands for. That is what people perceive the Volvo brand to be. If BMW is The Ultimate Driving Machine, then Volvo is The Ultimate Safety Machine. But Volvo really does build very safe cars, you might argue. We don't deny that. The Volvo brand's reputation was built on decades of making safe cars.

We have met people who have had serious accidents in Volvos and they assured us that if you have ever had an accident in a Volvo, you will never ever buy any other car. Especially after you have seen how badly damaged the other car is compared to your Volvo. Isn't that proof that the better product wins? Volvo is clearly the superior product in this case. It built its reputation by consistently building safe cars. Yes, and it continues to make very safe cars even today but that doesn't mean that nobody else can make safer cars than Volvo.

A lot of manufacturers these days can wave around crash test ratings that are as good as, if not better than, Volvo's. And not all of them are as big or as expensive as a Volvo. Renault is one manufacturer that has very good crash test ratings. In the Euro NCAP crash tests in 2000, the Volvo S80 scored four stars.[16] The Renault Laguna became the first car to score five stars – in 2001. So Renault can claim that their cars are among the safest in the world. But can Renault occupy the pigeonhole in your mind that is marked "safe cars"? Not a chance. Renault can spend hundreds of millions of dollars advertising their five-star Euro NCAP score but it will not change people's perception of Renault and Volvo.

When safe cars are mentioned, what comes to mind? Volvo. Renault is probably perceived as avant-garde, individualistic and Gallic but when safe cars are mentioned, Renault is not a brand that will spring to mind as easily as Volvo.

---

[16] www.euroncap.com

WHAT ABOUT QUALITY?

We are not suggesting that quality is unimportant in brand building. Undeniably, quality is indeed very important because you obviously can't build a strong brand based on hype, hot air and smoke and mirrors – not in the post-dot.com world anyway. Your quality must be at least as good as that of your competitors'. But quality alone is not enough to build a brand because quality can be copied. It can be reverse-engineered. To build a strong brand, you need to build a very strong perception in people's minds first. Remember, while perception can be changed, it cannot be reverse-engineered. That's the beauty of it.

Jacky grew up around Mercedes-Benz and Toyota cars because many of his relatives and parents' friends owned them. As a budding car enthusiast, he naturally paid very close attention to every car that he came in contact with. Over the years, he noticed that nothing ever seemed to go wrong in a Toyota – until recently. In other words, Toyota actually made very high-quality cars, even in the days when they were labelled as Japanese tin cans.

But Mercedes-Benz was seen by most people as the quality benchmark in those days – during the seventies and eighties. Mercedes-Benz cars were not only high quality but they created the perception of quality by using higher-grade plastics in the interior, making their doors heavy and needing a firm shove to close, styling their cars to look like they were hewn from solid billets of steel and pricing the cars out of the reach of ordinary motorists. Quality is important but the perception of quality is equally important.

BUT I DON'T WANT MY BRAND TO BE STEREOTYPED!

A lot of people don't like the idea of stereotyping or pigeonholing their brands because they think that if the brand becomes too closely identified with a category or product, it will be difficult for that brand to be extended to other categories. This kind of thinking will push companies to try to diversify their brand to the point where it loses focus (more of this in Rule No. 4). If you want to build a strong brand, you need to get your brand stereotyped. If you are Harley-Davidson and the stereotype of your brand is that it is a "rebellious brand" – the brand of motorcycles for outlaws – then keep it that way. Don't try to be the brand of motorcycles that is so easy to ride that even grandmothers can do it. Make full use of that stereotype. After all, there are a lot of law-abiding citizens who like the Harley image and style. They will buy it.

Businesspeople are generally uncomfortable with stereotypes but if you want to build a strong brand, you need to get it stereotyped. You need your brand to be strongly identified with a category, product or service. If you don't, your brand is weak. Brands cannot stand on their own. You need to attach a category or a meaning to that brand. If Volvo was not so closely identified with safe cars, the Volvo brand would be weak. A brand is an idea that you own in the mind. The idea that Volvo owns in the mind is safe cars.

Volvo is doing fine but its compatriot, Saab, is not doing so well. Although Saab makes excellent cars, it has a weak identity. While you know exactly what a Volvo is – a very safe Swedish tank – do you know what a Saab is? Because the Saab brand is not so strongly stereotyped, it is a weak concept in many people's minds. Saab is trying to make a comeback by tapping on its aerospace heritage. Saab used to make Viggen fighter jets and is trying to get its brand stereotyped as "fighter jets for the road". We think that is a good strategy but it remains to be seen if Saab can execute it successfully. However, the latest Saab 9-5 seems to be trying very hard to be a big, luxury car. We are not sure if that will work out well.

So, do you know how your brand is perceived? What does it stand for? Which pigeonhole in the mind does it occupy? If it is filed under the pigeonhole called "Miscellaneous", then you are in big trouble because if your brand doesn't stand for anything, it is weak.

Of course, a brand that is very closely tied to a category will die when that category dies. That's the way things are. Polaroid was so closely tied to the instant photography category that when the category died, the brand died. But the alternative is to have a weak brand. The choice is yours. Personally, we would rather have a strong brand that can dominate one category than a weak brand that straddles many categories because you can always launch a new brand if your current category becomes obsolete.

The next question is, how do you anchor your brand in the minds of your customers? How do you own a strong perception in people's minds? How do you get your brand locked comfortably into a pigeonhole in the mind? How do strong brands like Coca-Cola, OSIM, Starbucks, NESCAFÉ, Intel, VISA, Microsoft, Apple, Singapore Airlines (SIA), Rolex and Volvo do it? They did it by being the first, and that is the subject of the next rule of branding in the following chapter. The best way to create the better perception is by being the first one. If you are the first, you can do a lot of things. If you come later, you will have to do different things.

PERCEPTUAL MAPPING – A MEASURE OF SUCCESS

We have written about this at length in earlier chapters but it is so important that we cannot emphasise it often enough. A lot of company executives – especially those with financial or engineering backgrounds – are still sceptical about branding because they think that since branding is something intangible, it cannot be measured. And if it cannot be measured, then how do you know whether the time, effort and money spent on it is worthwhile?

As branding is a battle that takes place in the mind, that is where you measure the success or failure of your branding programme. If you already own a brand that has been in the market for a few years, then you need to undertake a Brand Audit, which is an exercise to find out how people perceive your brand versus your competitors' brands. You can measure a number of key attributes to see how you fare. For example, you can do a perceptual map of your brand in terms of price versus quality, reliability versus speed and so on.

That is the before picture. Then you undertake a branding programme to improve how people perceive your brand. After the branding programme is concluded, you measure people's perceptions of your brand again. If it has improved, then the programme has been successful. If nothing has changed, it's back to the drawing board. Rule No. 6 of branding will show you the best way to change perceptions of your brand. It is not easy but it can be done.

In A Nutshell

Perception is reality in branding. It doesn't matter what you say your brand is. All that matters is what other people perceive your brand to be. You operate the same way as a customer, so you can expect your customers to operate the same way as you. To win the battle of branding, you need to win in the only battlefield that matters – the minds of your customers. If you can win in the mind, you can win in the marketplace. The brand is just an idea that you own in the minds of your customers, and that idea is shaped by customers' perceptions of your brand. You need to create not just a high-quality product or service that is comparable to your competitors', you also need to create a better perception. The winner is not the one with the better product or service but the perception that it has the better product or service. The reason why perception is so important these days is because the quality gap between the best and the worst has narrowed so much thanks to technological advancements and hypercompetition.

Edward Bulwer-Lytton, a famous English author, wrote this sentence in 1839:

THEPENISMIGHTIERTHANTHESWORD

We read the sentence as "The Pen Is Mightier Than The Sword". Many of you will read it some other way. We are not going to say you are wrong regardless of what Edward Bulwer-Lytton intended the sentence to be because your perception is all that matters here. When you are trying to build a brand, your customers' perception is all that matters. And to create a strong perception, pay attention to Rule No. 2 of branding in the next chapter.

CASE STUDY
Perception Is Reality – InfoTech

The Global Information Technology Evolution And Challenges

The rising prominence of technology across the globe is evident at a glance in the market capitalisation of the largest firms in the world. In 2009, Google moved from 35th to 10th position in market capitalisation. Apple, which was not ranked in 2008, followed close on the heels of Google in 11th position, showing a gain of nearly 150 per cent in market capitalisation in 2009. The rankings reveal a changing mindset and an increasing emphasis on technology in our modern world.

A widely publicised media release by Gartner Inc, a top information technology (IT) research and advisory company, on 30 November 2010 predicts several IT trends for IT organisations and users in 2011 and beyond. These predictions highlight changing business and lifestyle trends that will shape the way businesses invest in information technology.

Bringing Forth A New Era In IT: InfoTech

Technology has always been the main driver of how people work, live and play. Indeed, it will continue to reshape the 21st century as new innovations are constantly being discovered. In South Asia, one company is determined to revolutionise the way technology is being used. InfoTech (formerly known as South Technologies) was established in Lahore, Pakistan, in 1987 by its founder and current CEO Naseer Akhtar, with a vision of helping customers simplify and manage business technologies. Since then, its clear vision and consistency has resulted in making the company one of the oldest in Pakistan as well as a highly trusted and credible business in many parts of Africa and Asia. Since its establishment, InfoTech has been focussed on creating a simplified approach to business technology. The company designs solutions that help customers solve problems by allowing them to focus on developing their businesses. This is an important variable given the extremely difficult markets in which these customers operate, namely the emerging markets in Africa and the Middle East. Due to its opportunity-driven approach, InfoTech has experienced tremendous growth in recent years.

In the past, large enterprises engaged multiple technology suppliers for their technology needs. Today, these same organisations are looking to engage suppliers that are able to provide end-to-end solutions wherever possible. This has given rise to cut-throat competition within a business sector that is fundamentally based on high levels of client contact.

Through progressive growth, InfoTech has been ranked as the largest IT consulting company of Pakistan in terms of size of contract value and staff. While size is an advantage when it matters; it is a disadvantage when it comes to being competitive. Here, the challenge for InfoTech is to stay competitive within its chosen market segments. In the longer term, this is not sustainable because of the limited financial resources of the economy in Pakistan.

Due to the rising competitive domestic market of Pakistan and the brand perception of InfoTech as an IT hardware reseller, InfoTech's board took the view that internationalisation was inevitable if the company wanted to grow to the next level. This decision was taken between 2005 and 2006 and brought about new challenges including the competitive landscape of global companies (quite a few were already partners of InfoTech, such as IBM). Other challenges were the lack of global projects among its track record, the lack of a unique offering, the level of strength in terms of client confidence and the company's visibility and reach. To top it off, from a country *perception* perspective, being a company from Pakistan had its own limitations. This is the first rule of branding. In the battle of the brands, the one that is able to create the best perception wins. On this perceptual challenge, Akhtar believed that being a company originating from Pakistan was both a catalyst and a challenge:

> *Firstly, let me describe how it has been a catalyst. We have been doing large amounts of business in Pakistan and that has given us the necessary experience to go international. Our teams are now the best skilled in Pakistan, and possibly the best in the region in some key areas; this has given us the edge to outperform other companies in international projects. Secondly, sourcing good human resources from Pakistan is cheaper than, let's say, Europe or other parts of Asia. This makes us very cost-effective as well, and that is a major factor when competing globally.*
>
> *On the other hand, being of Pakistani origin sometimes becomes a challenge, especially these days due to the perception of Pakistan and the on-going security and political situation here. International enterprises are hesitant to award contracts to Pakistani companies due to their apprehension regarding resource mobilisation, general operation and, importantly, support of the provided solutions.*

Unfortunately, only bad news makes news and for someone sitting outside Pakistan, news is the basic source of information. So international markets have quite a different perception of Pakistan from what the reality on ground is. Hence, the biggest challenge we face right now is the confidence of international markets. Due to the perception of Pakistan being a terror-ridden state, people are hesitant to engage with Pakistani companies, whereas the people and enterprises here are the same as they were before.

We are doing our best to change this perception by constantly going out there, meeting with key personnel and conducting workshops and seminars, to make the world realise that Pakistani IT companies are as good as others and are willing to go the extra mile for their customers.

The Strategy

With the need to break away from its domestic perception as a Pakistani IT hardware reseller, InfoTech's adopted strategy in treating these perception challenges was two-pronged:

- To develop a global brand.
- To further develop and establish a footprint of global offices in strategic locations in emerging markets.

Akhtar and his management also understood that perception is further built with experience. In the context of InfoTech, the experience was to be found only in its people. The ability to attract and retain some of the best global talent to help fulfil its regional footprint strategy for Asia and Africa was critical. In this regard, InfoTech mapped out both internal and external strategies to better anchor talent.

With the strategic intent of establishing a footprint of global offices in strategic locations within emerging markets, it was decided to keep InfoTech's headquarters and global delivery centre in Lahore and set up offices in strategic locations overseas. In so doing, it would be easier for the company to better understand the needs of its potential clients in view of close proximity.

The Execution

InfoTech took a three-step approach in overcoming its challenges.

STEP 1: ESTABLISHING A SENSE OF PRIDE AND CONFIDENCE IN INFOTECH'S PEOPLE
Akhtar is increasingly aware of the importance of developing InfoTech's human capital. He understands that InfoTech's business model is driven by the human factor. One such critical focus is creating an environment that supports all employees to enhance their sense of pride in what they do through results and achievements:

I pride myself in ensuring that I keep my people highly motivated through being goal driven because what gets measured, gets done. What gets done gets rewarded publicly.

STEP 2: SETTING UP A FOOTPRINT OF TALENT AND GEOGRAPHICAL REACH
In terms of talent development and management, the company administered a Perception Audit to better understand how their consultants and shared services staff viewed the company. An external consultant was appointed to provide an independent review. The exercise revealed that InfoTech was highly associated with (1) the leadership abilities of president and CEO Naseer Akhtar, (2) a good working environment and (3) strong relationships with clients. Management understood that the close association of InfoTech to its CEO, although gratifying, provided various perceived risks. Therefore, an HR policy was adopted to ensure the slow and steady emergence of a strong pool of new and promising leaders within the organisation. In addition, externally, the company began to actively engage the Lahore University of Management Sciences (LUMS), especially within the IT and business faculties, with the goal of developing its student capabilities through internships and further build its reputation as an employer of choice. The management of InfoTech regards this as a long-term investment towards talent development.

In terms of extending its footprint, two offices outside of Pakistan were immediately set up – one in Singapore to serve the South East Asian markets and another in Dubai to address the Middle East and Africa. This structure provides the company with the reach to and presence in its chosen markets. Within each region, the company's IT engineers are constantly on the road, talking to customers so that they can understand the most complex and burgeoning IT needs of each respective country.

STEP 3: BUILDING THE BRAND OF "INFOTECH – BRILLIANTLY BUILT"
InfoTech embarked on a brand strategy formulation exercise with the objective of finding out how clients perceived the company. The findings, although not entirely congruent, were indeed remarkable. The positive associations the InfoTech brand

carried included strong leadership, good relationships with customers, forthrightness, responsiveness, willingness to help customers, forward looking and highly supportive of its clients' efforts.

In its effort to develop a long-term strategy of being a global knowledge integration firm and taking the above into consideration, the board of the company crafted the vision of "A Knowledge Integration Company Renowned for its Brilliantly Built Solutions". It was then determined that the best-fit strategy for InfoTech was to differentiate itself through the personality trait of "BRILLIANCE" since most of its customers believed that the company's employees are brilliant when it comes to IT problem solving. Once such a perception is formed in the mind, it is very hard to change – something that is good for InfoTech. Consequently, InfoTech took the position as the provider of "Brilliantly Built Solutions". As the IT space is mature, its brand positioning strategy was to occupy this new category of solutions. To dramatise this further, the brand tagline "Brilliantly Built" was introduced to be permanently coupled with the trademark.

INFOTECH
BRILLIANTLY BUILT

The determined corporate positioning defined InfoTech's priorities, approach, objectives and strategies and allowed the company to embark on its marketing journey by formulating action and business plans with its vision as "A Knowledge Integration Company Renowned for its Brilliantly Built Solutions". Every marketing message rolled out of the company embodies its brand values of trust, professionalism, credibility and high-value delivery. As these values propagate good relationship drivers, the communications roadmap was determined to be dyadic in nature.

Since marketing InfoTech is a dynamic and evolutionary process, the company's marketing efforts and communications gradually replaced diverse, limited-focus promotional tools. Brand management was used for initiating and maintaining a continuing dialogue with stakeholders (external, in particular). Here, InfoTech's marketing communications messages were integrated such that all touch-points of the corporate brand received by a customer, principal or staff member were relevant to that particular stakeholder. These touch-points included the following:

- Online marketing channels (e.g. e-marketing campaigns, emails, blogs, podcasts, Internet, etc)
- Offline marketing channels (e.g. newspapers, magazines, public relations releases, advertisements, etc).

While remaining attuned to current marketing processes, InfoTech's integrated marketing communication messages were crafted in a stakeholder-centric manner to maximise effectiveness in engaging the stakeholders. As Akhtar has pointed out to his staff in all three offices:

The InfoTech brand is only as good as its people and what would enable us to be effective in building a strong brand is our transformation into brand ambassadors – when each one of us knows and embraces InfoTech for our "Brilliantly Built Solutions", we will inevitably conduct ourselves in ways that will enhance the company's reputation.

The company understands that for a service-based business, the brand is achievable only with people – brilliant people. Combining business process knowledge, highly skilled and dedicated intellectual human capital and a collaborative working culture, every employee of InfoTech stands ready to be appraised by his/her clients. The company believes that this is the only way to build credibility. These same people set the brand apart because they are each trusted and credible with high professional bearing, committed to their relationships with customers as they deliver high value.

Today, the perception of InfoTech as a backward Pakistani company is rapidly diminishing. Customers in South East Asia, the Middle-East and Africa associate the company with one that is global in its business model. This perception is very much a reality today.

B2B

CHAPTER
09

Rule No. 2 –
Fortune Favours The First

THE notion that being first gives you a strong competitive advantage is a controversial issue that usually splits opinions right down the middle. Whenever we mention the importance of being first, there are usually company bosses who will strongly disagree with us. Sometimes, there is an uneasy silence in the room – mainly because many people don't believe in the first-mover advantage school of thought anymore. They point out that there have been quite a number of first-mover failures and that is true.

Some university professors have pointed out to us that there are as many first-mover failures as there are first-mover successes so it is no surprise that many people are not sure that being first is important, especially Singapore company bosses who are typically more risk averse.

A lot of company bosses we have met actually feel that there is no need for a brand to be first in the market in order to win because the first mover is usually the one that bears the biggest risk if that market fails to develop. One company CEO told us, "Guys, no need to be first. I tell you why. First to move means first to die. Have you never watched those combat movies? The first ones to land on the beach are usually the ones who get blown to pieces."

Many companies that we have spoken to have shared with us harrowing stories of how their attempts at being first ended in heartbreak and abject failure because of the following reasons:

1. The more established competitors moved in to copy their ideas or innovations and because these larger players had more financial muscle, they eventually managed to steal the market. Yes, it's a cut-throat world out there.

2. The cheaper players also moved in with copycat products that were not as good but priced so much lower that many customers were swayed by the low prices.

3. Customers just didn't believe that the new innovations that they had launched would really work.

What we discovered in almost all the cases we have encountered is that the companies in question did not *package* their first-of-its-kind product or service well. When we talk about packaging in this context, we are not referring to product packaging. We are talking about these companies not wrapping their new innovations in the right brand strategy and then executing that strategy consistently. Yet many company bosses are still allergic to the idea of being the first mover – citing the three reasons above over and over again.

In some rare instances, the first movers did not succeed because they were actually way ahead of their time. Sometimes, you can launch a product that the market is not ready for. Apple launched the Newton – probably the world's first PDA – but it was too early for the market. Business users were not ready for it. Jacky used to work for an education software company that launched a very advanced e-learning programme in 1995 for the Singapore market but it was too early for the market. There are risks involved in being the first mover, we will grant you that. We will also tell you that sometimes luck – in the form of being in the right place at the right time with the right product – also plays a part. No businessman who is truthful will tell you that luck is not important.

LET'S PLAY FOLLOW THE LEADER

Due to their bad experiences of being the first mover, quite a number of CEOs have argued with us that the right strategy to use is to let others make the first move, see if the market catches on and then move in quickly with a better and cheaper product to overtake the first mover. These company bosses think that it is better to sit back and learn from the mistakes of the pioneers before entering the market themselves. This is called the fast follower strategy. Many companies do it. They look at what the market leaders are doing and then they move quickly to copy and launch their own cheaper versions.

If you are one of those people who think like that, we have bad news for you. On paper, the make-it-better-and-sell-it-cheaper strategy seems like the most logical thing to do but the reality is quite different. Johnny-Come-Lately brands seldom make it big if they adopt this strategy. That alone should be enough to warn you that this strategy is not viable. Many have cited Samsung as the perfect example of a brand that uses speed to overcome the disadvantages of not being first. One of the most visible Samsung products in the market today is its sleek and sexy mobile phones. Yet, despite all of Samsung's speed, it still lags behind Nokia (the first mover in digital mobile phones) with a 35 per cent market share and Motorola (the first mover in analogue mobile phones) with a 22 per cent market share.

Samsung did well to move up the ladder despite being late in the mobile phone market but do you have any idea how much money and time Samsung invested in research, development, innovation, design and marketing? You probably don't have that kind of money, resources or time, so do not try to do a Samsung.

But what about those brands that made it to the market first but still failed? We agree that being first in the market is no guarantee of success but being first in the market gives you the licence to establish your brand in the minds of customers before anyone else does – and that is what really matters because, as we have established in earlier chapters, the real battlefield of branding is in the mind.

SURVIVAL OF THE "FIRSTEST"

If you study the history of brands, you will find that the first brand in the market usually becomes the leading brand, and remains the leading brand for a very long time despite stiff competition. That is usually true unless the first brand makes a fatal mistake and allows its competitors to overrun it.

Coca-Cola

Coca-Cola was the first cola in the market. It was invented in 1886 by Dr John Pemberton, a pharmacist from Atlanta. The name came from coca leaves and kola nuts. By 1895, this fountain soda drink was available throughout the United States and the company started exporting it in 1898. Coca-Cola is over 120 years old but it is still the No. 1 cola brand in the world, and also the most valuable brand according to *BusinessWeek*. Coca-Cola's brand value in 2009 was pegged at US$68.7 billion (S$ 88.3 billion). Coca-Cola is still No. 1 despite an impressive challenge mounted by Pepsi (which we will talk about in Rule No. 5 later).

In 2009, according to *Beverage Digest*, Coca-Cola outsold Pepsi in the US market with a market share of 17 per cent versus 9.9 per cent. Being first also allows Coca-Cola to establish itself as The Real Thing. And who in the world wants to drink the fake thing? Everybody wants the real thing. That is a big plus for companies with first-mover advantage.

CNN

CNN was the first cable news network in the market. Broadcasting veteran Ted Turner launched it in 1980 despite criticism. Today, cable news stations abound across the world. Many came but none managed to wrest away the top spot from CNN, which is broadcast to over 200 countries around the world. For example, Singapore's Channel NewsAsia got into the market very late compared to CNN and the others. Naturally, its share of the global cable news market is small compared to CNN. But Channel NewsAsia has carved out its own niche despite being late – it is the *Asian* news network.

IBM

IBM was the first computer company in the market, established in 1911. Who is No. 1 in the computer industry today? IBM – by a huge margin. Is IBM better? Not necessarily. It is definitely great and we have always used IBM laptops but it may not be the best. But it got there first. And despite the stiff challenges mounted by nimble and innovative new competitors like Dell, Sun Microsystems and HP, IBM is still king of the hill. Why? It got there first. It got into people's minds early and planted the IBM flag there. That flag is still there today. Because IBM got there first, it became very successful early on and it leveraged on that success to move quickly and decisively into other areas like IT consulting and business process outsourcing (BPO).

TSMC

Taiwan Semiconductor Manufacturing Company (TSMC) was the first semiconductor foundry in the world. Is TSMC the best semiconductor foundry in the world today? Maybe. Maybe not. But it did get into the market first before its chief rival – United Microelectronics Corporation (UMC) from Taiwan – and Singapore's own Chartered Semiconductor. Despite the extremely cut-throat semiconductor market, TSMC is still No. 1. In 2009, it had a net profit of S$3.9 billion from a sales turnover of S$13.1 billion, giving it a whopping net profit margin of 29.8 per cent.[17] And 2009 was a bad year, especially for the electronics sector. Our clients who supply to this industry reported a drop in sales that averaged 30 per cent. Some companies that we have met reported a drop of 80 per cent in revenue.

In the first three months of 2010, TSMC reported a sales turnover of

---

[17] www.hoovers.com/company/Taiwan_Semiconductor_Manufacturing_Company_Limited/cycsyi-1-1njea5.html

S$4 billion compared to S$1.7 billion for the first three months of 2009. The net income for the first quarter of 2010 was S$1.5 billion, giving it an even more impressive net profit margin of 37.5 per cent.[18] And this is just for the first three months.

In stark contrast, Chartered Semiconductor posted a net loss of S$131.3 million on a sales turnover of S$2.3 billion in 2008 – the last year that the company's financial data was publicly available. The company was acquired by GLOBALFOUNDRIES that year and is no longer listed on the Singapore Exchange. Although we do not doubt the technical capabilities of Chartered Semiconductor, we believe that because TSMC got into the semiconductor foundry business before anyone else, it helped it to establish a strong position in the market before competition showed up. Being first in the market certainly didn't hurt.

Oracle

Oracle got into the relational database management system (RDBMS) first in 1977. Despite stiff competition from IBM and Microsoft, Oracle has managed to hang on to its No. 1 position. The 2009 figures published by research firm Gartner for worldwide RDBMS market share showed that Oracle has a 48 per cent market share.[19] It has more market share than its four closest competitors combined. Now that is impressive.

Is Oracle the best database software in the world? We don't really know. After experiencing an Oracle-based customer relationship management (CRM) software, in a previous organisation that he worked for, Jacky was not overly impressed as he found that the system was not user-friendly. But what Jacky thinks doesn't really matter because Oracle got there first and will probably remain No. 1 for a long time.

THE FALLACY OF THE FIRST-MOVER ADVANTAGE

Before you get overly excited with the idea that being first in the market is all that it takes to be successful, let us warn you that being first in the market is no guarantee that you will make it big. As many of our clients have correctly pointed out, there are many brands that got into the market first but have failed to become No. 1. Nevertheless, that doesn't mean that the brands that beat them were better.

---

[18] www.tsmc.com/english/e_investor/e01_financials/e0103_result.htm

[19] 'Market Share: RDBMS Software by Operating System, Worldwide, 2009' by Colleen Graham, Bhavish Sood, Hideaki Horiuchi and Dan Sommer, 30 April 2010. www.oracle.com/us/products/database/number-one-database-069037.html

As mentioned earlier, being first in the market in itself is of no use if you don't use this advantage to get into the mind and establish a position there before your competitors come along. Branding is a battle that is won or lost in the mind. So the brand that gets into the mind first will usually win in that category unless it violates the rules of branding or that category becomes obsolete. Being first in the market only gives you the licence to get into the mind first. If you don't exploit the licence that your first-mover advantage gives you, then you are giving competitors an opportunity to establish their brands in the minds of customers even though they entered the market late.

That was what happened to Creative Technology in relation to MP3 players. Creative Technology was first in the MP3 player market but Apple got into the mind first. Guess who won the MP3 player war? Although Creative Technology was first in the market, it squandered this advantage by not getting into the mind first. Creative *did* get into the mind first in another category – the sound card. Creative's Sound Blaster sound card was first introduced in 1989 and it soon became the industry standard.

So, even if you do get into the market first, your job is only half done. To win the branding war, you need to fully exploit this first-mover advantage and establish yourself in the customers' minds first. If you don't and somebody else does, then the battle for No. 1 is lost as far as your brand is concerned. If you are lucky enough to be the first in the market, do whatever is necessary to flood the market with your products and get into the mind first.

The companies we mentioned earlier that made the first move and failed did not fail because the first-mover advantage is no longer a relevant competitive and branding tool. They failed because they didn't jump into the battlefield with all guns blazing. They hedged their bets. They did a bit of this. They did a bit of that. They call it "testing the water". We call it "a lack of conviction". If you want to turn your first-mover advantage into something that can build a powerful brand, you need to drop everything else to concentrate on using your first-mover advantage to establish the brand in the only place that matters – the minds of your customers. Fail to do this and you will exit the market with a whimper.

Having said this, we also understand that being the first mover is not a game that everyone can play. In the battle of brands, there are always three categories of players – the leaders, the followers and the also-rans. Not everyone can be the leader but everyone can be a follower or an also-ran. It takes a certain kind of mindset. It takes conviction. It takes courage. That is why the great brands are the great brands. They strategise. Then they jump in with both feet. Yes, not all first movers are successful but we never said it's easy building a brand.

THE FIRST MAN IN SPACE

The first man in space was Yuri Gagarin, the Russian astronaut. He blasted into space on board the Vostok 1 on 12 April 1961. You have probably heard of Yuri Gagarin because he was the first man in space.

Who was the second man in space? The American astronaut, Alan Shepherd. Your mind is probably a blank right now. Alan who? That's the problem with being No. 2 – nobody remembers you. But Shepherd also scored a first. He was the first American in space. Big deal. Who cares about that?

All people want to know is who the first man in space was and that is Yuri Gagarin. Being the first American in space is not really something that is important enough, so hardly anyone remembers Alan Shepherd. So if you are not first in the market, what do you do? What do most companies do? To find out, turn to Rule No. 3 of branding. But read the rest of this chapter first for background information.

THE FIRST MAN TO FLY SOLO ACROSS THE ATLANTIC OCEAN

At 7:52am on 20 May 1927, Charles Lindbergh gunned the engine of the Spirit of St Louis and directed her down the dirt runway of Roosevelt Field, Long Island. Thirty-three and a half hours and approximately 5,790 km later, he landed in Paris as the first person to fly solo across the Atlantic Ocean.

The second person to fly across the Atlantic Ocean solo was Bert Hinkler. Hinkler was not the first so he had to be better – and he was. He crossed the Atlantic in less time and used less fuel compared to Lindbergh. But who is remembered more by people? The first pilot or the better pilot? The first pilot, of course. If you are first, you can get into the mind first and once you have established a position in the mind, it is hard for another person (or brand) to dislodge you. Hinkler was better (he flew faster) and cheaper (he used less fuel) but unfortunately for him, Lindbergh got into the mind first.

WHAT IS THE STRATEGY MOST COMPANIES USE?

Most companies are not first in the market, so they try to use the Bert Hinkler strategy. They study what the leading brands are doing, and then they reverse-engineer the product to make it better and sell it cheaper.

You would think that such a strategy would work but it doesn't. We know it goes against the grain of conventional marketing wisdom but that is how the game of branding is played. The leading brands in any market, industry or category are usually the first brands into the market. And they will remain the leading brand for a very long time unless they shoot themselves in both feet.

The examples below from the beverage industry illustrate the power of being first:

- What is the leading cola? Coke. What was the first cola? Coke.
- What is the leading energy drink? Red Bull. What was the first energy drink? Red Bull.
- What is the leading sports drink? Gatorade. What was the first sports drink? Gatorade.
- What is the leading pepper cola? Dr Pepper. What was the first pepper cola? Dr Pepper.
- What is the leading natural fruit drink? Snapple. What was the first natural fruit drink? Snapple.

Are these the best drinks in their category? Not necessarily. Are they the cheapest? Not necessarily. But they were there first. End of story.

THE DANGER OF MARKET RESEARCH

Most of the new brands being launched nowadays are created to serve an existing market rather than create new markets. That is why you get so many me-too products out there in the marketplace today.

We are not against market research. In fact, we do a lot of market research in the course of our work but market research alone will not help you create the next big brand. Market research can only tell you the size of an existing market and what customers have bought (or not bought). It cannot help you to create a new market. If you cannot create a new market for your brand, your brand cannot grow. The reason is very simple. If you launch a brand that is designed to serve an existing market, that market will already have been dominated by some big players and a lot of smaller ones. It is tough launching a brand into a market that already has so many battle-hardened competitors.

Xerox

This is one of the most famous cases that every first-year marketing student is taught. Market research would have killed the 914 – Xerox's first plain paper photocopier. Because the market research showed that nobody was willing to pay US$0.05 for each plain paper copy, the researchers concluded that the plain paper photocopy market did not exist – not at the kind of prices that Xerox needed to charge.

Of course the market was non-existent! Nobody had bothered to create this market yet. Customers indicated that they were not willing to pay 5 cents a copy but at that time nobody had actually given them the choice between a cheap but terrible thermal copy and a sharp, easy to handle, easy to sort but more expensive plain paper copy.

Xerox ignored the research and launched the 914 in 1959. The rest is marketing history. The Xerox 914 was launched to create a new market, not to serve an existing one. The existing market was the thermal paper photocopier market. If Xerox had launched a thermal paper copier, it would have run into stiff competition. But it didn't. It created a new market – the plain paper photocopier market.

Not only that, Xerox put in a lot of resources to dominate this market. It concentrated its efforts on making Xerox the No. 1 in the photocopier industry. It didn't test the water. It jumped in with both feet. And won big. We are often asked by companies how much they should invest in driving home any first-mover advantage that they have and the answer is you must spend enough. How much is enough? The rule of thumb is this: If you are serious about it, then make sure that you don't get outspent by competitors. That doesn't mean you splurge. Not at all. You still need to plan very carefully how and where you spend your marketing dollars but you have to spend enough.

Coca-Cola

Coca-Cola has one of the slickest marketing machines in the world. But even Coca-Cola managed to shoot itself in both feet when it let market research run amok. Market research showed that an overwhelming majority of people preferred the taste of a new soft drink formula that it was testing – called new Coke – to the original Coke formula. So it went ahead and did away with the original Coke.

In our opinion, that was the biggest blunder in Coca-Cola's history. Some marketing experts have even gone as far as saying that it was the single biggest marketing blunder in history. People protested and boycotted new Coke. The company had no choice but to revive the original Coke and rename it Coca-Cola classic.

Part of the problem, as the marketing books will tell you, is that Coca-Cola did not take into account the emotional bond that people have with the original Coke but that is not all. New Coke was actually launched to serve an existing cola market. And the incumbent brand in that market is the original Coke. New Coke did not create a new market for itself. Diet Coke, on the other hand, was a different story because it was launched to serve a new and hitherto non-existent market and hence Diet Coke had a lot more success.

Lexus

If Toyota had done – and it probably did – its market research properly, it would have found that back in 1989, nobody was willing to pay US$35,000 (S$44,968) for a Japanese luxury car because that was simply unheard of. If you forked out US$35,000 (S$44,968) in 1989, the car had better be German in origin.

But of course people would say that. They had never been given the choice of a US$35,000-(S$44,968-) Japanese luxury car before. Lexus went ahead anyway and launched the first generation LS400 to compete head-on with the Mercedes-Benz S-Class and BMW 7 series in the United States. It was a big hit. Lexus has been the best-selling luxury car in the United States since 2000. In 2005, over 300,000 Lexus cars were sold in the United States.

You can still do your market research but bear in mind its limitations and be careful how you interpret the findings. Market research can only tell you all about an existing market and what people have done in the past and are doing now. It cannot predict the future for you. If you are doing market research, perhaps you should find out what people are not doing instead of what they are doing and capitalise on that.

THE PARADOX OF LOGIC

Typical market research will tell you that customers want a better product at a lower price. So companies duly deliver better products at lower prices. But this strategy almost always never works. Why won't it work even though it was what customers said they want? Time and time again, you will find that what customers say they want and what they actually buy are two different things.

How many times has your own company launched a better and cheaper product than the leading brand and yet failed to make a dent in the leading brand's market share? The reason for this seemingly weird phenomenon is what we call The Paradox Of Logic. There is a discrepancy between how companies think and how customers think.

At the start, both companies and customers think the same.

"The best product should be the No. 1 brand."

Thereafter, the thinking diverges. Companies think that if they have the best product, they will be No. 1. Therefore, they should concentrate on making better products than their competitors. Customers, on the other hand, think that the No. 1 brand has the best product. If you are not No. 1, then you don't have the best product. They don't really care that the No. 1 brand usually became the No. 1 brand because it got into the market first!

All of us adopt either a company mode of thinking or a customer mode of thinking in different situations. But how we think in our capacity as employees or managers of an organisation with a product or service to sell is very different from how we think in our capacity as a customer.

When you are trying to sell something, you think like a company — if I have a better product than the leading brand, I will win. When you are trying to buy something, you think like a customer — the leading brand must have the best product. You should think like a customer all the time — even when you are trying to sell something or especially when you are trying to sell something.

Ask yourself whether you would buy whatever it is that you are selling. Be honest. Very often, you will find that if you had been the customer, you might not have bought your own product. Why? Because you are not the leading brand. A bitter pill to swallow but that is the truth that we are very often faced with.

CHECK YOUR ZIP

If you are wearing trousers, check your zip now. Not because we think your fly might be open, although that is a distinct possibility. Chances are, you might find that your zip is made by YKK. YKK is the leading zip brand. If you are a potential customer and we approach you with our J-Wil brand of zip, which we claim to be better, lighter, more durable and cheaper, you know what you would say to us, don't you?

"If your J-Wil brand of zip is so good, why aren't you the leading brand?"

That is a really difficult question for marketing people to answer and no matter what you say, the answer will seem quite weak. That is why it is important to be first. What if you are not first? Are you doomed? No. Fortunately, there are other rules of branding to help you out. In the next chapter, we will look at the third rule of branding – the power of a new category.

If we are not the first in zips, the next best thing for us to do is to create a new category of zips. Perhaps we can create self-closing zips – a new category – and that would give us the ammunition to use against YKK. That would allow our brand of zips to be first in the mind in a new category of zips called "self-closing zips".

In A Nutshell

If you want to create a strong brand, you need to own an idea in the minds of your customers. That idea is shaped by your customers' perception of your brand, so you have to create a great perception for your brand. The easiest way to do that is by being the first in the market. If you are the first in the market, you can get into the minds of potential customers before competitors show up. Being first in the market is just a licence to get into the mind first. That licence has an expiry date. If you fail to exploit this licence, your competitors will punish you for it. First-mover failures fail not because the concept of first-mover advantage is outdated or flawed. It is because they fail to use their first-mover advantage in the market to firmly establish their brands in the minds of customers. If you are first in the market and you use this advantage to establish the brand in the mind, then it will be difficult for competitors to unseat you. You will have a strong brand because you stand for something in the minds of customers. The first brand in the mind usually gets to choose what *idea* it wants to stand for because all the ideas are available.

The reason why companies choose the Better-And-Cheaper-Strategy is because most companies are not first in the market. This strategy doesn't work although it seems like a great idea because of what we call The Paradox of Logic. Customers think that the No. 1 brand – regardless of the reason why it became No. 1 – must be the best brand because all of us have been conditioned since young to think that No. 1 is the best. Companies think that if they have the best product or service, they will be No. 1 but the only opinion that matters is that of the customers. You should also be aware of the dangers of market research. Market research is good but you must know when to ignore it. If you are the first in the market, you will find that market research will often show you that the market size is zero. Of course it is. No one has done it before. And when you are the first mover, drop everything else to concentrate on driving home that first-mover advantage. If you are not first, turn to Rule No. 3 of branding for help.

CASE STUDY
Fortune Favours The First – Swee Hong

The Engineering And Construction Industry

Despite Singapore's small land area of 704 square kilometres, it is forecasted that the engineering and construction industry will grow at a compound annual growth rate (CAGR) of 2.6 per cent between 2009 and 2014, bringing the total value of the industry to S$8.7 billion by the close of 2014.[20] The largest segment of the construction and engineering industry comprises non-residential building, which accounts for approximately 60.4 per cent of the total industry, with the other 39.6 per cent in civil engineering.[21] It is expected that growth in non-residential building in Singapore will slow down in the coming years given the completion of the two integrated resorts, Resorts World Sentosa and Marina Bay Sands, as well as the Marina Bay development. However, it is expected that higher public construction activity and relatively higher civil engineering activity will slightly offset the drop in non-residential development.

Swee Hong – A Solid Foundation In Engineering And Construction

Founded in 1962 by Mr Ong Koh Bee under the name of Chop Swee Hong, Swee Hong is one of Singapore's leading civil engineering companies with a Grade A1 contractor (the highest-possible ranking) in the Civil Engineering (CW02) Category. This allows the company to tender for Singapore public projects of unlimited contract value. Consequently, Swee Hong is one of the main district construction contractors for government agencies in Singapore. The company's core capabilities lie in the engineering and construction of roads and highways.

Since its establishment, Swee Hong has grown from humble beginnings to a company that currently has over 100 skilled and semi-skilled workers. The company's current Managing Director, Mr Ong Hock Leong, is the grandson of the founder and his vision is to build upon the company's legacy of diligence and growth and stretch the Swee Hong brand into untapped international markets to seek new growth avenues.

Recently, the company has been involved in Gardens by the Bay and Seletar Aero Drive, both major projects in Singapore. Its repeated success in winning government contracts from the Singapore government is an illustration of the high level of trust and reputation it has built up over the years as a civil engineering company.

---

[20] Industry Profile, Construction & Engineering In Singapore, from www.datamonitor.com
[21] ibid

Ong, however, was aware that in order to remain competitive and expand the business, Swee Hong could not depend solely on the local market for two simple reasons: stiff competition and the island's limited land area. Foreseeing that the engineering and construction industry in Singapore will plateau following the completion of Marina Bay Sands, Resorts World Sentosa and the Marina Bay development, there was an urgent need for Swee Hong to look for new ways to grow its business.

Consequently, Ong decided to take a two-pronged approach. Firstly, he decided to strengthen the company's capabilities in tunnelling technology. Secondly, it should venture abroad and compete for regional projects.

Venturing out of its comfort zone was not an easy task for Swee Hong as its focus on government tenders has worked well. Having built a long-standing reputation as a reliable supplier to the Singapore government, it would have been easy to take the view that there was little need to market the company to secure projects. Ong, however, recognised the dangers of depending solely on Singapore for business. He did not want Swee Hong to be perceived as a brand confined to the Singapore market, but instead as a regional brand capable of handling sizeable regional projects. Yet the reality was that the company to date had not made a conscientious effort to communicate its brand, both locally and abroad.

This gave rise to the first brand perception challenge that Swee Hong faced – to reposition itself as a regional civil engineering and construction company capable of offering a suite of tunnelling services. This challenge involved the creation of a Swee Hong brand that would appeal to international developers, urban planners and governments. What was also needed was a marketing communications roadmap to guide Swee Hong's communications efforts to strengthen its brand within chosen markets.

The second brand challenge that Swee Hong faced was to modernise the organisation from a brand perspective so that it remains relevant in the 21st century.

The third challenge that Swee Hong faced was the lack of brand awareness in overseas markets. This would hinder Swee Hong from winning overseas projects, especially when the company has to compete with local players entrenched in their respective markets.

In a three-month long perception audit, it was found that the Swee Hong brand was strongly associated with an experienced civil engineering company specialising in infrastructure, particularly road building. This was consistent with Swee Hong's long and established track record in road building projects. Therefore, although the company had not actively communicated its brand in the past, its repeated success in tendering, winning and completing civil engineering jobs in Singapore created the strong association between the Swee Hong brand and civil engineering works.

While the strong association to being an experienced civil engineering company specialising in road building continued to generate new business opportunities, it also limited Swee Hong's growth into other desirable areas, such as tunnelling. Given that the strategic intent of the company is to go beyond road building by offering a wider range of civil engineering services, the company had to find a way to disassociate itself from being a pure road builder and becoming a fully fledged civil engineering company with strong tunnelling capabilities.

The Strategy: Position Swee Hong As "FIRST WORLD CITY BUILDERS"
Engineering and construction companies such as Swee Hong not only have to be equipped with cutting-edge technology but also be regarded as exceeding the demands of modern engineering and construction by offering innovative methodologies through technology. As part of its strategic intent, the company has set its vision on being the first tunnelling company in Singapore to provide advanced tunnelling technology to first-world aspiring cities and their respective governments. Ong understands that fortune more often favours the first:

> *Swee Hong has identified that there is a growing demand for tunnelling technology and services in many parts of Asia, This is why we see an emerging need for high-value tunnelling technology solutions in Asia.*

As a proponent of constant improvement and innovation, Swee Hong devotes a substantial amount of resources into technology. For instance, the company has developed an innovative tunnelling capability called "trenchless technology". Unlike conventional methods that require digging a trench, Swee Hong's trenchless technology allows tunnels to be dug without having to close off major sections of the surface area for trenches. This reduces traffic congestion associated with tunnelling.

Swee Hong was also the first company in Singapore to acquire and own tunnelling machinery. The company owns three Herrenknecht tunnelling machines imported from Germany, which cost S$48 million.

The Execution

The Perception Audit also suggested that while Swee Hong's reputation was found to be good, it lay mainly in the Singapore market, particularly in the government tender space. In order to become more competitive when bidding for engineering and construction projects abroad, Swee Hong had to evolve its brand into one that appeals to overseas buyers and then create a marketing strategy to effectively communicate the brand. Although its reputation is strong in the Singapore market, it is important that this reputation be made relevant and communicated to international clients. Hence, the first order of the day was to establish a distinct identity that clearly spelt out the differentiation and long-term strategy of the company.

Having established the identity, the next step was to enhance the Swee Hong brand in a manner that would help the company achieve its growth and organisational objectives. Within its markets of operation, whether local or abroad, Swee Hong then began communicating its differentiation.

In order to communicate the differentiation and associate Swee Hong to the attribute of "trust", a tagline that was short, unique and informative was formulated. Trust can be defined in several ways; in the context of Swee Hong, trust is defined by the number of government projects it has won over the last 48 years. The stringent criteria associated with Singapore government tenders suggest that only the most trusted and reliable company gets selected. Using this logic, the portfolio of government projects won and completed successfully by Swee Hong is a testament to the high level of trust associated with Swee Hong. It was also noted that in recent years, Swee Hong has been actively involved in the construction of structures that are transforming Singapore into a first-world city. This includes work on Gardens by the Bay and Sentosa South Cove. Taking this one step further, Swee Hong has been trusted not just for civil engineering works but for transforming Singapore into a first-world city. It is by this reasoning that the tagline "First World City Builders" was created for Swee Hong. This tagline communicates three things: (1) Swee Hong is different from its competitors due to the high level of trust it has gained in the market, (2) Swee Hong is in the business of engineering and construction and (3) Swee Hong is an enabler of first-world city living.

SWEE HONG
FIRST WORLD CITY BUILDERS

The differentiation strategy was complemented by Swee Hong's brand positioning – Builders of First World Cities for First World Living. This positioning had very strong international appeal, especially to emerging economies that are currently undergoing rapid urbanisation. More importantly, its positioning was complemented by its differentiation, which is based on trust. In essence, the evolved Swee Hong brand is one of an established civil engineering company that has the knowledge and expertise of building first-world cities.

As a result, Swee Hong has chosen to adopt a marketing-led philosophy to enable it to win market share and capture and retain the hearts and minds of current and prospective customers. It has pursued an aggressive marketing path to communicate its brand to chosen markets. The company has taken it upon itself to meticulously craft messages that are relevant to each stakeholder yet consistent with the overarching Swee Hong brand.

However, evolving an organisation at a rapid rate comes with side effects. One such side effect is people acceptance, i.e. the "getting-used-to" effect. Consequently, a brand operationalisation roadmap was also devised to communicate its brand to client segments through various communications platforms. A one-day workshop was also conducted to train and align every employee to the new brand.

Marketing as an activity is becoming more important to the company as it strives to build its capabilities in tunnelling technology and the accompanied services offered. Swee Hong recognises that this effort will increase its appeal to its customers and by doing so will stay ahead of regional competition. Building Swee Hong's brand is no longer the sole prerogative of its marketing department; Ong has made it everyone's responsibility so that marketing efforts are conceived, developed, planned, executed, reviewed and improved in a focussed manner. The company is today beginning to be recognised as a "First World City Builder". With this position, it continues to ensure that all of its visual and physical elements, i.e. from its people to services and processes, work together following the one vision that has made the company the leader in its category of tunnelling technology.

B2B

CHAPTER 10

Rule No. 3 –
Create A New Category

IN the war of brands, fortune favours the first. We have shown that the easiest way for a brand to become No. 1 is by getting into the market first because being first allows that brand to establish itself in the minds of customers before anyone else does. Being first in the market is a licence to own whatever idea that you want the brand to stand for in the minds of customers so that is something that brand builders should aim for.

What if somebody else got into the market first? What do you do? You have three options. One, you can roll over and give up the ghost. That is quite easy to do but not a whole lot of fun. Two, you can just copy what the leading brands are doing but we all know that's not going to build you a great brand. Three, you can create a new category so that your brand can be the first. Creating a new category allows you to be first in something. It is the same as being the first in the market. Somebody once said that the best way to predict the future is to create it. The best way to be the first in an overcrowded marketplace is to create something new that you can claim to be the first in.

The first person to fly solo across the Atlantic Ocean was Charles Lindbergh. As a result, he has a place in the minds of people. The second person to fly across the Atlantic Ocean solo was Bert Hinkler. Despite being faster and using less fuel than Lindbergh, Hinkler never had much hope of being as famous as Lindbergh because people are not interested in who is better, they are interested in who is first. Ironic as that may sound – given that we have always been conditioned since young to be better, to do better – that is how people function. So, what chance does the third person to fly across the Atlantic Ocean solo have of getting into the mind? Practically zero.

But the third person to fly solo across the Atlantic Ocean is probably even more well known than the first. How is that possible when most people don't even know who No. 2 is? We are quite certain that you have heard of Amelia Earhart. But she is not just the third person to fly solo across the Atlantic Ocean. She is the *first woman* to fly solo across the Atlantic Ocean. Amelia Earhart became famous because she set up an important new category. Her case also illustrates why new categories can be so powerful.

The first man in space was Yuri Gagarin, the Russian astronaut. Although Alan Shepherd, the second man in space, set up a new category for himself – the first American in space – that category wasn't interesting enough or important enough to make him famous. When you set up a new category, that new category has got to be important and interesting. Being the first American in space is no big deal because the first American in space is still just another human being. Being the 100-year-old man (or woman) in space might be interesting. Being the first Siamese twins in space might be interesting. Being the first human clone in space might be interesting.

Who was the 58th man in space? Neil Armstrong. He is probably the most famous astronaut in history, even though he wasn't the first man, woman, American or chimpanzee in space, because he created a new category that he could own. He was the first man to step foot on the moon. Who was the second man on the moon?

If you are not the first in the market, you can set up a new category within the industry that you are in so that you can be the first to own a particular idea. This rule has helped to build many successful brands in the past and can help you in your quest to be a stronger brand.

BUILDING A NEW CATEGORY IN COMPUTERS

IBM is the 800-pound gorilla in the computer industry. Although IBM has sold its PC business to Lenovo and moved on to more lucrative stuff such as consulting, it is still a multi-billion giant in this industry. What was the idea that made IBM a killer brand in computers? The mainframe computer. IBM leveraged its strength in mainframes to become the No. 1 brand in computers. So, how do you compete with IBM? How do you become a strong computer brand given such a fearsome competitor? You set up a new category for yourself.

Dell became a strong brand by creating a new category called "computers direct". Dell did what nobody had done – or has managed to do since – by selling computers direct to customers. Many people predicted that Dell would fail because that was not how computers were supposed to be sold. But Dell is one of the most successful computer companies today because of this new category. By selling direct, Dell could sell cheaper. By selling cheaper, Dell managed to get many consumers to buy from it. These consumers were, in turn, influencers or decision makers in the companies that they worked for. When they found that the cheap computer they had bought for home use was actually quite good, they bought or recommended the computer to their colleagues. And Dell found a backdoor into the corporate market. Very clever.

Cray became a strong brand by creating a new category called "supercomputers". These are super fast computers that can perform billions of calculations per second. If you are running a research centre anywhere in the world, regardless of whether it is in the public or private sector, you probably want to have one of these Cray supercomputers – provided, of course, that you can afford the price tag.

Silicon Graphics became a very strong brand by creating a new category called "3D computers". The next time you watch an animated movie, like one of those blockbusters from Pixar or DreamWorks, think of Silicon Graphics. Hundreds of these machines are usually required in the production of one animated movie. Movies are not the only applications that Silicon Graphics machines are used for. Any job that requires 3D rendering can be done using one of these computers.

At this point, you must be thinking that setting up a new category is going to be a difficult and expensive affair. Nothing good ever comes cheap but that doesn't mean that all new categories require such a huge investment of time, money and resources. However, if you are a B2B company, creating a new category will invariably be more expensive than if you are a B2C company because B2B products and services are usually more expensive to begin with. And B2B products and services are usually more technical in nature. Nevertheless, it can be done and if you are not the first in your market and still want to build a powerful brand, then you probably need to develop a new category.

PITCHING YOUR BRAND INTO UNCONTESTED MARKETS

There is an alternative strategy to building a strong brand and that is to find new geographic markets that you can dominate. These new markets are invariably in emerging countries that are often ignored by the big brands because the purchasing power is lower, and these big brands naturally want to focus on large markets with strong purchasing abilities. Many Singapore companies are more competitive than the local brands in these emerging markets but not as strong as the top global brands. In an open market, these Singapore brands might get caught in the middle, which is not the place to be. However, in an emerging market with few or no top global brands, they can do well.

One of Singapore's home-grown electronics and home appliances companies is AKIRA. You will not find this brand widely available in Singapore. Its target market is actually the African continent where competition from the top Japanese and European brands is not as intense and local competition is by and large non-existent. AKIRA has done well in its target markets in Africa but that doesn't mean that it was a walk in the park. You still need to have the first-mover advantage. You still need to get into these markets early and develop them patiently over time.

Food Empire is another Singapore company that has become very successful by targeting emerging markets such as Eastern Europe and Central Asia when it first started. The company is listed on the Singapore Exchange although most Singapore consumers might not have heard of the company. But the strategy has yielded good results for Food Empire. In many of the markets it operates in, Food Empire's MacCoffee 3-in-1 coffee brand is now the best selling. It was hard work according to the company CEO, Mr Tan Wang Cheow, but it helped Food Empire build a strong brand in these markets.

Pitching your brand into an uncontested geographic market might be a viable alternative to setting up a new category but you also need to move fast. You need to get into the market fast and establish your brand in the minds of your customers quickly before serious global competitors show up. Bear in mind also that these emerging markets have their own problems in terms of purchasing power, infrastructure, distribution channels, etc.

DO YOU WANT TO LEAD OR FOLLOW?

If you don't have the first-mover advantage, you can create a new category that you can lead in or you can follow the market leaders. Creating a new category is hard work, it is risky and in such a hypercompetitive market, it is hard to find new categories as you will discover that whatever new category you can think of will have been taken by someone else.

When Jacky was a student at the University of Wisconsin – Madison, his advertising professor, Scott Cooper, once told him, "If you want to be successful, you have to work very, very, very hard. You have to work much harder than the other guys." At that time, Jacky thought to himself, "Why should I work so hard? I just need to work smart." It was as if Scott Cooper had read his mind (or he has had too many smart-alec students like Jacky) when he continued by saying, "You may think that you are smart but trust me, out there in the business world, there are many guys who are as smart as you, and the only way you can win is by working harder than them." Fantastic advice. And something that is relevant to our discussion here. You've got to work very hard at finding or defining or creating a new category. Being smart helps but there are many people in your industry who are just as smart as you so you've got to work harder.

The alternative is to just follow the market leaders. You won't become a big brand but you can still earn a decent living. Which route you take depends on what you want to do and your risk appetite but history seems to suggest that creating a new category reaps bigger rewards than competing in an established category and playing the follow-the-leader – or more appropriately, copy-the-leader – game.

Starbucks was the first gourmet coffee chain in the United States and it is the No. 1 coffee chain in the world today, with 16,635 stores worldwide in 2009, up from the 12,440 stores in 2006 when we wrote the first edition of this book. Starbucks' revenue in 2009 was US$9.8 billion (S$12.6 billion), which is much higher than the US$7.8 billion (S$10 billion) it recorded in 2006.[22]

Southwest Airlines was the first budget airline to be established. It made its first scheduled flight in 1971 and despite the difficulties faced by the American airlines industry, Southwest has been profitable even during downturns. In 2009, despite the state of the American economy, Southwest still managed US$10.3 billion (S$13.2 billion) in revenue and US$99 million (S$127.2 million) in net income after tax.[23] Although this is a far cry from the US$645 million (S$828.7 million) in net income it earned in 2007, Southwest Airlines is still a strong brand in the airline industry and it got there because it set up a new category.

If you think Southwest's performance is pathetic, then you have to look at it in relation to the rest of the industry. In 2009, Delta Airlines recorded US$28.1 billion (S$36.1 billion) in revenue and made a loss of US$1.6 billion (S$2.1 billion).[24] In 2009, Continental Airlines recorded US$12.6 billion (S$16.2 billion) in revenue and made a loss of US$2.2 million (S$2.8 million).[25] In 2009, American Airlines recorded US$19.9 billion (S$25.6 billion) in revenue and made a loss of US$1.5 billion (S$1.9 billion).[26] What are the lessons that we can learn from this? Firstly, don't start an airline as it is not a good business

[22] http://investor.starbucks.com

[23] www.southwest.com/investor_relations/if_financials.html

[24] www.southwest.com/investor_relations/if_financials.html

[25] www.continental.com/web/en-US/content/company/investor/docs/continental_ar_2010.pdf

[26] http://phx.corporate-ir.net/phoenix.zhtml?c=117098&p=irol-fundIncomeA

to be in. Secondly, if you want to start an airline, then don't follow the leaders. They look rather lost – and loss-making as well. Create a new category just like Southwest did.

- Red Bull was the first energy drink and chalked up an estimated S$3.4 billion in sales in 2005.
- Zara was the first just-in-time fashion store and, today, Zara has 760 stores in 55 countries.[27]
- eBay was the first online auction website.
- YouTube was the first video sharing website.
- Montblanc was the first premium pen.
- Caterpillar was the first construction equipment company.
- Microsoft was the first operating system for PCs.

The list goes on and on.

Companies need to remember, however, that it takes time to build a category into a big business. You simply cannot force a category to grow. Just like growing a plant, growing a category takes time, effort and patience. You cannot force-feed the category or it will die, just like a plant that is overfed with fertilisers and water will die. Starbucks did not achieve overnight success. It took close to 10 years before the company cracked the US$50-million (S$64.2 million) mark. But after that, sales just exploded. Likewise with Zara. It was 13 years before it opened its first store outside of Spain.[28]

PROMOTE THE CATEGORY, NOT THE BRAND

Companies must always remember that they need to promote the category, not their brand. Nobody is interested in the brand. People are interested in categories, especially new ones. And when you promote a category, you are naturally seen as the leader. And as the leader in your category, it is your job to promote and expand the category. Anita Roddick did not promote The Body Shop. She promoted the category pioneered by The Body Shop – natural ingredients for cosmetics. And when that category grew, The Body Shop grew along with it.

As you promote the category, competitors will appear on the scene. That is almost as certain as death and taxes. But you need not worry if your market share starts to shrink as competitors join in. In the beginning, Coca-Cola had

---

[27] All figures for Red Bull and Zara are from Hoover's Inc, 9 March 2006.

[28] Al Ries and Laura Ries, *The Fall of Advertising and the Rise of PR*, Harper Business, 2004, p.103

100 per cent of the cola market. But because it promoted the category so aggressively, it grew and as it grew, the category became very attractive to competitors. Hordes of brands entered the cola market and Coke's share dropped as a result but that is all right because 30 per cent of a S$5-billion category is still far better than 100 per cent of a S$100-million category. Today, Coca-Cola has a lot less than the 100 per cent it had in the beginning but its sharply reduced market share now is still worth a lot more than its original 100 per cent share.

Keep promoting the category. That way, you will keep yourself ahead of the pack. You will be seen as the market leader. If you are perceived as the market leader, that is what you are. Remember Rule No. 1? Perception is reality. And perceptual leadership can often be translated into actual sales leadership.

CURRENT MARKET SIZE IS NOT THAT IMPORTANT

One of the biggest mistakes that marketers make (something that we ourselves were guilty of on countless occasions in the past) is to ask, "What is the size of the market?" But isn't that what they teach you in business schools? One of the first things you learn is that you need to find out the potential size of the market. Yes, we know that but we maintain that market size is really not that important.

First of all, if you want to build a powerful brand, you need to set up a new category that you can dominate. When you set up a new category, the answer to the question of how big the market is right now will most likely be a resounding "ZERO". So market size is really not relevant in this case. Every new category will have a market size of zero as its starting point.

Don't let that discourage you. Most of the big, successful global brands today started with a market size of zero because they created a new category but they promoted their category, grew that category and ultimately dominated it.

If you have figures regarding the size of the market in question, then it is probably the wrong market for you to build a new brand in. If you know the exact market size of a category, then it is an existing market and existing markets are usually dominated by a few big, powerful players. What you need to do is to create a new category (new market) instead of launching a me-too brand into an existing market – unless the brand that you launch into the existing market can be effectively differentiated.

Remember that the market size of new categories is always zero. Look at the following examples.

Walkman

What was the market size for portable cassette players before the Walkman came along? Nothing. It was a new category. Sony eventually sold 340 million units of the Walkman cassette player in its lifetime. The Walkman brand name became a generic term for this category and even entered the *Oxford English Dictionary*.[29]

Dell

What was the market size for computers sold directly to end users before Dell came along? Non-existent. It was a new category. Dell set up this new category and promoted it aggressively. It eventually became the biggest seller of PCs as this category grew rapidly.

Gulfstream

What was the market size for private business jets before Gulfstream came along? Probably not even worth mentioning. But Gulfstream promoted the category steadily and, today, the private business jet category has become a lucrative one.

Starbucks

What was the market size for gourmet coffee before Starbucks came along? Miniscule. Nobody paid US$3 (S$3.90) for a cup of coffee before Starbucks arrived on the scene. And if Starbucks had asked the question, "What is the market size for coffee that costs US$3 per cup?" it might have been discouraged from venturing into this new category.

Xerox

What was the market size for plain paper photocopiers before Xerox was launched? What market? There was no such market before Xerox launched the world's first plain paper photocopier, the Xerox 914 series.

Lexus

What was the market size for expensive Japanese luxury cars before Lexus was launched? There was no market. Before Lexus launched the LS400 in 1989, there was no such thing as a luxury Japanese car that could compete with the established players. If you wanted a luxury car before 1989, you would

---

[29] *Evening Standard* (London), 21 July 2004

have bought a Mercedes-Benz, BMW or Audi. The landscape has changed considerably since Lexus crashed the party.

THE MOST VALUABLE BRANDS ARE BUILT THROUGH NEW CATEGORIES

If you look at the 10 most valuable brands in the world according to *BusinessWeek*'s 2009 list of the '100 Best Global Brands', you will find that all of them were launched not to compete in an existing market that was already dominated by strong players but as new categories.[30]

1. Coca-Cola

Brand Value: US$68.7 billion (S$ 94.8 billion)

The world's most valuable brand wasn't launched to serve an existing market. Coca-Cola pioneered a new category of soft drinks in 1886 called cola. What was the market size of the cola category in 1886? Zero. But Coca-Cola promoted that category aggressively and consistently. When that category grew into a multi-billion dollar industry, guess who became No. 1? Not Pepsi, even though blind taste test after blind taste test demonstrated that respondents rated Pepsi as the better-tasting cola. That is how crucial a new category can be.

2. IBM

Brand Value: US$60.2 billion (S$83 billion)

IBM didn't start out as a computer company. In fact, IBM made all kinds of office machines (hence the name International Business Machines) like calculators and electric typewriters. And IBM wasn't even the first in the mainframe category that made it famous. The first mainframe computer on the market was UNIVAC but, as discussed in Rule No. 2, being first in the market is no use unless you use that advantage to get into the mind first. IBM concentrated all its resources on the mainframe. It got into the mind first and the rest is mainframe history.

3. Microsoft

Brand Value: US$56.6 billion (S$78.1 billion)

What Coca-Cola did for low-tech brands, Microsoft did in high tech. It is the 800-pound gorilla in the software jungle. How did Microsoft become so big and powerful? It was the first in a category called "16-bit operating system for personal computers". The rest were 8-bit systems at the time. Although Microsoft is trying to do all kinds of things these days, what really propelled the

---

[30] *BusinessWeek*, 17 September 2009

brand to the top initially was the 16-bit operating system, which found its way into IBM PCs and, subsequently, other computers.

4. General Electric

Brand Value: US$47.7 billion (S$66 billion)

Thomas Alva Edison didn't make a better, longer lasting and cheaper candle or paraffin lamp. He created a new category called "the electric light bulb" that was probably as revolutionary as the invention of the wheel and, in today's context, the birth of the Internet. His company eventually became General Electric (GE) and although it is a highly diversified company today, mention GE and light bulbs will still come to mind. That was the new category that launched the GE brand that is now 118 years old and still going strong.

5. Nokia

Brand Value: US$34.8 billion (S$48.1 billion)

Mention Nokia and what comes to mind? Mobile phones. But Nokia didn't invent this category, you might point out. Motorola did. Yes, but like IBM before it, Nokia dropped all of its other businesses such as pulp and paper, radios, tyres, rubber footwear, cable and electronics manufacturing, chemicals, machinery, television and IT to try and dominate this new category. That is why it managed to dominate the category. Despite stiff competition from Samsung, Sony Ericsson, Motorola and others, Nokia is still No. 1 with a market share that hovers around 35 per cent.

6. McDonald's

Brand Value: US$32.2 billion (S$44.6 billion)

McDonald's was the first fast-food hamburger chain – a new category that built McDonald's into the world's biggest fast-food chain, with more than 31,000 restaurants in over 100 countries. Who would have thought the simple hamburger could have resulted in such a big success. That is the power of a new category.

7. Google

Brand Value: US$31.9 billion (S$44.1 billion)

Since Google burst onto the scene with a new category – an Internet search engine that does nothing but search – people around the world no longer search for information on the Internet, they Google it. Many of Google's competitors at the time of its launch did a lot of other things besides search. Take a look at Yahoo!'s website today and you will know what we mean. Google is in danger of going down that path. Jacky – whose default home page is Google – has been increasingly irritated by Google because it seems that the Internet search giant is starting to lose its focus and has been adding a lot of things to the website that do not enhance the user experience. But Google's new category made it the No. 7 most valuable brand in the world.

8. Toyota

Brand Value: US$31.3 billion (S$43.2 billion)

What new category did Toyota create? The first reliable car. A Toyota may not be the most exciting or stylish car on the road but it was super reliable even by Japanese standards and apparently that is what millions of people want. After the massive worldwide recall that Toyota mounted in 2009 over faulty brake and accelerator pedals, the brand's reputation for reliability that you can take for granted has taken a major hit but if Toyota can fix the problems and regain its previously unassailable position at the top of the J.D. Power and Associates 'Initial Quality Study', it can still maintain its position as one of the top automakers in the world.

9. Intel

Brand Value: US$30.6 billion (S$42.3 billion)

Intel used to make memory chips when it first started but competition from the Japanese, Taiwanese and Koreans forced prices down. This category quickly became a commodity. Intel wisely dropped its memory chips business and focussed on a new category – the microprocessor. The microprocessor made Intel famous. And this time around, Intel wisely spent resources on building up the Intel brand of microprocessors to prevent this category from being commoditised by brutal price competition.

10. Disney

Brand Value: US$28.4 billion (S$39.2 billion)

What new category made Disney famous? Animated cartoons. Characters like Mickey Mouse, Donald Duck, Pluto, Snow White and Chip 'n Dale burnt the Disney brand into the minds of millions of people. Mention Disney today and you will still think of Mickey Mouse. Disney wasn't launched to serve an existing market. It created a new market. And as that category grew, so did Disney's fortunes.

THE QUESTION YOU MUST ASK

One of the most important questions that brand owners and marketers must ask is this: Is my brand serving an existing market or is it creating a new market? If you are serving an existing market, you will be faced with powerful, entrenched competitors. You won't be making a lot of headway but if you are all right with being a small player, go ahead and do it.

But if you want to build a brand, you need to create a new market. Set up a new category that you can own. Promote that category (not the brand) relentlessly. It is not an easy job. It takes years but that is how valuable brands are built. It is not too late for you to start but you better get a move on before all the possible avenues are closed by the relentless march of new brands from countries like China and India.

For example, Lenovo, Haier and Huawei are already giants in computers, home appliances and networking systems respectively in China. Furthermore, given China's huge domestic market, these top brands already have a size advantage even before they venture overseas so you have to move faster in your brand building efforts.

You can't possibly compete with China on cost. Not many countries can. Therefore, you have no choice but to rely on the intangibles and the most important intangible that you can own is the brand. So start thinking of new categories that you can possibly set up and dominate.

HOW DO YOU CREATE NEW CATEGORIES?

1. Break Things Apart

You don't need to own the final product in order to build a powerful brand. The easiest way to set up a new category is to take a complete product and break it apart. Look at the individual components or functions. Pick one to focus on. Many big and successful brands have been built this way, both in high-tech as well as low-tech.

The computer industry provides many examples of brands that were built by taking out specific functions or components from a computer.

- Palm took the organiser function out of the computer and created a new category – the PDA. Palm is the leading brand of PDAs today.
- BlackBerry took the e-mail function out of the computer and created a new category – the portable e-mail computer. BlackBerry has become the leading brand for portable e-mail computers.
- Creative Technology took the sound card out of the computer and created a powerful component brand around this category.
- NVIDIA took the graphics chip out of the computer and built a powerful brand around it. Its GeForce graphics chip is used by almost every major computer maker in the world.
- Intel took the microprocessor out of the computer and built a brand that is even bigger and more profitable than established computer brands like Dell.
- Asus took the motherboard out of the computer and built a powerful brand around this category.

We suspect that most people base their computer purchase decisions partly on whether that computer has all the right brands of components like an Intel Pentium CPU, a GeForce graphics chip, an Asus motherboard, a Sound Bláster sound card, etc.

In the low-tech sector, the department store has spawned many component brands that have become bigger and more successful than the department store brands that inspired them. Look at a typical department store like Robinson's, Takashimaya, Seiyu, Isetan, JC Penney or CK Tang. Each has many different departments selling all kinds of things. What happened to these different departments? The specialists came, took each department out one by one and turned it into a separate category. The brands listed below all started out as specialists. They decided early on to focus on just one of the department store's many offerings and make it big in that category. Instead of being everything to everyone, the specialist brands decided to focus on a specific area and that subsequently made them very successful.

- G2000 took the affordably-priced men's and women's business wear department out and turned it into a new category.
- Giordano took the casual clothing department out and turned it into a new category.
- Americaya took the shoes department out and turned it into a new category.
- Victoria's Secret took the lingerie department out and turned it into a new category.
- Royal Sporting House took the sporting goods department out and turned it into a new category.
- Aussino took the bedding department out and turned it into a new category.
- Gap took the high-end casual clothing department out and turned it into a new category.

The list goes on. That is one way for you to create a new category for yourself. Look at the final product, take it apart and try to figure out which component or function you can turn into a category that you can dominate. And make your brand stand for that category. The possibilities are not limited only to the computer industry and the retail sector that we have cited as examples.

2. Evolution

Evolution is one of the ways that new categories are created. The process of evolution is usually linear and the advent of a new category usually does away with the existing category. Look at typewriters. First of all, there was the mechanical typewriter. And Remington Rand was a powerful brand in the mechanical typewriter category. Then came a new category called the electric typewriter. The electric typewriter was a natural evolution of the typewriter category.

But Remington Rand did not move fast enough to dominate this category. Brother became a more successful brand than Remington Rand in this new category. And this new category eradicated the existing category of mechanical typewriters.

After this came the word processor, which was again a natural evolution of the electric typewriter. This new category practically killed the electric typewriter and made Wang into a powerful brand. But Wang, in turn, fell victim to a new category called personal computers, which was dominated by Compaq.

3. Divergence

Another way to create a new category is through divergence. Divergence refers to the process whereby a new category diverges from the original category. Divergent categories can usually co-exist with the original category.

An example of divergence at work can be found in the software industry. Microsoft was the original software company and stands for operating systems for PCs. But over time, other software categories diverged from this original category. Today, you have all kinds of divergent software categories existing side by side with Microsoft.

- Symantec in anti-virus software.
- Trend Micro in Internet security.
- Ad-Aware in anti-spyware.
- Intuit in financial software.
- Oracle in database software.
- SAP in enterprise resource planning software.
- ACT! in contact software.
- Linux in open source operating systems software.
- Siebel in customer relationship management software.
- Datastream in asset management software.

WHAT DO YOU USE YOUR NEW CATEGORY FOR?

If you have a new category, that means there must be an old category. Therefore, you should use your new category to attack the old category. What you are trying to tell the world is that your category is the latest thing. It is next generation and it is going to make the existing category obsolete.

The Sony Boombox was the first portable music player. Remember those big boxes that people used to carry on their shoulders while they danced their way down the street? New category. It was a major hit. Then Sony created a new category called the portable cassette player under the Walkman brand. The Walkman made the Boombox obsolete as a portable music player.

What Sony did here is a classic example of a company attacking its own category and making it outdated before a competitor does. And this is a good thing because it pre-empts the market and stops competitors from establishing a foothold with their own new categories. After that, Sony again attacked itself with a new category called the portable CD player. The Discman became a big hit. Sony's drive petered out after the Discman and this allowed Apple to seize the initiative. Apple attacked Sony with a new category called the MP3 player and the iPod made the Discman (and everything else) obsolete.

So if you are Sony or Creative Technology, how do you attack Apple? With a better, cheaper, features-loaded, longer battery life MP3 player? No. If you want to succeed against Apple, you need to create a new category and attack the MP3 player as a category. Make the MP3 look last generation. Make it obsolete. That is how you attack Apple.

Intel and Microsoft are two other classic examples of companies that continuously create new categories to maintain their brands' leadership positions. Intel launches new categories of microprocessors with lightning speed and clockwork regularity: 286, 386, 486, 586, Pentium I, Pentium II, Pentium III, Pentium IV, Pentium D, Celeron, Centrino, Xeon and Core Duo. As a result, it is difficult for any other brand to attack Intel and make its category obsolete.

But AMD found a way with a new category. AMD decided to focus its efforts on dominating a category that is fast becoming very important in the Internet era – server chips. AMD's 64-bit Opteron server chip managed to chalk up impressive growth, going from less than 1 per cent market share to over 22 per cent in less than two years.

Microsoft, likewise, maintains its leadership by launching new categories to make its existing categories obsolete. Windows 95 was quickly followed by Windows 98, Windows 2000, Windows NT, Windows ME, Windows XP, Windows XP Pro, Windows Vista and now Windows 7. Although all these sub-brands fall into the operating system category, they can be viewed as new categories within "operating system".

CATEGORIES COME AND CATEGORIES GO

It is possible that one day your category will become obsolete. And it is much better for you to be the one making your category obsolete than for a new upstart to do it for you. When your category starts to become obsolete, you need to jump ship. Find a new category to anchor your company. Don't hang on to the obsolete category for too long. And most importantly, don't bring your existing brand name (which is tied to the old category) into the new category. That is a recipe for disaster.

Kodak invented digital photography in 1976. That was the beginning of the end for film photography. It took a long time, yes, but it was bound to happen. Kodak had a new category that would make the old category obsolete but Kodak made two big mistakes that hampered its efforts to dominate the digital photography category.

Firstly, it did not use the new category to aggressively attack the old category. That allowed other companies like Canon, Sony and Olympus into the game. Secondly, when Kodak finally jumped onto the digital camera bandwagon, it chose to keep the Kodak name, which stood for film, not digital cameras.

Many years ago, when Jacky was working in the marketing department of an education software company, he missed the opportunity to use a new category (e-learning) to attack the old category (conventional classroom learning). Although the company marketed its brand of education software very aggressively, its campaigns would have been more successful if it had been geared towards making the existing way of learning look outdated and prehistoric instead of competing with the other brands that began appearing in this new category.

It is not an easy task but that is what the category pioneer needs to do. Promote the category. If a category pioneer does not actively promote the category, then it is fighting the wrong war. Remember that.

In A Nutshell

History has shown us that strong brands can be built through the creation of a new category. Many of the top global brands that you see today were not the first in their industry but they each created a new category that they could be the first in. These companies also promoted the category aggressively. When you promote a category, you are seen as the category leader – a very important thing. When you promote the category, you "own" it. When you promote a category, it will grow and your brand will grow with it. But a growing category will attract competitors and they will erode your market share. Don't worry about that. Keep promoting the category. Long term, if you can maintain a 40 per cent market share, that is good enough. Plus, if the category grows, your 40 per cent will definitely be more than the 100 per cent that you had in the beginning. There are three ways to create a new category. One, break things apart and see what component or function you can take out and make into a new, separate category. Two, evolution. This is the natural progression of a category. When a category matures to the point that it can't mature anymore, a new category usually comes along to replace it. Three, divergence. This is when a new category is created that co-exists with the original category. Keep in mind that categories can grow, mature and die. If your new category starts to die, recognise the signs early and then save your company by launching a new category along with a new brand.

CASE STUDY
Creating A New Category – Kansai

The Paint And Coatings Industry

The global market for paint and coatings was valued at S$91.3 billion in 2006 and is expected to grow to S$131 billion by 2012. The decorative paint market alone is projected to be worth S$65 billion by 2013, as reported by industry research firm The Freedonia Group Inc.

Paints for a myriad of applications will continue to be widely used as the world becomes more industrialised and advanced over time. You can imagine the global rivalry and within it, a highly competitive environment. The situation in Singapore is no different. Global leading brands such as AkzoNobel, Jotun, Nippon and Kansai, as well as many other lesser-known brands, all have a piece of the market. From the product perspective alone, it is common to note that it is quite difficult for the average consumer to tell one paint brand from another in terms of quality. Hence, perceptual differentiation is a critical success factor when buying paint. That is why next generation products within new categories are an important feature in this business.`

Going Aggressive In Decorative Paint – Kansai

Established in 1963, Kansai Paint Singapore ("Kansai") is a joint venture between Kansai Paint Co Ltd and Mr James Lim, a Singapore entrepreneur with decades of experience in the paint industry. It is important to note that Kansai Paint Co Ltd was founded in 1918 and is Japan's No. 1 paint and coatings company.

With over 45 years of experience in Singapore, Kansai is an established company with modern manufacturing facilities. As Kansai Paint's decorative paint technology was developed entirely in Singapore, Kansai Paint assigned Kansai, Singapore to spearhead the group's decorative paint expansion plans in order to fully exploit the commercial potential of this product range.

Kansai seeks to further boost its market share in the Asia Pacific region by focussing on the lucrative decorative paint category. Unfortunately, while it is evident that this category has a lot of growth potential, it is also a highly competitive one with many entrenched competitors such as Nippon Paint, AkzoNobel, Jotun and SKK.

As the leading paint and coatings company in public sector repainting and private sector repainting, Kansai desires to continue strengthening its position in these two markets while, at the same time, build upon its strengths and track record to enter two new segments – the new construction painting market for both the public and private sectors.

For the private residential sector, the two common methods used to secure business is through open tenders (an extremely price-sensitive segment) and pitching to existing condominiums' Management Corporation Strata Title (MCST), the management committee that decides which vendor will be used for the condominium's repainting job. Open tenders will be the typical mode of entry to the private residential sector's new construction painting market. The company is not yet a big player in this sector and hence needs to focus on strategies that can help penetrate it. As part of its strategy, Kansai also has to focus on ways to enhance its competitiveness when marketing to the MCSTs.

The Strategy: Creating A New Category In "Decorative Paint Systems"

Having a great brand reputation and track record is insufficient for Kansai as the other leading global paint brands that have a presence in Singapore are equally reputable. In view of this, the company has been on an innovation path to develop new products or further enhance the performance of existing ones. This strategic intent continues to ensure that the company stays ahead of its competitors in terms of quality and ease of application yet without compromising performance. In an interview with Mr James Lim, the Executive Chairman of Kansai Paint Singapore, he said:

> We want to create a paint system for the decorative market and this must be a system that lasts. It is very easy to paint a small section of the home or a wall in the kitchen. But when it comes to painting a building, it's a very different game all together. Specific surface conditions need to be achieved so that paint can be best applied. This includes the cleanliness and dryness of the surface, which must first be achieved. The chemical combination of the primer, first and second coats of the paint must also be administered in a systematic way. At Kansai, we have developed a proprietary system that will outlast other paint brands when it is administered in the proprietary manner that we have developed.

Since it is generally almost impossible to determine product quality differences between paint brands, it is natural for customers to gravitate towards either the strongest brands or the cheapest brands. A formidable player relative to its key competitors, Kansai is neither the most accepted brand nor the cheapest brand. Without a clear differentiation strategy (which enables the company to command its desired price) or structural cost advantage (which offers customers the lowest price), Kansai faces the uphill task of attracting new customers and retaining existing ones.

In 2010, the company employed a leading brand consulting firm to evaluate new opportunities for the Kansai brand in Singapore. In order to enhance and strengthen the Kansai brand in the decorative paint sector vis-à-vis other brands, the company first had to be evaluated against its competition. Within this process, rigorous research was conducted on the industry and on four of Kansai's major competitors. The industry and competitor analyses were crucial in uncovering the fact that Kansai could leverage on a professional paint system to deliver optimum paint performance – something very much needed by the market as a result of cost consciousness.

At the same time, through a series of market studies and product evaluations, it was determined that Kansai held high-market performance in various specialised product classes. These products were well accepted by specialist paint application companies, specialist firms that provide painting services to the residential market. It was also ascertained that when a combination of products was deployed in specific circumstances and measured conditions, its products would generally outperform most products in the market. This was clearly a winning discovery.

This discovery quickly led to the launch of "Décor", a new product brand for Kansai's decorative line. In consideration of Kansai's real and perceived perception of being a provider of professional paint systems, as well as an evaluation of its competitors' strengths, the recommended differentiation strategy for Kansai was to own the attribute of "professional". Here it is important to note that Kansai sells paint to professional paint applicators who, in turn, provide painting services to customers. Hence, the "professional" attribute of Décor gave more weight to the applicators' profession – a tactical move to drive home the need for specialist applicators. The tagline "The Paint System That Lasts" served to encapsulate and dramatise this differentiation strategy. Executive Chairman James Lim had this to say:

> Décor will be our new offering to the decorative paint market. We believe that the durability of decorative paint and its performance is found not just in one tin of paint. Here at Kansai, we have developed a proprietary paint system that involves systematic and professional applications. What this does is that when our products are used in a proprietary manner, the durability of the paint actually lasts longer. To emphasise this, we are putting our name behind this promise by providing our customers with a better warranty period. This is the reason why we have started this new category and in so doing, Kansai Singapore

is now the first company in this space. We know this is what our customers want because Décor meets two very important factors: High Product Performance and Cost Savings Due To Durability.

In terms of market competitive advantage, most paint brands that sell into the decorative segment market themselves well through either their wide range of colours or coating protecting ability. However, none focussed on performance. Here, Kansai opted to adopt the divergence strategy in creating a new category of "systems" within the paint category.

The Execution

The definition of Décor's product position is essential in determining Kansai's priorities, approach, objectives and strategies for its decorative paint products. This new category allows the company to formulate clear action plans to guide Décor on its journey to penetrating the decorative paint market segment.

With the mission to expand its presence in Singapore by increasing paint projects in the repainting sector as well as developing new paint projects in the new construction painting sector, Décor's preferred future is succinctly summarised in its new vision, "Beautifying Buildings For All Time". To achieve this, Décor, as a product brand, seeks to offer customers cost savings, convenience and continuous performance when they purchase decorative paints as a unified bundle since it is currently common practice for specialist paint applicators to buy various products from different brands.

However, a brand is not a brand until it is well known. The Décor brand will only work well in today's overcrowded, hypercompetitive market if it is effectively dramatised and well-articulated to all its various stakeholder groups. Having established the relevant strategies to differentiate and strengthen the new Décor brand, a sound Integrated Marketing Communications (IMC) strategy was developed. This IMC strategy provided a highly effective and cost-efficient platform for Kansai to communicate the Décor product brand to internal and external stakeholders by determining both the content and method of communication. Here, Décor's stakeholder groups were mapped out and stakeholder-centric brand messages were crafted in a customised way. These stakeholder touch-points include both online marketing channels and offline marketing channels.

Since the implementation of Décor's marketing activities requires a gradual but dynamic process, all brand messages and marketing communications have to be greatly enhanced in order to replace the current promotional tools which are limited in scope and reach. Aside from these, it is also necessary for Kansai to initiate and maintain a continuing dialogue with internal and especially external stakeholders. As a result, an implementation roadmap was developed to ensure that Kansai communicates and implements the formulated strategies for Décor in a clear, consistent and constant manner.

The creation of the new brand "Décor – The Paint System That Lasts" clearly articulates Kansai's determination to differentiate its decorative paint from other players in a way that is relevant to its customers and defensible against the competition in the long run. Bringing clarity to Décor, the new product brand also minimises the risk of customer confusion with the company's other product lines. The long-term growth strategy for Décor to be a highly differentiated product brand of decorative paint is well-manifested in its crystal clear and well-thought-out differentiation, positioning and integrated marketing communications strategies.

B2B

CHAPTER
11

Rule No. 4 –
The Power Of Focus

IN the battle between generalist and specialist brands, the specialists usually win because they are highly focussed. When you are focussed, two things happen. One, you actually become very good at what you do because that is all that you do. Two, other people will perceive you to be very good at what you do since that is all you do. Remember that in branding, perception is reality. Besides being good, you need to create the perception that you are good. And focus is a very good way for brands to create the perception that they are good at something.

WHICH IS THE BETTER BRAND?

Who makes the better air-conditioner? Daikin or Sanyo? Most people we know will automatically say Daikin because that is all that Daikin does – air-conditioners. Sanyo, on the other hand, makes a lot of things. While it is entirely possible that Sanyo air-conditioners are as good as, if not better than, Daikin units, the common perception is that Daikin has got to be better because it is an air-conditioner specialist. That is why Daikin is able to charge a premium for its products.

Who makes the better watch? Seiko or Guess? Well, Seiko may not be a very hip brand but most people will think that Seiko makes a better watch than Guess because Seiko only makes watches. Guess makes all kinds of things and because of that, people tend to perceive it as less superior to a specialist watch brand like Seiko. After all, how can you make clothes, fashion accessories and watches, among other things, and be good at everything? That is how people perceive things. However, people do still buy Guess watches because they regard them as fashion accessories rather than watches per se.

Who makes better sunglasses? Ray-Ban or Prada? Most people will say Ray-Ban because Ray-Ban is highly focussed on sunglasses. Most people are not experts in sunglasses technology but that doesn't matter. Ray-Ban is focussed on sunglasses so people think that Ray-Ban must be better when it comes to sunglasses.

Who makes better off-road vehicles? Land Rover or BMW? Most people will say Land Rover because Land Rover is a highly focussed off-road vehicles specialist. Yet how many people actually go off-road? Not that many. But whenever people talk about serious off-road driving (even people who know very little about off-road driving, like us, for instance), the Land Rover brand will always come to mind because the reasoning is if it is focussed on off-road driving, it must be good.

Who makes a better golf club? Nike or Titleist? Wilson is an avid golfer and has tried all kinds of golf clubs. He finds Nike golf clubs quite good but when he had to buy a set for himself, he decided to buy Titleist. When asked why, he said that Nike is famous for sports shoes, not golf clubs. Titleist is famous for golf clubs. Therefore, no matter how good a Nike golf club is, he will never buy it because there will always be this nagging feeling that because he is not buying from a specialist, he may not be getting the best. Some golfers would probably buy Nike but we believe that most would prefer to go with the specialist brands like Titleist or Callaway.

Who makes better vacuum cleaners? Dyson or Electrolux? Most housewives we spoke to who have actually heard of both these brands said Dyson because it is a highly focussed vacuum cleaner brand. Electrolux, on the other hand, makes a lot of things other than vacuum cleaners. Besides being highly focussed, Dyson vacuum cleaners are also highly differentiated because of their striking design and innovative technology.

Who makes better computer servers? Sun Microsystems or HP? Most people would say Sun Microsystems because it is a more focussed brand while HP makes a lot of other things such as desktop computers, laptops, printers, digital cameras, handhelds, software, plasma televisions, DVD players, etc.

Who makes a better beer? Heineken or Budweiser? Although both companies are focussed on beer, we believe more people will see Heineken as a better beer because Heineken only makes one kind of beer – lager. Budweiser has so many types of beer that it is no longer easy to order a Budweiser. Tell a bartender, "Give me a Heineken," and he will know exactly what you are talking about. Tell him, "Give me a Budweiser," and he may ask, "Which one? Budweiser, Budweiser Select, Bud Light, Bud Ice or Bud Ice Light?" In the end, the confused customer will probably say, "Oh, never mind. Just give me a Heineken." Or the guy might just say, "Ah, give me a Tiger Beer."

FOCUS REQUIRES SACRIFICE

A curious thing happens when a brand becomes successful. It will gradually lose focus. Jack Trout, the father of positioning, calls it FWMTF, which stands for "Forgot What Made Them Famous". It happens to successful companies all over the world and across all types of industries. We call this The Wardrobe Phenomenon. Have you ever noticed that no matter how neatly you arrange your wardrobe (or your cubicle at work), it will get messy over time? It happens to everyone, even people who are pathologically neat, like Jacky. The same thing happens to companies once they become successful. They get messy. They lose their focus. They start line-extending their brand into every area – some related to their core business, some totally unrelated.

For a lot of companies, once they become successful, they plan for an IPO. There is nothing wrong with that. But the problem arises when these newly listed companies go on an acquisition spree in the name of growth. Many of these acquisitions have nothing to do with the company's core competency. As a result, the company starts to lose its brand identity.

If you need any convincing, just take a look at the companies listed on the Singapore Exchange. Many of them are so diversified that you cannot describe what they do and what they do becomes no different from what other listed companies do. A property company may decide to go into the food and beverage sector. A trading company may decide to enter the health care sector. Everybody is jumping into everyone else's business.

What made GE so successful? The electric light bulb. And once it became successful, it expanded its focus and went into all types of business. Look at GE today. Can you really describe what it does? It is not easy. But GE had a huge head start over most companies. Competition wasn't as keen as it is today. And GE only diversified after it became huge and rich. If you try to do a GE today and you are not already the No. 1 in whatever it is that you are doing, all we can say is a heartfelt "Good luck, buddy."

What made IBM successful? The mainframe computer. And once IBM became successful, it expanded into all kinds of business. Look at IBM today. It is a very diversified conglomerate with a finger in every pie. But IBM is like GE. It got a very early start in the computer industry and became very big and successful before it ventured into systems integration and then consulting. But if you look at IBM, it has evolved. It dropped the PC business to focus on services – systems integration and consulting.

What made BMW successful? Making the ultimate driving machines. And once it was successful, it started to lose focus. BMW has launched a new range of SUVs and MPVs. Can these behemoths drive like a real BMW? Jacky test drove the first generation BMW X5 4.4 and found it to be a highly compromised vehicle. It is tall and heavy (over 2,000 kilogrammes) so BMW had to fit very stiff suspension to make it handle remotely like a BMW. But it only serves to ruin the ride and still doesn't make the X5 handle as well as a regular BMW saloon or station wagon for that matter.

The typical CEO will look at these companies and say, "Look, these companies are successful brands. And see how line-extended they are? Why shouldn't we do the same thing?"

If you are thinking along these lines, you need to read the next paragraph carefully.

If you want to become a successful entrepreneur like Sir Richard Branson, what do you do? Buy expensive houses, drive flashy cars, wear high-end tailor-made suits, travel by private jet, entertain guests on your own exclusive island? If you do that, you will end up making a big hole in your bank account. And you will probably go bankrupt. If you want to be successful like Richard Branson or Li Ka Shing, don't do what they did after they became successful. Look into their pasts and study what they did before they became successful. Emulate what they did in order to become successful.

The same applies to brands. A lot of successful brands today are unfocussed and heavily line-extended but that doesn't mean you should do the same. What made these brands successful in the first place is usually a single-minded focus on one thing and one thing only. These brands narrowed their focus in order to become successful. Plus, a narrow focus is necessary for a company that is still trying to become a global brand because it has limited resources and can't possibly do everything. You need to focus. Pick your battles carefully.

But focus requires sacrifice. In order to have a focus on one thing, you cannot focus on other things. That is the price you have to pay to build a focussed brand. A lot of companies are reluctant to make this sacrifice because they are afraid that being focussed on one thing will mean that they could possibly lose out on opportunities in other areas. Fear and greed are the two factors that usually drive companies to diversify. Sure, when you diversify your business, you diversify your risks but at the same time, you will also dilute your brand's power. If you want your brand to stand for something in the minds of your customers (and the mind is where the branding war is won or lost), you need to focus. And focus requires sacrifice.

- FedEx focussed on overnight letters when it first started. That focus imprinted the brand in people's minds. FedEx owns the pigeonhole in the mind that is marked "overnight letters". But being focussed on overnight letters meant that FedEx had to give up all the other things that it could possibly do. Was the sacrifice worth it? According to the FedEx 2009 Annual Report, FedEx had a net profit of US$105.8 million (S$135.9 million) on a sales turnover of US$38.3 billion (S$49.2 billion).[31] Considering that the logistics business is capital intensive and ultra-competitive, we would say that it is worth it. Only when FedEx became successful based on this single-minded concept of overnight letters did it expand into other areas. The lesson of FedEx is this: When you are first starting out, narrow your focus; sacrifice everything else. Once that narrow focus has made you successful and famous, then you can branch out into other areas.

- Domino's Pizza focussed on pizza delivery. That means it had to give up dine-ins, takeaways, sandwiches, pasta, etc. But that sacrifice helped Domino's to dominate the category known as "pizza delivery" and it is second only to Pizza Hut worldwide. Not bad.

- Microsoft focussed on operating systems. That meant Microsoft had to sacrifice other types of software that it could have ventured into. But that focus built Microsoft into the dominant operating system brand in the world as well as the most successful software company. Now Microsoft is trying to get into all types of software and even game consoles and MP3 players. But remember that what made it successful in the first place was the resolute focus on operating systems.

- Sun Microsystems focussed on Unix-based servers. Although that meant that the Sun brand could not stand for other types of servers, Sun eventually became a powerful global brand because of that focus on Unix servers.

- Intel focussed on microprocessors. Intel had to sacrifice all its other businesses including the memory chip – its staple for decades. But today, Intel owns over 80 per cent of the world market for microprocessors

---

[31] www.fedex.com/us/investorrelations

and is the world's ninth most valuable brand. With its current CEO Paul Otellini, Intel is trying to branch out into other areas. While it is too early to tell if it will be successful, Intel risks diluting the power of the Intel brand by broadening its focus.

- TSMC focussed on semiconductors. It was the world's first semiconductor foundry. Being focussed meant that TSMC could not do what a typical contract manufacturer like Flextronics, Beyonics or Foxconn does today, which is everything under the sun. But that sacrifice has been well worth it because TSMC is an extremely profitable brand. In 2009, TSMC had net profits of S$3.9 billion on a sales turnover of S$13.1 billion, which translates to a huge margin of 29.8 per cent. In 2009, the NASDAQ-listed Flextronics made a loss of US$6.6 billion (S$8.5 billion) on a turnover of US$33.5 billion (S$43 billion), a margin of minus 20 per cent.[32] Flextronics' turnover is 247 per cent higher than TSMC but TSMC is making a lot more in terms of profit. There may be a lot of reasons why TSMC is more profitable than Flextronics but without doubt its focus is one of them. TSMC is a highly focussed brand. This focus not only makes it good at what it does, it also creates the perception that TSMC is good at what it does.

FOCUS ON CARS

In 2004, Mitsubishi had the dubious distinction of being the only Japanese car company to lose money. In fact, on a sales turnover of US$30 billion (S$38.6 billion), Mitsubishi Motors Corporation lost a whopping US$2.6 billion (S$3.3 billion).[33]

And according to business information database Hoover's (a Dun & Bradstreet subsidiary), Mitsubishi Motors Corporation did even worse in 2005 with a net loss of US$5.1 billion (S$6.6 billion) on a sales revenue of US$24.9 billion (S$32 billion).[34]

Does Mitsubishi make bad cars? No. Mitsubishi is, in fact, quite an innovative car company. It pioneered the Lanchester balancer shafts that quells vibration in four-cylinder engines and makes them run very smoothly. Even the original Porsche 944 had a pair of Lanchester shafts in its 2.5 litre four-cylinder engine. Mitsubishi also pioneered direct injection petrol engines that produce 20 per cent better fuel consumption compared to normal petrol

---

[32] www.nasdaq.com/asp/ExtendFund.asp?symbol=FLEX&selected=FLEX

[33] www.hoovers.com

[34] www.hoovers.com

engines. These days, most petrol engines use direct injection. But Mitsubishi is an unfocussed brand. That is why it does not have a strong hold on the mind.

Over the years, Mitsubishi's financials have improved. If you look at the table below, the company was profitable in 2008. We did not use 2009 figures because that was an unusually bad year for automobile manufacturers because of the deep recession. But among the Japanese car makers, it was still the least profitable both in terms of absolute profit and in terms of margin.

Table 5: Japanese Car Makers' Profitability In 2008

Brand	2008 Sales (US$ million)	2008 Net Profit (US$ million)	Net Profit Margin (%)
Toyota	263,028	17,187	6.53%
Nissan	108,503	4,835	4.46%
Honda	120,318	6,015	5.00%
Mazda	35,004	925	2.64%
Suzuki	35,272	808	2.29%
Daihatsu	18,941	389	2.05%
Mitsubishi	27,011	350	1.29%

(Source: www.hoovers.com; www.daihatsu.com)

Toyota seems like another unfocussed company as it makes all kinds of cars and trucks but its focus is actually on reliability. Toyota stands for reliability. That focus made the brand powerful. For decades, Toyota was so focussed on reliability that it would even settle for a car design that looked boring if that design was easier to build and resulted in better reliability, fit and finish. Toyota's ascension to the position of the world's largest car manufacturer has taken some toll on the company's focus. You probably remember the massive controversy surrounding faulty Toyota brake and accelerator pedals in 2009. We are sure these faults will be fixed and Toyota will regain its reputation for reliable cars but the loss of focus on what made Toyota such an admired brand cost the company dearly in 2009.

Nissan is starting to find a focus. In recent years, Nissan has begun to make distinctive-looking cars. You may or may not like the looks but they definitely stand out from the crowd. We are talking about cars like the March, Latio, 350Z, Murano, FX45, G35, Leaf, Qashqai, 370Z, GT-R, etc.

Honda has always been focussed on engines. Honda is widely acclaimed as one of the best engine makers in the world. We are not too crazy about the looks of recent Honda cars, which are yawn inducing, but their engines are definitely top of the line.

Mazda is focussed on sporty cars. Take a look at Mazda's line-up. Every single one looks sporty, even their MPVs and SUVs – traditionally the most boring of vehicles.

Suzuki is focussed on quirky SUVs.

Daihatsu is focussed on small cars.

Getting back to Mitsubishi, what is a Mitsubishi? It is a refrigerator, an air-conditioner, a bank, a car and a computer chip, among other things. Mitsubishi has a weak brand because it stands for so many things that it stands for nothing. It has no hold on your mind unlike a focussed brand.

Diversification, line extension and brand-stretching strategies will ultimately damage the brand. Of course, in the short term, you will see an increase in sales because you have more products to sell but, over time, a line-extended brand loses its power because it stands for so many things that it will start to lose its distinctive identity.

FOCUSSED BRANDS MAKE MORE MONEY

The table below shows you the total revenue and net profit/loss for focussed versus unfocussed brands over a period of 10 years (1996 to 2005). You will find that focussed brands tend to be more profitable, even though their revenue may be smaller in comparison to diversified brands.

Table 6: Profitability Of Focussed Versus Unfocussed Brands From 1996 To 2005

Brand	Core Business	10-Year Revenue (US$ million)	Net Profit/Loss (US$ million)	Net Margin
Sony	Video game players, TVs, DVDs, MP3 players, cameras, camcorders, phones, laptops, etc.	556	4.8	0.9%
Nintendo	Video game players	43	5.9	13.9%
Samsung Electronics	Microchips, mobile phones, MP3 players, DVDs, LCD panels, cameras, computers, colour monitors, DRAM, SRAM, etc.	333	34	10.3%
Intel	Microchips	247	52	20.9%
Hitachi	Semiconductors, PCs, elevators, TVs, robots, power plant equipment, metals, wires, cables, etc.	719	(1.7)	(0.2%)
TSMC	Semiconductors	28	7.8	27.9%

(Source: www.hoovers.com, 2005)

While it is evident that Samsung Electronics did well despite being an unfocussed company, it still made less money than Intel. Samsung's turnover was 35 per cent higher than Intel's but, comparatively, Intel's net profit was 53 per cent higher than Samsung's.

While you may argue that Samsung's net profit was still fantastic no matter what and it is therefore all right to copy its strategy, you need to bear in mind that you are not Samsung. Samsung has always spent heavily on R&D, innovation and design, and it is willing (and able) to sustain these efforts over a very long period of time. In addition, Samsung introduces a lot of innovative products every year. For example, Samsung was among the very first to introduce colour LCD monitors for mobile phones. Do you have the time, money, expertise and people to do all the things that Samsung does?

We decided to update the data in the table on the previous page with the financial data from 2007 to 2009 to see how these brands have done since.

Table 7: The Profitability Of Focussed Versus Unfocussed Brands From 2007 To 2009

Brand	2007 – 2009 Revenue (US$ million)	Net Profit/Loss (US$ million)	Net Margin	Net Margin (1996 – 2005)
Sony	246,210	2,246	0.9%	0.9%
Nintendo	43,942	6,939	15.8%	13.9%
Samsung Electronics*	292,786.70	20,774	7.1%	10.3%
Intel	111,047.00	16,637	15%	20.9%
Hitachi	312,084.80	(9,829)	(3.1%)	(0.2%)
TSMC	29,265.30	(9,176)	31.4%	27.9%

(Source: www.hoovers.com, 2010)
*Samsung figures are for 2006 to 2008

If you look at the data from 2007 to 2009, it would suggest that focussed brands generally make more profits. Regarding Sony versus Nintendo, Sony's net profit margin has remained unchanged but Nintendo's actually improved from 13.9 per cent to 15.8 per cent – aided no doubt by the success of Wii. Because Nintendo is focussed only on making video games, it could come up with the highly innovative Wii before anyone could make such a concept work.

Regarding Samsung versus Intel, both companies have seen their net profit margins drop, no doubt because of the recession, which typically hits electronics companies very hard, but Intel's profit margin is still double that of Samsung's.

Regarding Hitachi versus TSMC, Hitachi continued to lose money. In fact, its losses widened from negative 0.2 per cent to negative 3.1 per cent. In stark contrast, TSMC continued to thrive and its net profit margin increased from 27.9 per cent to 31.4 per cent.

Yes, we are aware that the second set of data is for three years and the first set is for 10 years but you can see a trend, can't you? Focussed brands tend to be more profitable even though they may have lower sales.

WHY DO COMPANIES REFUSE TO FOCUS?

Most companies refuse to focus because they think it is too risky. What if the category becomes obsolete or does not take off? Andy Grove, the founder of Intel, has this to say, "Put all your eggs in one basket and watch that basket carefully." If you refuse to focus out of the fear that you may fail, then you will find it hard to build a strong brand. Intel started out by making memory chips. Intel became the No. 1 memory chip maker but competition from the Koreans, Japanese and Taiwanese made the memory chip a commodity. That could have killed Intel because it was so focussed on memory chips and couldn't match the Asian companies on cost.

But Intel refocussed and put all its effort into microprocessors in 1985. It gave up the memory chip market completely. But the difference this time around was that Intel built a brand around its microprocessors. You remember the famous "Intel Inside" campaign? Intel is less susceptible to price competition now because it has built a strong, focussed brand around its microprocessors. Intel, in effect, built a brand out of what should have become a commodity like memory chips. Normally, we would recommend that when companies change their focus, they do so with a new brand because the old brand probably has too much baggage attached to it.

In Intel's case, it was all right to continue using the Intel brand because:

1. The memory chip is a commodity.
2. The memory chip belongs to a low-interest category.

So, nobody really identified memory chips with the Intel brand. Furthermore, Intel never really put in enough effort to tie the Intel brand to this category. While this made Intel's memory chip business susceptible to price competition, it also allowed Intel to refocus the brand more easily. The microprocessor is still regarded as a chip. This made it much easier for Intel to refocus its brand on this new category.

HOW DO YOU FIND A FOCUS?

You have to make a judgement call. Let's say you are an unfocussed company with multiple products or services. You need to decide which one has the most potential and focus on developing that into a category leader. For example, you have a portfolio of all these products and services under your brand:

- Pulp and paper
- Radios
- Tyres
- Rubber footwear
- Cables
- Electronics
- Chemicals
- Machinery
- Telecommunications
- Television
- Information technology

You are highly unfocussed. What do you do? You need to be ruthless. You cannot have it all. Don't be greedy. Which of these categories do you think has the greatest potential? Which one of these do you want to dominate? Once you have decided, sell off or close down all the other divisions to focus on the one category that you have decided on.

That was what Nokia did. In fact, the example given above was, in actuality, Nokia, which was founded in 1865 and over time became very unfocussed. But Nokia decided that it wanted to be a leader in mobile communications. Consequently, it sold off everything else to focus on mobile phones. It poured all its resources into becoming the No. 1 mobile phone brand in the world and launched its first digital mobile phones in 1993. Today, Nokia is still No. 1 despite stiff competition from Motorola, Sony Ericsson and Samsung.

Although Motorola was the father of the mobile phone category, it lost the lead to Nokia because Nokia became a specialist. That focus burned the Nokia brand into people's minds.

In the first quarter of 2010, 314.7 million handset units were sold worldwide according to a key insight report by Gartner that was published on pluggd.in – an online magazine for start-ups.[35] The table opposite shows the various brands' unit sales and global market share. Nokia is in the lead despite stiff competition from other players.

---

[35] www.pluggd.in/mobile-handset-sales-worldwide-nokia-297/

Table 8: Unit Sales And Market Share Of Handset Makers

Company	1Q 2010 Unit Sales ('000)	1Q 2010 Market Share (%)
Nokia	110,106	35.0
Samsung	64,897	20.6
LG	27,190	8.6
RIM	10,553	3.4
Sony Ericsson	9,866	3.1
Motorola	9,575	3.0
Apple	8,360	2.7
ZTE	5,375	1.7
G-Five	4,345	1.4
Huawei	3,970	1.3
Others	60,418	19.2
Total	314,654	100.0

(Source: www.pluggd.in)

The other way to find a focus is to create separate brands for the separate businesses that you have within the company. In the case of Nokia, if it had wanted to keep some of the original businesses that it had, it could have created new brands to park those businesses under. That would have maintained the focus. One brand for one business.

CAN YOU BE FOCUSSED AND STILL NOT DO WELL?

We have often been challenged on this point. Among the 10 rules of branding, this is the one that very often gets CEOs all charged up in disagreement. Their thinking is different. Some of our clients have pointed out that Chartered Semiconductor is a focussed company but it is not doing as well as its Taiwanese rivals, namely TSMC and UMC. Why is that so? Does this invalidate the rule of focus? No, it does not. TSMC and UMC are also highly focussed brands and that is one of the reasons why they are so successful. When you have two major competitors with first-mover advantage and they are highly focussed, you have to do something else to build the brand.

Chartered is indeed a focussed company but it was neither the first to enter the semiconductor foundry category nor was it the second. Chartered is a brand that was launched into somebody else's category. TSMC was the pioneering brand in this category. It was the first semiconductor foundry in the world. UMC followed closely behind. Once the No. 1 and No. 2 spots have been firmly established, it is hard for a No. 3 brand to establish itself as the lion's share usually goes to the top two brands.

Focus is important but category leadership is even more important. The best time to establish yourself in a new or emerging category is right at the start. Many companies wait until a category is established before they jump in with a better, cheaper product. By then, it is already too late. So if you are already highly focussed but you still have a problem building the brand because you don't have category leadership, what can you do? Differentiate. Rule No. 5 of branding is on the power of differentiation, which will be covered in the next chapter.

In A Nutshell

Two things happen when you focus. You become good at what you do because that is all that you do. And other people will also perceive you to be good at what you do since that is all that you do. This is the way the mind works. Focus is an important rule of brand building. When you compare focussed companies against diversified companies, you will find that diversified companies generally have higher sales. That should come as no surprise because if you have more things to sell you will have – everything else being equal – more sales. However, it is the focussed brands that make more money. We have met many companies that believe that they are focussed but they are not. We like to ask, "What is the area of focus for your brand?" And very often we get answers like, "We have four areas of focus – property development, food and beverage, waste management and investments." If you have this kind of "focus", you have no focus at all. To be focussed, you need to sacrifice. That means you have to give up something to be good – and to be perceived as good – at something else. If you are in property development, food and beverage, waste management and investments, you need to sacrifice three of them if you want to have a focus. Alternatively, you need to create four separate brands – one for each of the businesses – and ideally four separate companies as well.

CASE STUDY
The Power Of Focus – Shao Fook Engineering

The Engineering And Construction Industry

The engineering and construction industry is predicted to grow at a CAGR of 2.6 per cent between 2009 and 2014. Furthermore, the industry is expected to be worth S$8.7 billion by the end of the same period.[36]

Singapore's engineering and construction industry, especially the oil and gas and offshore and marine industries, will be fuelled by the rising demand for energy by the rapidly urbanising economies of China, India and numerous South East Asian countries. Accounting for 5 per cent of Singapore's gross domestic product (GDP), it is estimated that the island will account for 3.81 per cent of Asia Pacific's regional oil demand by 2014, and the demand for oil in the region will continue to outpace supply expansion.[37] In 2010, it was reported that eight out of 10 of the world's top pharmaceuticals and all of the top 10 medical technology companies have established their regional headquarters in Singapore.[38] The global focus on Singapore as a pharmaceutical hub for companies' Asian operations suggests great potential in Singapore and the region for the engineering and construction of pharmaceutical facilities.

Within these industries, engineering and construction complexities exist when it comes to joining large structures and complex equipment. The movement of such behemoths requires the process of complex lifting. As this type of lifting is a safety and engineering hazard, it requires highly specialised engineering skills.

A Focus In Lifting To Greater Heights – Shao Fook

Shao Fook Engineering Pte Ltd ("Shao Fook") was established in 1989 to provide specialised contract engineering services in industrial steel fabrication works and the installation of industrial equipment and machinery. A large part of the engineering services provided by Shao Fook involves complex lifting procedures for the construction and maintenance of oil refineries, petrochemical plants, industrial plants and pharmaceutical plants as well as for factory expansion.

Traditionally, Shao Fook has been a contracted provider of specialised engineering services that are ancillary to a main engineering and construction project. In other words, Shao Fook operates as a sub-contractor to the main contractor of the project, providing specific engineering services in the area of steel fabrication and installation.

[36] Industry Profile, Construction & Engineering In Singapore, from www.datamonitor.com
[37] Singapore Oil & Gas Report Q4 (2010) from Business Monitor International
[38] www.sedb.com/etc/medialib/downloads/industries.Par.44136.File.tmp/Biomedical%20Sciences%20Factsheet%202010.pdf

While its business model has kept it profitable over the last two decades, Shao Fook's management foresaw that rising competition and cost pressures would continue to erode the company's margins as a sub-contractor. Furthermore, the barriers to entry in the sub-contracting market are low, resulting in an ever-increasing pool of competitors.

Operating in a high-cost centre, the company soon realised that it could not continue to compete solely on price. In addition, rising competitiveness in the sub-contracting market led to a strategic need for Shao Fook to grow its business beyond this market and look to partner other companies to co-bid as main contractors for projects as margins are generally high. With this in view, the constant temptation to diversify was high but the company's management continued to concentrate on its area of expertise by focussing on new innovative ways of lifting and moving large structures and equipment.

Foreseeing a growing regional oil and gas industry, Shao Fook identified several key international markets that it wanted to target. These markets engage in oil and gas activities that require the kind of contract engineering services that Shao Fook is known for. Operationally, there was an intention to establish a direct presence in these markets with either a subsidiary or an associate company. In an interview with Shao Fook's executive chairman Mr Chong Ooi Min, Chong elaborated:

> From a customer perception perspective, we now need to concurrently build our brand in our chosen overseas markets to generate interest and awareness. This requires a strategy that differentiates us from competitors in these overseas markets as well as a marketing strategy to communicate the Shao Fook brand effectively and generate the desired perceptions in these markets. At the turn of 2010, we realised that we face some perception challenges.

The first challenge was that Shao Fook's brand was largely unseen by the end-client because the company is a sub-contractor. As a result, the level of awareness of the Shao Fook brand was significantly low in the end-client market.

The second challenge was that the company garnered new business through pull factors such as referrals, its track record and known expertise rather than push factors such as active marketing communications. While pull factors are important, Shao Fook realised that it was also critical to establish push factors, especially if it wanted to grow its business beyond its current borders.

The Strategy

In mid-2010, the management of Shao Fook knew that the company needed to overcome these perception challenges in order to help the company achieve its growth objectives. They realised that the business needed to identify its differentiation and, further, market its position. As stated by Chong:

> Throughout the life span of Shao Fook, we had many opportunities of doing different things from general construction works to engineering projects. Where we continue to excel, it has always been in the area of moving complex structures and equipment. This core competency was discovered in the earlier years of Shao Fook and I think our clients appreciate that we can do these complicated tasks well.

Therefore, the company took it upon itself to administer four key strategic tasks:

- To find out its customers' perceptions of its brand.
- To determine the company's key differentiation.
- To identify key markets.
- To market its differentiation to its chosen markets in an integrated way.

One of the key findings that emerged was that Shao Fook was perceived by the majority of its customers, employees and suppliers to be focussed in its specialisation. This specialisation was found by its stakeholders to be in the function that Shao Fook fulfils – specifically, equipment erection and installation. This finding was consistent with the company's reputation of providing equipment installation services for main contractors. Therefore, customers and suppliers who have experienced the Shao Fook brand associate it strongly with engineering capabilities in lifting.

The findings also provided Shao Fook with the viable strategic options that the company could take to position and differentiate itself in the market. However, these strategic options needed to be verified and tested with factors external to the company. Differentiation is a relative concept; therefore, an in-depth understanding of Shao Fook's key competitors in each of its chosen markets was necessary in order to create a distinct Shao Fook brand.

The analysis of Shao Fook's competitive landscape highlighted that communications employed by most competing brands were sporadic and inconsistent. It also revealed that none of the competing brands actively communicated a point of differentiation based on its engineering capabilities. This gave Shao Fook the opportunity to carve a niche within its focus that it could dominate, an area that no other brand had laid claim to.

Hence, the company decided to differentiate itself through its focussed area of specialisation in complex lifting. As stated in the accompanying chapter, focus requires the concentrated discipline of being an expert and getting to the top of the game. Being focussed also means that a company, in this instance Shao Fook, will not and cannot dilute the brand by going into other business activities using the same brand. With this focal point, Shao Fook's corporate position (which charts the long-term direction of a company) was determined.

The Execution

Operationally, Shao Fook has expressed its commitment to working towards its vision through the development of advanced techniques in complex lifting; the adoption of industry best practices for safety, communications and project management; the hiring of technically competent people and the establishment of a system to train and retrain its people.

Externally, the company took bold steps to operationalise its long-term organisational strategy. One key observation was the tone of voice used by the company to communicate the corporate brand online. The descriptive copy used to describe the focussed specialisation within construction engineering was both *functional*, i.e. supporting the technical skills and complex lifting techniques required for Shao Fook's specialisation, and *symbolic*, i.e. supporting Shao Fook's position as a leading specialist in the category of complex lifting. This was consistently applied to all communications materials across all stakeholder groups.

What was also notable was the company's convergence in brand communications. This extended to a commitment to all employees that the company would relentlessly pursue innovation and productivity in the area of complex lifting within construction engineering. All members of staff were aligned to the new Shao Fook brand position, an important move as most of the company's customer touch-points are through employee-client interaction. That is why it is pivotal that Shao Fook's employees are aligned in the way they behave and in the messages that they send out to customers. On this, Chong had the following to say:

The company is committed to pursuing two things to create sustainability. Firstly, it is to establish a pool of strong talent highly knowledgeable in construction engineering, particularly in the field of complex movements and lifting. We will do so by upgrading our people and attracting new talent into the firm. Secondly, we will have to acquire new technology to help us do our work better and faster. We will do so through internal project trials with existing systems and machines. From an outside-in approach, we will scout the world for new technology and systems to improve the way we work. I strongly believe that if we execute these strategies, our brand as a focussed company in complex lifting will quantum leap.

Today, Shao Fook remains a highly profitable brand that is synonymous with complex lifting and recognised by customers as a unique company providing specialised engineering services. The brand is also gaining headway in regional markets as a specialist in complex lifting in the oil and gas, pharmaceutical and land-based industries.

B2B

CHAPTER
12

Rule No. 5 –
Differentiate Or Sell Cheap

TAKE a look at the vans below. They are both new and they both come with a three-year warranty. Which one would you buy?

We are quite sure it would be the one on the right because you probably can't tell the difference between the two except that the one on the right is cheaper by $5,000. If you can't see any difference between the two, why would you pay more for the one on the left?

This example illustrates a very important principle in business acquisition. There are two ways for you to secure business and that is what Rule No. 5 is all about – differentiate or sell cheap.

SELLING CHEAP

If you are not differentiated, meaning that you cannot create any perceived differentiation in the minds of your customers, you will have to sell cheap. Selling cheap is not a bad thing unlike what many brand consultants will have you believe. If you can sell something cheap enough, you will find many buyers.

Don't be afraid to sell cheap. We always tell our clients that if you can sell cheaper than your competitors and you can maintain that price advantage, then you will always have business. There are two types of buyer – people who want to buy from the strong (meaning highly differentiated) brands regardless of price and people who want to buy from the budget brands. It is entirely up to you who you want to target as customers.

BRANDS THAT PILED THEM HIGH AND SOLD THEM CHEAP

While computer companies such as IBM, Compaq, HP, Packard Bell, Texas Instruments, Acer and the rest were busy trying to build strong brands out of what is fast becoming a commodity, Dell took a different route. Dell was busy trying to commoditise computers by selling them cheap. When Michael Dell started Dell in his dorm room in 1984, he knew that he had to do one of two things – he could either differentiate his brand or sell it cheap. He sold it cheap, and Dell is still highly affordable today.

Once, Jacky was attending an IT fair and a client asked him to check out the prices of computers for her while he was there. Jacky could only manage to get the price lists for two computer brands as the place was extremely crowded. So, he called the client to tell her that the place was too crowded and he was taking a break. The client told him, "Oh, never mind. It's too much hassle for you. I will just buy Dell. Can't go wrong with Dell when it comes to price."

Dell is one of the two most successful PC companies in the world today, along with HP. And it is a strong brand despite selling cheap because it owns a powerful idea in the minds of its customers – cheap PCs. In the financial year ending January 2010, Dell recorded a sales revenue of US$52.9 billion (S$68 billion) and a net profit of US$1.4 billion (S$1.8 billion), or 2.7 per cent.[39] The net profit margin may not seem fantastic but considering the recession, we think Dell still did well to turn a profit.

Walmart is the world's biggest retailer. Its turnover in the financial year ending January 2010 was US$408 billion (S$524.4 billion) – that's 408,000,000,000.[40] The net profit was US$14.8 billion (S$19 billion), or 3.6 per cent. How many companies in Singapore, no matter how successful, can generate an annual turnover that is equal to Walmart's *net profit*? Even the likes of Keppel FELS – an extremely successful Singapore company and the world's No. 1 builder of oil rigs – recorded a sales turnover of US$8.7 billion (S$11.2 billion) in 2009.[41] That gives you an idea of Walmart's scale. What is Walmart's secret? It is captured in the tagline that Walmart has used for many years – "Everyday Low Prices". Walmart sells it cheap.

IKEA is the Swedish furniture giant that also sells cheap but has managed to become very successful. Today, it is a very strong brand as well as a great showcase for Sweden. Since IKEA was founded in 1943 by Ingvar Kamprad, it has grown to become the world's top furniture company. Today, it has 267 stores in 25 countries, employs 123,000 employees and generates an annual

---

[39] www.hoovers.com/company/Dell_Inc/ryrsyi-1-1njea5.html#income

[40] www.hoovers.com/company/Wal-Mart_Stores_Inc/rrjiff-1-1njea5.html#income

[41] www.hoovers.com/company/Keppel_Corporation_Limited/hjksyi-1-1njea5.html

turnover of $21.5 billion (S$38.9 billion).[42] That's huge considering how difficult and competitive the furniture industry is.

As we stated above, IKEA's secret lies in its low prices. That was proven by Jacky when he accidentally damaged a bookshelf that he had bought from IKEA in 2000 after using it for at least eight years. So, he went back to IKEA to buy the same bookshelf and discovered that the price had actually dropped. He knew because he still had the original receipt and the replacement that he bought was not on sale. IKEA could sell cheap and became very successful because of it.

The point is, you don't have to think that if you sell cheap, you cannot become successful. Many strong brands have been built using low price as a strategy. However, that doesn't mean that selling cheap is easier than finding a way to differentiate your brand in the minds of your customers. Selling cheap can sometimes be even more difficult than finding a way to differentiate your brand.

YOU NEED TO HAVE STRUCTURAL COST ADVANTAGE

Before you run off thinking that you can just try to sell cheap and win, you have to remember that it is not easy to sell cheap because the market is full of competitors who are ever ready to undercut you on price. You may have faced such competitors before. Maybe it was a strategy that you once used against your competitors. You can generate a lot of business by selling cheap. You can even build a strong brand using a low-price strategy. However, to do it successfully, you need to be able to maintain that price advantage in the long run. You need to have a structural cost advantage.

As the name suggests, structural cost advantage is something that is built into your business model. That is why it is called structural. It is part of you. It is how you do business. Many companies have told us that they have relocated their factories to low-cost countries but that is not structural cost advantage. Structural cost advantage does not come from moving to a low-cost country. It does not come from squeezing your suppliers. It does not come from cutting your employees' wages. It does not even come from improving your productivity and efficiency. These tactics can easily be copied by your competitors. There is nothing structural about them.

Dell has a structural cost advantage because of the way it does things. Dell sells direct to its customers. Because of Dell's direct sales model, it cut out the middlemen and the savings have subsequently been passed on to customers.

---

[42] www.ikea.com/ms/en_IE/about_ikea/facts_and_figures/index.html

However, that structural cost advantage came at a high price. Computers are complicated products and not the easiest items to sell direct. Therefore, Dell had to develop a strong technical support call centre to help its customers with various issues. It wasn't exactly easy to perfect this direct sales model. Perhaps that is one of the reasons why no one else has succeeded at doing the same thing as Dell. In contrast, books are not complex. Amazon.com is another company that sells cheap – it used to price its books up to 30 per cent cheaper than anyone else – and still managed to become big and successful.

Walmart's structural cost advantage is economies of scale. As it is so big, it can force prices down. You might be thinking that this is nothing new. That it's a no-brainer. If you are big and buy in bulk, you can get a better deal but when Walmart started, it was small. It definitely didn't have structural cost advantage then. How did the founder of Walmart, the late Sam Walton, do it? Well, he was a shrewd entrepreneur. He decided right from day one that he would only open Walmart stores in smaller towns with populations of 50,000 and below. His reason behind this was that the only competition would come from the Mom-and-Pop stores. Therefore, it would be easy for Walmart to win. It used this strategy to grow to a size whereby it had enough bargaining power to drive prices down to a level that the other large retailers could not match. The way Walmart ran its business resulted in its structural cost advantage. However, getting it right was also not an easy thing.

IKEA's structural cost advantage is in the way its furniture is designed. Right from day one, IKEA decided that its furniture had to be designed in such a way that it could be flat-packed. Furniture is bulky and because of that, it takes up a lot of space and that makes it expensive to transport and store. By designing its furniture to be flat-packed, IKEA actually made the furniture easier and cheaper to manufacture, store, transport and assemble. This resulted in huge cost savings for the company. These days, all the other furniture manufacturers have adopted flat-packed as the way to go. Because of IKEA's flat-packed philosophy, it sometimes puts constraints on how creative its furniture designs can be but that is one price you pay in order to maintain that cost advantage.

If you don't have a structural cost advantage, you have to find a way to differentiate. If you don't have a structural cost advantage and you can't differentiate your brand, then your days are numbered. We have come across companies in the past that were stuck in such a situation and yet they were unwilling to invest in ways to differentiate themselves. For such companies, our recommendations were always – and will always be – milk the business for all you can or sell it off while you still can. In other words, take the money and invest in another business. The reason we recommend that is because if you cannot differentiate and you can't sell cheap, you will die. Your competitors will force you out of the market.

STRUCTURAL COST ADVANTAGE ALSO REQUIRES DIFFERENTIATION

It seems that you can't run away from differentiation because even structural cost advantage requires you to be different – maybe not at the brand level but in your business or operating model. All the companies that have managed to achieve structural cost advantage have gone out of their way to be different.

Dell did it differently. When everyone else was selling computers using the traditional retail model, Dell sold direct to end users. In those days, critics would have laughed at Michael Dell and said, "That is the dumbest thing we have ever heard. Nobody sells computers that way. They are too complicated to be sold direct." Dell proved them wrong.

Toyota did it differently. It implemented the just-in-time manufacturing system when all the other car manufacturers had no idea what it was all about – because nobody manufactured cars that way. The just-in-time system gave Toyota its structural cost advantage because it didn't need to have large inventories of parts and that created huge savings.

Amazon.com did it differently. Instead of having a physical bookstore, it created a virtual one. The display shelf is limitless and the cost is low.

Southwest Airlines did it differently. Unlike other airlines, it focussed on budget travellers. It only runs the Boeing 737, which has made it easier to train crew and carry out maintenance, and when you have a fleet of over 600 Boeing 737s, you can imagine the kind of discounts that you can get from Boeing. It doesn't have expensive reservation systems. It doesn't fly to expensive hubs; all flights are direct to the destination. All these things gave Southwest Airlines its structural cost advantage and made it very successful. Today, all budget airlines operate using the Southwest model.

You can sell cheap and still be very successful but you need a structural cost advantage and that cost advantage comes from doing things differently. And it is going to require a lot of hard work, creativity and persistence to get it right. If you think it is easier for you to get a structural cost advantage, then go ahead and do it. If you think it is easier to differentiate your brand, then that is the route you take.

Based on experience, we can tell you that trying to find a structural cost advantage is even harder than differentiating a brand. Differentiating a brand is all about creating the right perception in the minds of your customers and there are things that you have which can be used to differentiate you.

WHAT IS DIFFERENTIATION ALL ABOUT?

In order to be different, you have to be unique. If you are not unique, it is impossible to achieve differentiation. The term Unique Selling Proposition, or USP, was first coined in 1960 by advertising genius Rosser Reeves. In his book, *Reality in Advertising*, Reeves defined USP as something that a brand can offer to its customers that the competition cannot, or does not, offer. It must be unique – either a uniqueness of the brand or a claim not otherwise made in that particular category.

In order to be different, you must find something that is unique about your brand, dramatise it and communicate it relentlessly at all customer touch-points or you have to claim something that might not be unique but appears to be unique because no one else in your category has made that claim. Several decades ago, when a relatively unknown American beer company advertised that all of its beer bottles were steam washed, it created the perception that it was unique – since its beer bottles were steam washed, its brewing processes must be very hygienic and therefore the beer must be good. A few years later, people found out that all beer bottles – in the United States at least – were steam washed. But since no one claimed to steam wash their bottles, it created the perception of uniqueness for this particular beer company.

When Otis incorporated remote diagnostics into its elevators that can warn of impending breakdowns, it created a USP that other brands did not have at that time.

When AT&T developed its self-restoring fibre-optic network that can automatically re-route data seamlessly in the event that a cable is accidentally severed, it created a USP that other telephone companies did not have.

When SK-II launched its range of cosmetics with a yeast-like substance called Pitera, it created a USP that other cosmetics brands did not have.

Only SK-II products are created with Pitera, which works very well in creating smoother skin. We know this, not because we use SK-II products (although we know of some men who do), but because we have seen the results in people who use SK-II.

When Xerox launched the 914 in 1959, it created a USP that other photocopier brands did not have. Xerox was the first and only automatic plain paper photocopier, which made it far superior to all the other brands that were still using thermal technology.

But a USP is not easy to find and even harder to defend, especially in these days of hypercompetition. If you have a USP, you can be sure that within a short span of time, your competitors will try to tear that USP apart, analyse it and reverse-engineer it to create something that is both better and cheaper.

QUALITY CANNOT BE A DIFFERENTIATOR

Quality is important. If your quality is not at least as good as your competitors, you won't even get a second look from customers. But quality is now a hygiene factor, meaning that it is something that is expected of you. It is a given. Even if you buy the cheapest product in a category, you still expect it to have a certain level of quality.

Yes, you can still make a quick buck and get rich fast selling sub-standard products or services but you won't be able to build a strong, lasting brand that can continue to generate value for you for many years. You know the saying that goes, "You can fool some of the people some of the time, and all of the people some of the time, but you can't fool all of the people all of the time." Abraham Lincoln never professed to be a branding expert but we think he would have made a great brand consultant. He got it right.

Furthermore, all your competitors also stand for quality. You won't find a competitor that is willing to take the opposite position and say it does not stand for quality. If everybody stands for quality, then nobody owns the idea of quality.

And thanks to the twin wonders of *benchmarking* and *modern technology*, the quality gap between the best and the worst has narrowed so much that it is no longer an issue. The worst car you can find will still have an acceptable level of quality. It will take you from Point A to Point B without breaking down. The worst TV that you can buy will still allow you to watch the programmes that you want. So, in that respect, it has acceptable quality. The worst computer that you can buy will still do its job as a computer. In the majority of cases, the worst of anything that you can buy will still get the job done, unlike in the past. So, quality has ceased to be a differentiator.

SERVICE CANNOT BE A DIFFERENTIATOR

As customers get more and more demanding, they expect to get good service even if they buy cheap products or services. Therefore, service has also become a hygiene factor. It is something that customers expect you to have. Furthermore, all your competitors will claim that they care about their customers and strive to provide the best standard of service to give their customers an unrivalled experience, etc, etc, etc.

Another problem that you face when trying to use service as a differentiator is that it is something that is delivered by humans. And humans are notoriously difficult to train and standardise. That is why service standards are extremely hard to maintain despite your best efforts. We are not saying that you shouldn't try. You should, of course. Your customers expect that of you. And it will harm your business if your service levels are not competitive. You just need to be aware that if you want to use service as a differentiator, your service levels need to be of a certain standard and, most importantly, this standard needs to be *consistent*. If you offer average service but it is consistent, it won't be as damaging to your brand as claiming to offer good service but, in reality, offering varying levels of service. But service is almost impossible to make consistent due to the human factor. That is why it is not a good differentiator.

As you grow, you will employ more and more people. The more people you have, the harder it is to ensure a consistent delivery level. That is why if you claim that your level of service is what makes you different from other companies, customers will be a lot less forgiving when you fail to deliver on that brand promise. We are not saying that you shouldn't strive for good service, we are saying that using service as a differentiator is not a great idea. Besides, if you provide great service, customers might still say, "So what? That's something you have to do anyway!"

PEOPLE CANNOT BE A DIFFERENTIATOR

People also cannot be used as a differentiator. That might sound really strange coming from us because running a brand strategy consulting firm means we have to have great people in the organisation in order for us to do our work well.

However, having good people is also a given. Customers expect you to hire competent, reliable and well-trained people to serve them. This is something that you cannot run away from. Therefore, if you want to differentiate your brand by saying, "Our People Make All The Difference", bear in mind two things – your competitors are also saying the same thing and your customers already expect you to have good people. Therefore, even if you have good people, it is hard to use them as a differentiator.

WHY IS IT SO DIFFICULT TO DIFFERENTIATE A BRAND?

There are three reasons why it is so hard to find a differentiating idea today.

1. The Market Is Hypercompetitive

Companies have an insatiable appetite for growth. Everybody wants to grow. In the search for growth, they will try to expand their range of products and services into categories that they were traditionally not competing in. You have probably done or are thinking of doing the same thing as well. Everybody is getting into everybody else's business in the name of growth. That is why over time, you will get more and more competitors.

For example, Company A might be in the business of selling paint, Company B is in the business of selling building materials and Company C is in the business of selling waterproofing products. Over time, as all three expand, they will very likely encroach on each other's businesses. Company A might reason that "Since we are selling paint and paint is a liquid coating that is applied to the exterior and interior walls of buildings and structures, we should also go into the business of selling waterproofing products since waterproofing products are usually liquid coatings." Suddenly, Company C has a new competitor.

Company B, on the other hand, might reason that since it is in the business of selling building materials such as mortar, bricks, cement, tiles and adhesives, it should also sell paint and waterproofing products because they are related to building materials. So, overnight, Company A has a new competitor and Company C has one more headache to deal with. Company C might respond by saying, "Since we are already selling waterproofing products, why don't we venture into fireproofing products so that we can offer our customers end-to-end water- and fireproofing solutions under one roof?" All of a sudden, the fireproofing industry has a new competitor. It goes on and on and on.

This hypercompetition makes it difficult to find a differentiating idea that is relevant, desirable and defensible as competitors will try very hard to take it away from you. And as you grow and start selling more and more non-core products or services, you will also dilute whatever brand idea that you originally might have had.

2. The Companies Are Hyperconfused

The second reason why it is hard for companies to differentiate is that many of them are confused as to what differentiation is and what makes a good differentiating idea. We have often come across CEOs, academics and consultants who can wax lyrical about the importance of creating a differentiated brand but are lost for words when asked how to create meaningful differentiation.

Many CEOs are even proud of the fact that they are able to offer customers the best of both worlds by being almost as good as the leading brands and almost as cheap as the entry-level brands. That is not differentiation. That is just an accident waiting to happen! When you put your brand in the middle of the road, you get run over by a truck marked "The Competition". Being stuck in the middle doesn't differentiate you. When you are stuck in the middle, nobody knows what you are. You are neither here nor there, neither this nor that.

3. And They Throw It All Away With Meaningless Slogans

To make things worse, companies often squander their differentiating ideas with meaningless slogans. So many examples abound everywhere you look. And it is not just unknown brands that are doing it. Many of the biggest brands in the world are in on the act too. We will just touch on two cases.

It seems that every Tom, Dick and Sally has a mobile phone. What is the best-known mobile phone in the world? Nokia. Is it the best? Maybe. Maybe not. So, why is it so well known? Because one in every three mobile phones sold is a Nokia. That is Nokia's USP. It is the best-selling mobile phone in the world. But is Nokia using that powerful USP? No. Nokia has a meaningless slogan – "Nokia. Connecting People."

Connecting people? Isn't that what all mobile phones are designed to do? If you have a mobile phone that connects people, that is not a USP! If Nokia is not connecting people, what is it connecting? The slogan Nokia should use is, "Nokia. No. 1 In Mobile Phones". Yes, it is not a sexy slogan but consumer psychologists tell us that 95 per cent of buyers are imitators – they buy what other people buy. So, sales leadership is a powerful USP. The typical buyer thinks, "If one in three people buys Nokia, it must be good. Why buy anything else?"

Nike is another brand with a meaningless slogan. But it is a famous slogan nonetheless. Take away the Nike name and logo and people around the world can still tell that "Just Do It" means Nike. Nike spends around US$650 million (S$835.1 million) a year in advertising to make sure that slogan remains famous but that slogan was not what made Nike into a strong brand. Do you have US$650 million (S$835.1 million) a year to spend on building a meaningless slogan into a brand? We don't think so.

So, why do people buy Nike? Because it is what serious athletes wear. When Nike co-founder Phil Knight started the company, it was because this former track star couldn't find a track shoe that was good enough for him. So, he made his own. And other serious athletes started buying his shoes and that was how Nike the company was born. Being the brand that is preferred by serious athletes was Nike's USP and that built the brand.

Today, Nike still has that USP. The best athletes in the world wear Nike. Never mind that Nike pays them to wear its brand. The fact is, Nike is worn by more athletes than any other brand. So, what should Nike's slogan be? "Nike. What The World's Best Athletes Wear."

If it is good enough for the world's best athletes, it should be good enough for you. In fact, that is the real reason why you buy Nike. Subconsciously, you know that Nike's quick-dry sportswear, for example, is probably not much different from what its competitors offer (and Nike stuff is not exactly cheap) but it is what the best athletes in the world wear, so why shouldn't you? Do you buy Nike just because it spends hundreds of millions to tell you to "Just Do It"? Not a chance. You are not that stupid.

A true USP is hard to come by these days. So, if you happen to find one, don't waste it with a meaningless slogan! We are not saying that Nokia and Nike are not strong brands. They are among the best brands in the world. And they are BIG. So, they can get away with meaningless slogans. You are probably nowhere near as powerful as these brands. If you use a meaningless slogan that does nothing to proclaim your USP, you will be torn apart by your competitors, unless you have clueless competitors.

THE 13 STRATEGIES FOR DIFFERENTIATION

In this section of this chapter, we will examine the differentiation strategies that will work in differentiating any brand in any category in any market. There are 13 strategies that can be used to differentiate your brand and these are the same strategies that we apply to every single one of our clients.

For a more detailed explanation of these strategies, you can choose to read our book *Killer Differentiators* but this section will give you a good idea of what each of these 13 strategies does and if you can use any of them. Of course, when we work on client projects, we go into great detail and dissect each strategy to see which one is the best for the client. Our greatest fear is a client that cannot be differentiated no matter what we do. So far, we have not come across such a client because what we have found is that every company – and that includes you and your competitors – has something that can be used to differentiate it. The only problem is that most companies don't make use of it. This is actually good news for us because very often, when we analyse our clients' competitors, we find that they too can be differentiated but they have not done so.

1. Sales Leadership

What do customers want to buy? They want to buy the best product or service that they can afford. Everybody wants the best but how do customers determine who the best is? Very often, customers don't have enough knowledge to judge which of the brands is the best. As they have so many options to choose from, it can become extremely confusing. Is the digital camera with 8.1 megapixels but a normal 25-mm lens the best? Or is the competitor with only 5.0 megapixels but a wide-angle 28-mm lens the best? You see how difficult it is? So, how do customers determine which brand is the best? And how do you create the perception that you are the best?

Customers often see the best-selling or the No. 1 brand to be the best. So, if you have sales leadership, you can create the perception that you are the best because if you are not the best, how can you be the best-selling brand? That's how people look at things. Well, that's how you look at things, too. Customers don't behave like this for everything that they buy but when they don't have perfect knowledge, they will assume the No. 1 brand is the best. You don't have to be the best-selling brand in the world to claim sales leadership as there are four types of sales leadership that you can use.

Market Leadership

If you are the leading brand in a market that is well known for the product you are selling, then you can use market leadership as a differentiator. Barilla may not have been the best-selling pasta in the world when it first started its export drive but it is "Italy's No. 1 Pasta" so that is the tagline that it has used to communicate its differentiating idea. Who knows more about pasta than the Italians? Nobody. So, if Barilla is Italy's No. 1 Pasta, then it must be the best pasta. We asked some of our Italian friends if Barilla is any good. They told us that they didn't know. When we told them that Barilla is the best-selling pasta in Italy so how could it not be good, they simply said, "For all you know, it is the best selling because it is the cheapest." They made a good point. We are not saying that Barilla became No. 1 because it is cheap but this could well have been the reason. However, the rest of the world doesn't care. If it is Italy's No. 1 Pasta, it must be the best.

DBS Bank could also have used this strategy. DBS Bank is not the biggest in the world but it is No. 1 in Singapore. Since Singapore has been widely acknowledged as one of the top financial centres in the world, being the No. 1 bank in Singapore would have been a great differentiating idea.

Category Leadership

You may not be the overall sales leader but you can be the leader in a particular category and that can be used as a differentiator. The overall sales leader in mobile phones is Nokia but that doesn't mean the rest of the players can't use sales leadership as a differentiator. BlackBerry could claim to be the category leader in smartphones. You can break down any market into sub-categories and if you have sales leadership in any of the sub-categories, you can use that to differentiate your brand.

Time Leadership

You can also claim sales leadership for a particular time period. For instance, Dell has lost its sales leadership to HP, which is now the best-selling PC brand in the world. But Dell might still have overall sales leadership if you add up the number of computers it has sold over the past 10 years. If Dell has that leadership, it can claim it and differentiate the brand effectively in this highly competitive market.

Proxy Leadership

You can use proxy leadership if you believe that you have sales leadership but it is very difficult for you to get accurate data because of the nature of the industry. In the event that you cannot compare your sales figures with those of your competitors' – because they are not available – you can publish your sales figures to create the perception that you are the sales leader. For example, if you say, "100,000 [Your Product] Sold. And Counting." it looks like you are a very successful brand. Perhaps your competitors have sold more but since they are not publicising their data and not claiming sales leadership, you can usurp that position. Should competitors confront you, it is even better because when they challenge your claim, it puts you in the spotlight.

2. Technology Leadership

Technology is something that we all need. It is like a second skin to us. But technology is not easy for the majority of people to understand. That is why companies that have a good grasp of technology are highly respected. If you have technology leadership, use it. You don't need to be a technology company to use technology as a differentiator. Gillette is not a technology company but it is the leader in wet shaving technology. Rolls-Royce is not a technology company but it is a leader in jet engine technology. GORE-TEX is also not a technology company but it is a leader in waterproof and breathable fabric technology.

Accuray makes medical equipment such as the awesome-looking CyberKnife, a radiosurgery device that is used to treat cancerous cells. The technology is nothing new, having been around for over 30 years. But what helps to differentiate the CyberKnife is its technology leadership. CyberKnife is the first to combine image guidance technology with advanced robotics and this gives the CyberKnife extremely high levels of accuracy and the ability to treat multiple areas all at the same time. This impressive technology leadership differentiated the CyberKnife effectively. Since its launch, over 80,000 patients have been treated using it.

3. Performance Leadership

There are some categories that are particularly sensitive to performance. If you are operating in such a category and you have leadership in performance, you can use that as a differentiator. You have to work very hard to ensure that you maintain your performance leadership because once you lose it, you lose your differentiating idea.

FedEx was established in 1971. It was late into the air courier services market – Emery Air got there first in 1946. But FedEx still managed to beat Emery by focussing on its higher performance. FedEx differentiated itself by being the delivery company that can get your letters and packages to your shipping destination by 10am the next day.

AMD differentiated its Opteron server chip on the basis of faster performance and became very successful. Whether it can continue to be successful depends on whether it can maintain this performance leadership in the face of a much improved Xeon server chip from Intel.

Sometimes, you need to change the measure of performance. For MBA programmes, many universities publish rankings. This has traditionally been the measure of performance. When we advised one university on how to differentiate its MBA programme, we recommended performance leadership as a differentiator. That idea was met with frowns. Someone said to us, "But we have never ever been ranked No. 1, not even in Asia, let alone the world. How can we claim performance leadership?" That was true but this university had something the other universities didn't. Its MBA programme was the only one in Asia that had been ranked in the Top 3 for 12 years in a row. So, our recommendation was to change the measure of performance from outright ranking to *consistency*. The communications was supposed to be along this line, "Everyone can get to the top once in their lifetime but only one MBA has stayed at the top 12 years in a row." That strategy was deemed a bit too radical by the university but it gives you an idea of what we mean about changing the measure of performance to your advantage.

4. The Next Generation

We have asked some middle-aged people why they went Rollerblading with their children despite the risk of having serious injuries if they fall. On top of that, they didn't look that stable on Rollerblades. They told us that they had to keep up with their children or risk being labelled outdated and not with it. Nobody wants to be labelled a dinosaur. The fear of being seen as outdated is a strong motivator for people to get the latest in everything. That is why being "next generation" can be a powerful way to build your brand.

Being the next generation is a great way of making your competitors look outdated. This gives customers a reason not to buy from them because they fear that they might be getting an outdated product. They might not buy from you as well but at least they will stop to think about it. The only downside is that the next generation brand must constantly innovate and re-invent itself so that it remains next generation. In other words, a next generation brand needs to constantly attack itself and make itself obsolete so that competitors can't.

Intel is a great example of such a brand. Intel has always been at the cutting edge of microprocessor technology. But Intel has had to constantly launch new versions of its chips at breakneck speed to stay ahead of the curve. It was not that long ago that we were using the now ancient 286 chip. Before long, the 386 came along and this was followed in quick succession by the 486, 586, Pentium 1, Pentium 2, Pentium 3, Pentium 4, Pentium D, the Core Duo and so on. In between, Intel also launched other categories like the budget-priced Celeron, the mobile Centrino chip, the Xeon server chip and Viiv.

5. How A Product Is Made

Very often, any product within a given category performs the same functions and provides the same benefits as the other products in that category. What differentiates it is very often found in the way the product is made.

Pizza is pizza, right? Could you really tell one premium pizza from another? Might be quite difficult. So what differentiates Papa John's pizza so effectively? The way its pizzas are made. Papa John's pizza dough is made with filtered water to ensure a purer taste. The difference here is actually in the process employed to make the dough.

Harley-Davidson is an American institution. A Harley-Davidson bike is almost entirely hand built by a team of dedicated and enthusiastic craftsmen. That makes it very different from the bikes manufactured by Honda, Yamaha, Suzuki and Kawasaki in ultra-modern factories with a high degree of automation where robots do much of the work.

6. Where A Product Is Made

The country of origin could be an important differentiator provided that country is well known for certain products. Germany is a country that is well known for precision engineering so if you are making your engineering products in Germany, you want the world to know about it. If you are making your pasta in Germany, then it might be a good idea to keep quiet on that front. This differentiator is important for smaller players. When you are big and well known, the country of manufacture becomes less important because people will think of you as a brand from that country even if your products are not made there.

Many BMW and Mercedes-Benz models are made in South Africa but they are still regarded as German cars. Nike products are made all over the world except in the United States but Nike is still seen as an American brand. Many Sony products are now made in China but Sony is still considered a Japanese brand.

If you are operating from a country that is not well known for the product or service that you are selling, what do you do? You need to seriously consider moving your base of operations to another country. If you are a Singapore company trying to sell high-end watches, you will need to shift your headquarters to Switzerland. Remember that where your product is made can work for or against you.

7. Attribute Ownership

There are usually between five and seven attributes within each category that are important to customers, and owning one of these attributes can be a great way to differentiate your brand. When we start a branding project for a client, we will usually determine what these attributes are from multiple sources such as in-depth interviews with the client's team, a review of academic journals on research that has been done in the client's industry, a review of business journals and so on. We will usually find around five attributes that are important to buyers. After that, we will attempt to determine, from the Perception Audit done on the client's customers, if our client owns any of these attributes as far as customers are concerned – or if these attributes are associated with competitors.

The set of attributes that is important to customers will be different from industry to industry. That is why you need to determine which attributes are important to customers. For one industry, it could be speed, price, reliability, after-sales service and track record. For another industry, it could be financial strength, brand reputation, personal relationship, flexibility and price. No industry has the same set of attributes.

If there is an attribute that is not owned by a competitor, you could try to own it but that also means that you might need to invest resources to ensure that your brand can stand for this attribute. For example, "zero downtime" might be an attribute that is very important in your industry and no one actually has a strong grip on this attribute. You could own that attribute but you would need to be able to deliver on that brand promise. The question you need to ask is, "What do I need to do to own that attribute? And can I do it?"

8. Personality

Personality can be a powerful differentiator but this is one differentiation strategy that we rarely recommend to clients because it is one of the hardest to get right. If you want to use personality as a differentiator, you need to ensure that the same personality is exhibited throughout the entire organisation and that kind of consistency is very hard to achieve. But if you can get it right, it can differentiate you.

Apple is a brand that is differentiated by its "cool" personality. Apple products are cool and Apple folks are cool. And that has a lot to do with Steve Jobs who is able to steer the entire organisation in that direction. Harley-Davidson is differentiated by its "rebellious" personality. This is the bike for the rebel in all of us. Virgin is differentiated by its "adventurous" personality. Virgin likes adventure. Virgin will venture into any new market and pick a fight with the established players.

If you want to use personality, you must first determine what personality you want to project. Then you have to decide if the CEO can project this personality and whether the CEO can align the entire company to this personality. If the answer is yes, then go ahead and try. But make sure you project a consistent personality. The last thing you want is for people to see your company exhibiting multiple personalities. Nobody likes to hang around people with multiple personalities and nobody likes to buy from schizophrenic brands either.

9. The Opposite Position

One of the best ways to differentiate yourself is actually not up to you, unless you are the category pioneer. Since most companies will not find themselves in the enviable position of being market or category leaders, how they differentiate their brands is entirely dependent on their competitors' strategies. So, if you are jumping into a category that is already populated by competitors, how you differentiate your brand will depend on what your competitors are already doing.

You can differentiate yourself by turning your competitors' strengths into weaknesses. In other words, you must get to know what your major competitor's strength is and try to discover if the very thing that makes your competitor strong is also a weakness that you can exploit by positioning yourself to be the exact opposite. This is especially important for a No. 2 brand. You have to take the opposite position from the leading brand. But taking the opposite position also applies to brands that are not No. 2 in their categories. The following case studies are excellent examples of how to take the opposite position.

Fast Food

McDonald's is No. 1 in fast food. But McDonald's strength lies in kids who form the bulk of their customers. In fact, the adults are there only because their kids want to go there. So, Burger King used to differentiate itself by being the brand for adults. That is taking the opposite position. That helped Burger King to become a strong No. 2 brand until it abandoned this strategy and started going after the kids' market. It lost its point of differentiation and things went downhill from there.

In-N-Out Burger is a highly profitable burger chain in California. What is its secret? It took the opposite position from McDonald's. McDonald's stands for mass-market burgers. In-N-Out stands for premium burgers. That point of differentiation has worked very well for In-N-Out.

White Castle is another hamburger chain that is quite successful. What is White Castle's secret? It also took the opposite position from McDonald's. While McDonald's burgers are round, White Castle serves square burgers called sliders. This may seem very trivial to a lot of people. Square burgers to take on round burgers? But it worked in White Castle's case.

Wendy's also took the opposite position route to success. McDonald's is the epitome of the modern fast-food franchise. Wendy's serves traditional style burgers and that has made Wendy's into a strong brand. McDonald's is modern. Wendy's is traditional.

But the best position is the one that Burger King pioneered but abandoned. Your customers are either adults or kids. If McDonald's is for kids and Burger King is for adults, that just about covers everyone in the market. That leaves very little room for other burger brands to manoeuvre.

Computers

IBM is the king of the computer jungle. Its strength lies in its corporate accounts. IBM sells through distributors just like every other computer maker. Dell differentiated itself by going after the consumer market with its direct sales model. This actually opened a back door for Dell into the corporate world because many consumers are also decision makers or influencers in the corporate world. Their positive experience with Dell at home translated into them buying or recommending Dell at work. Taking the opposite position helped Dell to become a powerhouse brand.

Cars

The toughest job for any car manufacturer is to go up against Mercedes-Benz, which has a stranglehold on the luxury car sector. But BMW cleverly took the opposite position. Mercedes-Benz is known for big, luxurious and comfortable cars. BMW focussed on smaller, lighter, nimbler cars that are sportier in appearance and sportier to drive. The general rule of thumb when we were growing up was this: for smaller premium cars, go for a BMW like the 3 series; for a bigger premium car, go for a Mercedes-Benz like the S-Class. That high degree of differentiation and BMW's consistent execution of this strategy of building "The Ultimate Driving Machine" over decades allowed the brand to become strong. In 2005, BMW managed to overtake Mercedes-Benz as the best-selling premium car brand in the world. According to a report in Reuters UK, that year, BMW saw a 10.1 per cent jump in the number of units sold to 1.13 million cars. Mercedes-Benz saw a smaller gain of 1.6 per cent to 1.08 million units.

Soft Drinks

Coca-Cola is "The Real Thing". So what does that leave Pepsi with if it takes the opposite position? The fake thing? That doesn't sound too good. But Pepsi found a weakness in Coke's strength. Coke may be the real thing but it is also a very old brand – established in 1886. So, Pepsi took the opposite position. Pepsi became the brand for young people – The Pepsi Generation. That allowed Pepsi to become a strong No. 2 brand.

10. Specialisation

This is a great strategy for a small company because people expect specialists to be small. This is actually the wrong mindset because specialists can become very big due to their specialisation. When you position your brand as a specialist, customers don't mind if you are small. When you specialise, two other things happen – both good. When you specialise in something, you tend to become very good at what you do because that is all that you do. When you specialise in something, other people also tend to think that you must be very good at what you do because that is all that you do.

General Electric was a specialist in light bulbs. That made it very successful and its success allowed it to branch out into all kinds of electricity-related products and services; and then into non-electricity-related products and services such as financial products and services. When you specialise, you become good and other people perceive you to be good. This will help you to grow and once you have grown to become a dominant brand in your area of specialisation, you can use your financial strength to branch out into other areas. But first things first. Become the best specialist in your field and dominate the category before you branch out.

11. Preference

Who prefers to buy from your brand can be used as a differentiator, especially if your customers are the who's who in their industry. For example, Marshal Systems – a fire and gas detection company in Singapore – differentiated itself based on preference. Marshal Systems is an SME but a few of its customers are giants in the offshore and marine industry, such as Keppel FELS, the world's No. 1 builder of oil rigs. So, Marshal Systems differentiated itself by being the brand that is preferred by these giants. It uses the tagline "Protecting Offshore & Marine Giants" to dramatise and communicate its differentiating idea.

12. Heritage

Heritage is a good way to differentiate your brand because if you have heritage – and in Singapore, if you have a 30-year history, you can apply for the Heritage Brand Award under the Singapore Prestige Brand Award organised by the Association of Small and Medium Enterprises (ASME) – people will perceive that you must have done something right to have survived for as long as you have.

But heritage is a double-edged sword. If you don't do it well, you are just going to end up looking old. That is why heritage must be modernised so that it still appears current. There was a period of time when Heineken advertised its beer as "Unchanged Since 1873", meaning that it still used the same formula so what was a great-tasting beer in 1873 was still a great-tasting beer. We seriously doubt that it was exactly the same but it created a positive perception for Heineken.

Don't ever use a tagline such as "Established 1932" because that is not relevant to customers today. So what if you were established in 1932? All that tells people is how old you are. Why is the fact that you have been around since 1932 important?

13. Design

Design has increasingly become a differentiator for brands since the gap in terms of quality, price, performance, benefits, function, etc, has narrowed dramatically today. Coca-Cola used the unique design of its Coke bottle to differentiate what is essentially a commodity. The iconic Coke bottle continues to be an identifier for Coca-Cola. Swatch used its unique watch design to differentiate the brand. Swatch entered the market relatively late but its unique design helped to establish the brand in the minds of customers. Porsche used the 911's unique design to prolong the life of the model. The 911 is the oldest sports car in the world and one of the best-selling of all time. Alfa Romeo used its achingly beautiful design to keep the brand alive through its darkest years. Milwaukee Electric Tool Corp. used its ergonomic design for power tools to help differentiate the brand from all the other power tool brands out there. Design is not just about the way things look but about how they work. If it is just about how it looks, then it is not design, it is *style*. Apple's products are successful not just because they look great but because they work very well too.

In A Nutshell

There are two ways for any brand to secure business. The first way is to be differentiated so that your brand can own a great idea in the minds of customers. The second way is to sell cheap. There is nothing wrong with selling cheap. It is a viable business model. Many companies have become successful by selling cheap, including some of the biggest brands in the world such as Dell, IKEA, Southwest Airlines and Amazon.com. However, you have to ensure that you have a structural cost advantage – something unique about the way you do business that allows you to enjoy a natural cost advantage and cannot be easily copied by your competitors. For instance, Dell's direct sales model, IKEA's flat-packed furniture design, Southwest Airline's one aircraft model policy and Amazon.com's virtual bookstore concept. If you can't sell cheap, you have to find a way to differentiate your brand using one of the 13 differentiation strategies listed in this chapter. If you can't differentiate and you can't sell cheap, then it is only a matter of time before your competitors force you out of the market.

CASE STUDY
Differentiate Or Sell Cheap – ParexDavco

The Building And Construction Industry

In recent years, the construction industry has been the fastest-growing industry with no sign of decline in the near future, as reported in 'Research and Markets: Worldwide Construction Industry – Opportunities in Developing Regions' (Nov 2010). Growing populations and rising income levels have led to the increasing demand for residential and non-residential buildings, notably in the developing regions. The global market size of the construction chemical market is expected to reach S$38.2 to S$44.6 billion by 2015.

According to 'Research and Markets: Singapore Construction Market Data & Forecast to 2013' (Jan 2010), Singapore accounts for about 0.9 per cent of the value of Asia Pacific's construction and engineering industry. The Singapore domestic construction market has also grown steadily since 2004. The total value of construction projects in Singapore in 2008 was S$26.6 billion, following an expansion at a CAGR of 24.1 per cent since 2003. This positive CAGR caused a double-digit annual growth from 2004 to 2008. The healthy level of construction output was sustained by robust activity in the residential, industrial and civil engineering building segments.

Within these industries, building materials such as tile and stone adhesives, waterproofing systems, technical mortars, coloured grouts and drymix products are fundamental to their development. Such materials are needed in heavy building and construction works, especially when it involves concrete structures. Within the process of building and construction, high-quality building material products are necessary to ensure that finishing surface materials are adhesively strong to ensure that buildings stay not just appealing, but also safe.

Differentiating Building And Construction Materials – ParexDavco

ParexDavco was established in 1985 and is a fully owned subsidiary of ParexGroup of France. The group is a global leader in the manufacturing, distribution and marketing of chemicals and materials for the building and construction industry, operating 46 industrial sites in 17 countries. The company's products – marketed under the brands of DAVCO, LANKO and PAREX – cover technical mortar, waterproofing, tile adhesives, façade and drymix products.

Having worked with internationally renowned pioneers in building and construction, ParexDavco understands its clients. By staying close to them, the company continues to focus on developing new products that exceed client expectations through research and development and advancements in manufacturing technologies.

Establishing differentiation is a challenge in the building materials business because such products are known to be a low-interest category hidden away from the eyes of the property consumer. This notwithstanding, high levels of competition still exist among many players who compete mainly on price. In an interview with Mr Micheal Pattison, the managing director of the company, Pattison had this to say:

> One of the many things that we as a company know today is that our products in terms of quality are highly regarded. However, it is not being used as a technical benchmark; and this is something we want to work towards. The ParexDavco brand in terms of awareness among the professionals in the building and construction industry in Singapore also needs to increase. Professionals in the industry refer to the opinions of other architects, engineers and contractors. These professionals are typically also the ones who specify the use of materials.

The Strategy

In this case, it is clear that the objective was to determine ParexDavco's key differentiation. This was a key challenge because its products were of a high quality yet the brand was not accepted as the specified benchmark. It was clear in Pattison's mind that the strategy had to elevate the brand to benchmark level.

At the close of 2009, Pattison commissioned a Perception Audit to find out how customers perceived ParexDavco's brand. An independent consulting firm was appointed for this purpose. The findings of the study revealed that engineers and contractors found its product quality to be consistent, providing long-lasting results, and more superior than other brands found in the market. In the aspect of customer relationship, the company's staff was viewed by customers to be knowledgeable and able to provide prompt and accurate product information. While these findings were well and good, the question of differentiation continued to linger. However, one factor remained clear throughout the customers' Perception Audit – while engineers and contractors did not list the brand as a benchmark, they did actually recognise the brand for its high quality and consistency. Many actually preferred the brand compared to others, even when ParexDavco was known to be slightly pricier. This was evident in the customer research findings. This fact brings justification to the concept of *preference* as a differentiating factor. Since leading engineers and contractors prefer ParexDavco, there essentially should be no reason why others in the building and construction business should not. The postulation was that Professional Specifiers had no knowledge that such preferences exist. Getting to the stage where ParexDavco is preferred by architects, engineers and contractors has not been an easy thing to achieve and management of the company knew that it was an opportunity for leverage.

At the same time, Pattison also knew that the company needed to work very hard to make sure that the brand remains the preferred choice of these building and construction thought leaders for many years to come. In view of this, Pattison and his team set out to chart the mission statements of the firm:

- **Product:** Undertake innovation programmes to develop a wider range of cost-effective foundation materials with consistent quality.
- **Process:** Adopt industry best practices for customer services, environmental friendliness and internal communications.
- **People:** Hire, train and retain technically competent people who always put themselves in their customers' shoes.

Pattison on the mission of the company:

Key customers in the business know that we have the best products in the market place; we achieve this through keeping our manufacturing base in Singapore. This helps us to manage and maintain a high level of quality in our manufacturing process. This makes it easy for us to develop products that the market needs because our customers' views and feedback matter most when it comes to our product development. This helps us to develop local product knowledge and competent technical and logistic support systems that meet their needs. This gives us the edge in maintaining our investment in local R&D whilst embracing a culture of exchanges in innovation, to and from ParexGroup globally.

The Execution

It was crucial for ParexDavco to create a relevant, desirable and defensible point of differentiation because if the brand could not be differentiated, the company would be forced to compete on price. When architects, engineers and contractors say that they prefer ParexDavco, it is a powerful differentiator because their preference makes the brand strong. They are thought leaders in the building and construction industry and their views count. Since ParexDavco is probably the biggest brand, this differentiation is all the more stronger. The challenge was how to communicate this preference in a clear and believable way. Here, as always, flawless execution in communications is key to achieving strategic success.

Even though ParexDavco's differentiator had been established, this differentiator would not be strong unless it was well dramatised and captured in a strong tagline. Hence, the following tagline was created – "Preferred by Professionals, Globally" – to enable ParexDavco's stakeholders to understand how the brand is differentiated very quickly.

PAREXDAVCO
Preferred by Professionals, Globally

Since the challenge was now to communicate this preference, the ParexDavco brand concept, or the tone of voice, was determined next. Management decided that the ParexDavco brand would carry a 70 per cent *symbolic* concept due to the company's global network of clients and offices and the fact that key thought leaders perceive the brand to be the best (if not one of the best) brand(s) in the market. The remaining 30 per cent would carry a *relational* concept since relationships are important in ParexDavco's industry.

Having established the relevant strategies to differentiate and strengthen the ParexDavco brand, a marketing communications roadmap was developed to help guide the company in the implementation of these strategies to ensure consistent message delivery. ParexDavco swiftly determined the right mix of media platforms to use to communicate ParexDavco's brand given its objectives and available marketing budget. Due to fragmentation in the media, it was important to determine the correct media to use to ensure proper targeting and maximise ParexDavco's marketing budget. The important stakeholder groups of the company were identified and key brand messages unique to each group were developed. A step-by-step guideline on the activities that ParexDavco had to undertake over the following 12 months was also developed.

In generating internal brand buying, the new corporate trademark and brand strategy were introduced and explained to all employees. This involved a thorough walkthrough of the brand, its values and how it was to be operationalised into everyday worklife and client contact protocols.

Today, the ParexDavco brand articulates the brand's differentiation in the marketplace – one that is perceptually defensible and relevant. The crafted tagline "Preferred by Professionals, Globally" communicates the knowledge attribute that ParexDavco owns and differentiates it from other building material manufacturers. It also illustrates the global brand that ParexDavco stands for.

The professionals' preference of the brand is a strong endorsement for ParexDavco. Coupled with the referrals obtained from existing clients worldwide, ParexDavco is able to reach out to the specifiers in Singapore and give them greater confidence in using the brand as a standard for specification. In addition, the internal alignment of its employees to the brand resulted in clients having higher brand awareness at every touch-point. Every employee of ParexDavco lives and breathes the brand and delivers consistent brand messages to his/her clients.

With the development of the brand strategy, ParexDavco is standardising its corporate identity and marketing collaterals to ensure consistency in design and content. Today, ParexDavco continues to serve an international clientele working on large projects around the region. Its Singapore market share has seen constant growth, with its products increasingly being used as a standard for specification.

It can clearly be seen that this differentiation strategy has provided the company with the platform to transform itself from a successful multinational business into a focussed and highly differentiated brand that provides the company with direction in its marketing and innovation activities. A stronger ParexDavco brand enables the company to withstand both local and foreign competition more effectively, thus growing the brand's market share and bringing long-term sustainability to the business.

B2B

CHAPTER
13

Rule No. 6 –
Brands Are Built With PR,
Not Advertising

WHEN was the last time you read an advertisement? And we are not talking about recruitment advertisements. More importantly, when was the last time you actually believed something you read in an advertisement? You probably don't really remember. The fact is, we are bombarded by so many advertising messages a day that we just tune out most of them.

Now, even if you do read an advertisement and it advertises a product at an unbelievably good price, you would still be sceptical, wouldn't you? If you see a new freehold condominium in a good location being advertised at a very low per-square-foot price, what would you think? You would probably think that in order to get that low per-square-foot price, you would have to buy the really big unit with a roof garden that is, for the most part, unusable. If you want the three-bedroom, 1,200-square-foot unit (like most people), it will probably cost you 50 per cent more in terms of price per square foot compared to the advertised price. We have been "conned" by such advertisements before so that these days, we take every advertisement with a pinch of salt.

Every time people read an advertisement, they will be thinking in the back of their minds, "Sounds good but what's the catch?" If it is an advertisement from a mobile phone service provider offering the latest model of mobile phone from Nokia or Sony Ericsson for an incredible price, the catch is usually this: You have to sign up for a new line for two years and have a suitable phone to trade in. But then again, you already knew that, right? That is why you always ask, "What's the catch?" when you read an ad.

Furthermore, people don't really pay attention to advertisements these days. Here is a typical scenario that happens at our branding workshops. When we ask the participants if they read advertisements, some will shake their heads. Others will answer with a degree of indignation, "Of course we read advertisements!" Interesting. But our follow-up question reveals something even more interesting. "Why do you read advertisements?" (At this point, these executives are looking at us as if we are two village idiots.)

A typical answer to the second question is, "We need to monitor what our competitors are doing, you know? That's what companies do. That's why we read advertisements diligently." Yes, we know. *You read advertisements because you need to monitor what your competitors are doing.*

Are you getting it yet? The only people who will diligently read your advertisements are your competitors. They will read every single word, look at every single picture, take note of the size of the ad, how many times it has appeared and where. Things like that. But your target audience, your customers, those people who really matter, don't pay attention to your ads. While you are busy reading your competitors' ads and they are busy reading yours, your customers are reading something else.

There are many companies out there bombarding you with print ads, TV and radio commercials, direct mail, e-mail ads, flyers, posters, bus/MRT/taxi ads, etc. Do you pay much attention to them? Did any of these ads motivate you to buy something? Did any of these ads even stick in your mind? Did any of these ads change the perceptions that you already have of the brands being advertised? Did any of these ads change the perceptions that you already have of the advertised brands' competitors?

Probably not.

According to Al and Laura Ries in their book, *The Fall of Advertising and the Rise of PR,* the average person is bombarded with 237 marketing messages in a day. That was in the year 2000. When we first read that book, we thought that the authors had got it wrong. We did not feel as if we were being bombarded by 237 marketing messages a day. After some reflection, we realised why. Our society is over-communicated. The media clutter is incredible. As a result, we tend to tune out most of the marketing messages that are targeted at us. That is really bad news for advertisers. The clutter is so bad that people just don't notice ads any more. The advertisements just fade into the background; they are just like wallpaper.

And what solution does the advertising industry recommend? Outspend the competition. In fact, one of the first things that advertising executives do is ask clients what their annual advertising budget is. The advertising industry has often warned clients about under-spending. We know because we used to work in advertising and marketing communications. But before you launch your next advertising campaign, there are several issues that you need to consider.

DO AS I SAY BUT DON'T DO AS I DO

Have you ever wondered why advertising agencies will happily recommend millions of dollars in advertising for their clients but they themselves do not advertise? When Jacky first started working in an advertising agency in 1996, he asked his boss during a brainstorming session why the agency did not advertise to increase its sales. His reasoning was that as the agency recommended advertising to its clients and if advertising was so good, how come the agency itself didn't advertise? How naive of him. Jacky's boss told him (very loudly) that the agency didn't advertise because first of all, the only people who would read the ads were the agency's competitors and, secondly, nobody would believe the ads. Jacky's immediate reaction in his mind was, "Huh? And we are still recommending advertising to our clients?"

After Jacky left that advertising agency, he couldn't get another job as a copywriter although he went for interview after interview. The problem wasn't that Jacky couldn't write creatively. That he could do reasonably well. The problem was advertising agencies only want to hire award-winning copywriters, art directors and creative directors. The first question that was usually directed at Jacky was, "How many awards have you won?" His standard answer – "None. I don't believe in awards. I believe in effective advertising campaigns that increase clients' sales." Saying something like that is the biggest mistake you can ever make when interviewing for a job in an advertising agency. Jacky was extremely discouraged back then because he had always thought that the aim of advertising was not to win awards but to increase the clients' sales.

Here lies the crux of the problem. Advertising agencies don't advertise because they know that no one is going to read their advertisements. Why? Advertisements have no credibility. Advertising is what you say about yourself and, of course, you will say good things about yourself, right? Where is the credibility in that? Well, credibility lies in what others say about you. Credibility lies in public relations, or PR. That is why advertising agencies are so focussed on winning creative awards. These awards create publicity and they use the publicity to win business. That is why a guy like Jacky who believes that awards are not as important as running effective advertising campaigns will never get a job in advertising.

If advertising is the lifeblood of a business as the advertising industry keeps repeating, why don't advertising agencies advertise? Why do they rely on PR to promote their brands? Some advertising executives that we have met tried to explain that advertising agencies don't need to advertise because their work speaks volumes and they need to hire award-winning copywriters, art directors and creative directors to ensure that their work is up to scratch. Well, we disagree. How do clients know your work is good? When you tell clients that you have won such-and-such award? And that is PR because that is somebody else (presumably a panel of experts) saying that you are good by giving you the award. Those awards usually generate positive publicity which helps to build the advertising agency's brand. The bottom line is, even advertising agencies use PR to build their brands.

HOW MANY ADVERTISING PEOPLE ARE TRAINED IN MARKETING?

We are not saying all these things to spite the advertising industry but advertising is part of marketing so it is important for advertising people to understand marketing if they want to run effective campaigns. But the advertising industry is more interested in winning creative awards. The next time an advertising agency makes a pitch to you, ask this question, "What percentage of your staff is trained in marketing?" It is a valid question. Jacky once attended an executive training programme called 'Measuring ROI in Branding', run by The Fournaise Marketing Group. The CEO of Fournaise, Jerome Fontaine, told the participants, who were all marketing managers, that they had better ask this very important question or they could put their advertising campaign at risk. His point is that if your advertising people are not marketing trained, how on earth can they be expected to run an effective campaign? We could not agree more.

Yes, you need to express your marketing messages creatively but if you don't even understand marketing, how can you come up with a strategy that has a chance of succeeding? We suspect the reason why there are so many shockingly bad advertisements out there is because the people who created the ads have no understanding of marketing.

THE "ADVERTISING IS AN HONEST PROFESSION" DEBATE

The following chart shows the results of the Gallup Poll Honesty Survey for 2004. The American public was asked to rank which professions they felt to be honest or dishonest. Results showed that nurses are perceived to be the most honest, with an honesty rating of 79 per cent. Car salesmen are perceived to be the most dishonest, with a rating of 9 per cent. Advertising practitioners are rated as the second most dishonest profession in the list – ranking even lower than lawyers, politicians and businesspeople!

So, if advertising is perceived as a dishonest profession, what are the chances of your potential customers believing anything you say in your ad? That is why you need to use PR to launch and build your brand. PR has credibility because it is what others say about you. People still believe what they read or see or hear in the media more than advertisements. But PR is not easy to manage. It is slow, it is hard to get and it is even harder to control – sometimes reporters say things about you that you don't want them to. But what choice do you have? PR has credibility, advertising doesn't. Hence, you need to rely on PR to build your brand.

We are not saying that advertising is redundant. On the contrary. Advertising does have a role to play but just not in building up a brand that is not well known. The role of advertising is actually to maintain a brand that has been built. When you see something that you already know being advertised, you are likely to be more receptive to the messages – provided, of course, that the messages are consistent with your perception of the brand. Advertising is great for reinforcing perceptions but not that great when it comes to changing perceptions. If you perceive Brand X to be "such and such" and the advertising tells you it is "so and so", you are not likely to change your mind.

Remember Rule No. 1 – Perception Is Reality. Research showed that advertising is not perceived as a very honest profession. That is why people will not perceive an advertisement to be a highly credible source of information unless the information being advertised is already in their minds. We are just telling you as it is.

Chart 1: Gallup Poll Honesty Survey 2004

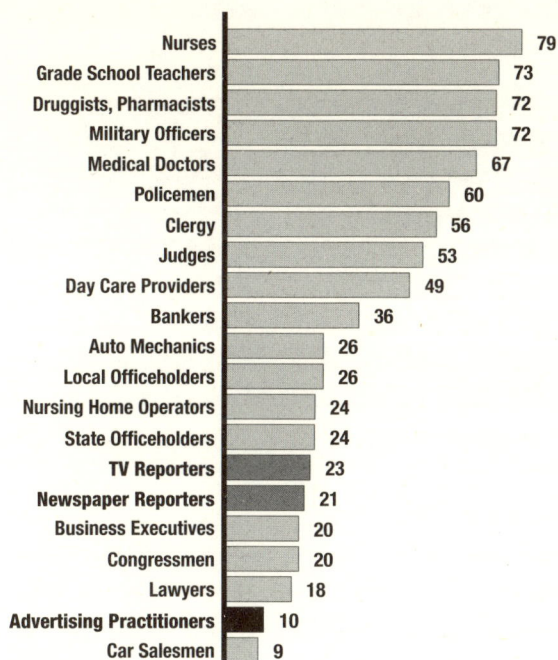

Profession	Score
Nurses	79
Grade School Teachers	73
Druggists, Pharmacists	72
Military Officers	72
Medical Doctors	67
Policemen	60
Clergy	56
Judges	53
Day Care Providers	49
Bankers	36
Auto Mechanics	26
Local Officeholders	26
Nursing Home Operators	24
State Officeholders	24
TV Reporters	23
Newspaper Reporters	21
Business Executives	20
Congressmen	20
Lawyers	18
Advertising Practitioners	10
Car Salesmen	9

(Source: www.gallup.com)

If you look at the 2008 Gallup Poll Honest Survey 2008 on the next page, you will find that advertising is still among the nine professions that are rated the lowest in terms of honesty and ethics. Yes, there are five professions rated as more dishonest than advertising – Stockbrokers, Congressmen, Car Salesmen, Telemarketers and Lobbyists – but that is not much comfort. This again reinforces the fact that advertising is not the way to build a brand.

Chart 2: Gallup Poll Honest Survey 2008
Least Well-Rated Professions For Honesty And Ethics 2008
■% Very High/High   ■% Average   ▨% Low/Very Low

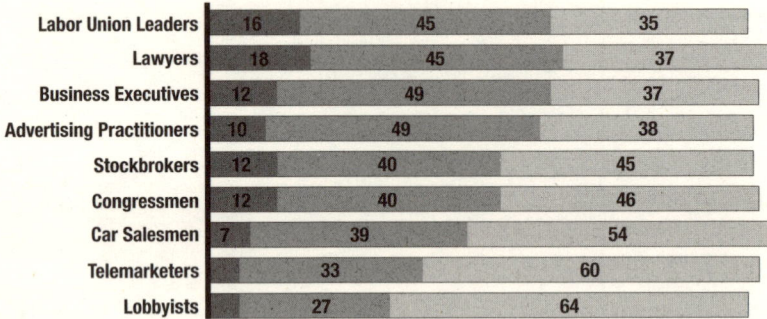

Profession	% Very High/High	% Average	% Low/Very Low
Labor Union Leaders	16	45	35
Lawyers	18	45	37
Business Executives	12	49	37
Advertising Practitioners	10	49	38
Stockbrokers	12	40	45
Congressmen	12	40	46
Car Salesmen	7	39	54
Telemarketers		33	60
Lobbyists		27	64

(Source: www.gallup.com)

HOW DO YOU GENERATE GOOD PR?

We are often asked by companies how they can generate good PR. Bear in mind that PR is basically what the media say about your brand so it has credibility, but PR is not easy to manage. We have outlined some questions below that might help but it is still no guarantee.

Question #1

Ask yourself if you have a new category or a next generation product/service that is new and interesting. People (journalists included) are not interested in what is better. They are interested in what is new. That is the reason why the PlayStation received so much media coverage when it was first launched. Have you seen a PlayStation ad before? Neither have we but the PlayStation sells millions of units a year. It was something new and interesting. Consequently, it received a lot of publicity.

Dell also received a lot of publicity because it was something new – the first computer to be sold direct to consumers. Gateway 2000, which came along later with the same concept, didn't generate the same amount of publicity. Why? It's not new. Dell got there first with the concept of direct sales.

Question #2

Are you differentiated? If you are a me-too, same-same kind of brand, forget about getting good PR. Nobody is going to be interested in you. "But we are better than the leading brand!" many companies will argue. Maybe you are but that's not enough. How are you different? That is more important. Microsoft dominates the market for operating systems. So how did Linux generate so much publicity? It was different from Microsoft. It was the first open-source operating system.

Question #3

Are you focussed? If you do everything under the sun, people will quickly lose interest in you. What does your brand stand for? What is your brand all about? The typical company that we meet will say very excitedly, "We are doing this! We are really good at that. We are also doing that other thing."

Are you interested in such a company? Probably not because in the back of your mind, you are thinking that this company can't be any good if it does everything under the sun. You need to find a strong focus if you want to generate good publicity. If you want the media to write your story, you need to give them an anchor – a really strong focus point – or the story will not be interesting.

NVIDIA focuses on 3D graphics chips. Every time a story is written about graphics chips, guess who is interviewed? NVIDIA, who else? Oracle is focussed on database software, so who do journalists quote when they are writing a database software story? Oracle.

Question #4

Are you comfortable in front of the media – whether it is an interview with a newspaper or on TV or radio? Many CEOs or business owners are not comfortable talking to the media. Some even shun the publicity whenever the media want to interview them. To us, that is a wasted opportunity. It is no different from speaking in public. Even if you think that you are not very good at talking to the media, you can train yourself to be comfortable. Some CEOs that we know are not very smooth in front of the media but that's all right because they really believe in what they do and they sound and look credible. There are professional training courses to help CEOs with this. We don't offer such courses but we often assist clients in preparing for any interviews. Thorough preparation can overcome nervousness so you need to be thoroughly prepared.

Does it have to be the CEO? The answer is usually yes because the CEO is the head of the company and the default brand champion. That is why it has to be him or her. It is not something that should be delegated until the company has become a global giant. When that happens, then it is all right for the CEO not to be at every media interview.

THE MILLION-MILE BMW

An example of a good PR campaign is the one that Mobil did in 1990 in the United States. Mobil wanted to find out how good its Mobil 1 synthetic engine oil really was. So it took a new BMW 325i (model type E30) and ran it for a million miles (1.6 million km) using only Mobil 1 synthetic engine oil. The test took four years to complete.

In 1994, the engine was dismantled and examined for wear and tear. The components looked almost brand new. Virtually no wear at all. That quickly resulted in a host of positive publicity for Mobil. Today, nearly two decades later, people still talk about that test in car clubs and online car forums around the world. Good PR has the potential to live for a very long time.

The Million-Mile BMW illustrates the importance of creating a dramatic story that will capture the eyes of the media and the public. It is not an easy thing to do and requires a lot of belief in your brand and commitment of time, money and resources. Mobil obviously believed that its product was superior and therefore was willing to do what it did. Of course, Mobil has a lot of money as well. Most of us don't have such deep pockets but that doesn't mean that you cannot create a dramatic story on a smaller budget.

For example, if you are selling LED lights and one of the key selling points is that LED lights generate very little heat, what do you do to inject some drama and interest into the brand? You can have a cooking competition. The person who can fry an egg in the shortest time will win the top prize. But the heat source can only come from an electric light. So, you can have a selection of halogen lights, spotlights and, of course, your LED light for the contestants to chose from. Whoever chooses to try and fry an egg using heat from your LED light would definitely not win but this would help to dramatise the low-heat aspect of LED lights. This would create a good story for the brand.

Of course, you would also do well to video tape the whole thing and send snippets of the video to your customers and distributors as well as post it on YouTube. Hopefully, this would create a viral effect and the video would be watched by millions around the world. We can't guarantee anything but this is a relatively low-budget way of creating a story. Yes, we know that *all* LED lights are low heat but as long as no one has dramatised this aspect for PR purposes, then you can still do it and gain some mileage. This is just an example.

THE 3M SAFETY GLASS

3M ran a very successful PR campaign that created ripples around the world. It put up a glass display at a bus stop. Then put what looked like tens of thousands of dollars in the glass display and stuck a small "3M Safety Glass" logo on the glass. A lot of people attempted to break the glass to get to the money. But none succeeded because 3M safety glass is really tough. One man even took a flying kick at the glass. The reporter who was there said that the glass wasn't even scratched but the man looked like he might have broken a few toes. That campaign generated a lot of publicity all over the world.

SO DOES THAT MEAN YOU DON'T NEED TO ADVERTISE?

On the contrary. Successful brands, be they consumer or business brands, are almost always launched and built with PR. Microsoft, IBM, Linux, Cisco, Oracle, SAP, Siebel, Intel, Dell, Xerox, Sun, Callaway, Yahoo!, Google, PlayStation, Volvo, Coca-Cola, Ben & Jerry's, Starbucks, Gatorade, Red Bull, The Body Shop and Zara were all built by PR.

But there comes a time when a brand runs out of PR potential. That's when you switch to advertising. Coca-Cola is heavily advertised today but in the distant past, Coca-Cola was built with PR. But the advertising has to be consistent with the perception that PR has already built up in the mind.

When Volvo launched the world's first three-point safety belt, the world's media praised it as a breakthrough in car safety. That built Volvo into the "safety" brand. In the nineties, Volvo tried to take on BMW in the performance sector. Volvo built a series of fast, turbocharged cars like the 850 T5. These cars were faster and cheaper than equivalent BMW models and Volvo advertised them aggressively. Did it work? No. Because people perceive Volvo as the safe car and BMW as the performance car, never mind that the Volvo is actually faster!

THE MOST IMPORTANT LESSON: Brands are born and built with a blaze of publicity but they need advertising to survive. However, the advertising messages must agree with the perception that PR has already sowed in the mind or the brand will lose credibility.

THE CHALLENGE WITH MANY PR PROFESSIONALS THAT WE HAVE MET

The one thing that strikes us as very strange about the many PR professionals that we have come across – whether they work for local or international PR agencies or for the PR department of a corporation – is that they don't see themselves as brand builders.

In our experience, PR people get uncomfortable when you talk to them about their roles as brand builders. What do they see their roles as? Issuing press releases to announce the company's financial results and organising events and road shows as well as managing crises (basically putting a positive spin on bad news). While those are important, PR professionals should play a more active role in building brands.

And to all the PR people out there, we strongly encourage you to read *The Fall of Advertising and the Rise of PR* by Al and Laura Ries if you have not done so already. It is a really excellent book on public relations and it will change the way you see your role and how you do your work.

In A Nutshell

We have nothing against advertising. Advertising has an important role to play in branding but that role is brand maintenance, not brand building. The reason is simple. Advertising is what you say about yourself so people will perceive that as biased. And perception is reality. So, they will take your advertisements with a pinch of salt. What a third party – such as the media – says about you will have more credibility. So, companies should focus their brand building efforts using PR once they have settled on their brand strategy. Brands – even the top brands in the world – eventually run out of stories to tell the media. That is when advertising kicks in to help maintain the brand. Brand maintenance is all about keeping the customers reminded of the brand and what it stands for. However, in terms of B2B companies where the number of customers they have is much smaller than for a comparable B2C company, advertising might not be necessary at all. The brand maintenance can be done on a one-to-one basis. For example, if you are a B2B company operating in an industry with a total of 300 customers who can potentially buy from you worldwide, then it wouldn't make sense to advertise because you can reach out to these customers/potential customers one-to-one. For a B2C company like Coca-Cola with a potential customer base measured in the hundreds of millions (if not billions), then advertising is necessary. Regardless of what you do, you have to keep the advertising message consistent with the idea that people already have of your brand or you will hit a brick wall. If you perceive Volvo as a safe car and Volvo advertises itself as "sporty", you are not going to believe that advertisement. If you perceive Toyota as reliable and it advertises the brand as "sexy", you are not going to believe it either.

CASE STUDY
Brands Are Built With PR, Not Advertising – CYC

An Overview Of The Fashion Industry

From 1995 to 2007, the luxury goods market grew on a worldwide scale. The CAGR was 11 per cent from 1995 to 1999 (commonly known as the period of the luxury industry boom), 1 per cent from 2000 to 2003 (a contraction) and 8 per cent from 2004 to 2007 (an expansion of the luxury industry in emerging markets).[43] Two main drivers that caused this development were principally the economic growth in South East Asia,[44] which created "the new rich", and the rise in the use of "new luxury" (luxury products for the mass affluent).[45] In the 2008 financial meltdown, the worldwide luxury goods market suffered, including fashion, perfumes and cosmetics, wines and spirits, watches and jewellery.

Many studies have shown that in the managing of luxury products, brand and marketing management is very important.[46] This is because fashion changes all the time and is a dynamic business based on trends and social evolution. For example, a fad 20 years ago can make a comeback and become the fashion of today. Thus, understanding the culture and the market in this industry is particularly critical for those in the fashion business. Studies have also shown that in the purchasing intention for fashion luxury goods, consumers buy luxury fashion goods mainly to match their lifestyle, thus satisfying their inner drives. This is the reason why lifestyle brands that have been around for a long time have a tougher task staying relevant.

In the Singapore context, shopping is often called the national pastime. The city-state of some 5 million people has continued to attract luxury brand retailers in droves while the rest of the world slowly shakes off the global economic crisis. From a fashion retailing point of view, Singapore has got, and attracts, more than enough local and Asian shoppers willing to spend on luxury fashion, a fact that is fitting for a country that has the world's highest density of millionaires and is positioning itself as a centre for luxury living. This has great implications for Singapore brands in the fashion business because as demands increase, so too will competition.

---

[43] Bain & Company, 'Osservatorio mondiale sui mercati del lusso' (2009) from www.altagamma.it/admin/contenuti/allegati/amministratori/altagamma/attivita/studiricerche/2009-10-19/Monitor_Altagamma_sui_Mercati_Mondiali_2009.pdf (accessed 28 March 2010)

[44] Vigneron, F. and Johnson, L.W., 'Measuring perceptions of brand luxury', *Journal of Brand Management*, Vol. 11, No. 6, 2004, pp. 484-506.

[45] Silverstein, M. and Fiske, N. 'Luxury for the masses', *Harvard Business Review*, Vol. 81, No. 4, 2003, pp. 48–57.

[46] Dubois, B., Czellar, S. and Laurent, G., 'Consumer segments based on attitudes toward luxury: Empirical evidence from twenty countries', *Marketing Letters*, Vol. 16, No. 2, 2005, pp. 115-28.

CYC – The Custom Shop

CYC Shanghai Shirt Company Pte Ltd ("CYC") was established in 1935 by Mr Chiang Yick Ching who migrated to Singapore with his wife, Madam Foo Ah Neok, to seek better fortunes. Mr Chiang and Madam Foo ran a small tailoring outfit in Swatow, Guandong, for three years before coming to Singapore.

By the 1960s, CYC's customer base had grown to Malaysia and Indonesia and the company had also launched a line of ready-made shirts. Before the 1984 recession, CYC had six branches and several sub-agents in Singapore. The company also owned a five-storey building in MacPherson with the capacity to make 20,000 shirts a month. The recession of 1984 hit the company hard and it also started losing market share to cheap imports.

In 1992, the torch was passed to CYC's third-generation management, headed by Mrs Fong Loo Fern, the founder's granddaughter. Mrs Fong continues to run the company today as its managing director. With the new management came a new corporate direction. Mrs Fong refocussed the company back to its core business – custom-made shirts – leaving the low-end market to the cheap ready-made imports.

A Great And Genuine Story Will Speak For Itself

For a company such as CYC – The Custom Shop, which has been in business since the 1930s, keeping the business story alive is a challenge. This is particularly so for this company because it is in a high-interest business – fashion.

In an attempt to revitalise CYC, Mrs Fong refocussed the business back to offering custom-made shirts and undertook a major revamp of the company's image. In 1994, the company opened an exclusive outlet in Singapore's prestigious Raffles Hotel. The brand of CYC began to move to new strengths and new heights.

In November 2001, Mrs Fong decided to create a vintage shirt museum. She made a public appeal for customers to donate their shirts so that they could be put on display. Much to her surprise, Mrs Lee Kuan Yew visited CYC and handed over three of the then Senior Minister's shirts. The shirts were more than 30 years old and were still in excellent condition. Mrs Fong said that one was a "retro-looking" shirt with blue polka dots that Mrs Lee described as the shirt MM Lee had worn on TV when Singapore became independent in 1965. This activity of creating a vintage shirt museum, which had originated without the intention of capturing any media attention, turned into the story of the town and almost every media platform carried the story in one form or another. Many today still remember this story and associate the CYC brand to this event. Mrs Fong on Minister Mentor's shirts:

I saw Mr Lee on TV at that time in a white CYC shirt with Philippine-style embroidery on the front. It was about 15 years old. This shows that he treasures what he has and he's frugal. For more than 30 years, MM Lee has bought CYC's shirts about once a year, and at most two shirts each time. Mrs Lee picks the fabric (usually Oxford cotton) and colour (pink is his favourite). Comfort and fit are more important to MM Lee. He commonly asked for a larger-than-normal collar, and so did Mr Goh Chok Tong, then the prime minister, whom Mr Lee introduced to CYC.

What ended up as a public relations activity had not been planned as one (while most such activities do require planning); instead it revolved around CYC's genuine desire of wanting to set up a vintage shirt museum. This genuine desire was a powerful endorsement for the company. It was one based on facts. While there was no intention to manage, control or influence people's perceptions of CYC, this PR event initiated a sequence of behaviour that probably led to the achievement of CYC's organisation's objectives in building a strong heritage brand. This, to a large extent, successfully created, changed and reinforced the opinions of potential customers through subtle persuasion.

Without meaning to do so, CYC leveraged on the power of the media through public relations. The extensive media coverage surrounding the story was an efficient way for CYC to reach its mass audience very quickly. It generated awareness of and, to some extent, demand for CYC's shirts. It also helped to develop a stronger, more controlled image of the brand. It further generated the perception that CYC was an active and progressive company, even though it had a rich heritage. All of these provided the company with a marketing advantage over its competitors. It was obvious that when Mrs Fong was interviewed, the values of the CYC brand, which had been imbued in the Chiang family for generations, were communicated. This, in turn, increased its reputation as readers felt that there was a sense of originality and genuineness in the brand. This gave the company increased recognition and visibility in the marketplace, especially with MM Lee's generosity, which provided third-party endorsement.

This media-driven event also provided CYC's customers with a better understanding of the value proposition of CYC and, what is more, the high level of service that the company provided. After all, if the political leaders of Singapore bought their shirts from CYC – The Custom Shop, then what the company did must be good enough for anyone.

Since this event, the company has seen an increase in its client base and profitability. In addition, it increased the profile of Mrs Fong, the spokesperson of the brand, and provided employee security within the company – all CYC staff know that what they are doing provides a meaningful future for themselves and for the company.

B2B

CHAPTER 14

Rule No. 7 –
You Better Have
A Great Name Or Else

DO not underestimate the power of a great name in building brands. By the same token, do not underestimate how detrimental a bad name can be to your brand. If you are one of those people who think that a name is just something that you slap on to your products so that you have a brand to call your own, think again. That name can make or break your brand.

Companies very often attribute failures to cut-throat competition, changing market conditions, insufficient marketing resources and everything else under the sun. But we have never seen a company attribute its failures (or successes) to the name. After all, a name is just a name, right? How important can it be?

Well, what if you have a name like Sum Ting Wong? We think it would be very hard for you to do business with anyone because they will think that there is something wrong with you. Can you imagine introducing yourself to a prospective client, "Hi! My name is Sum Ting Wong and I would like to introduce to you the next generation of…" Your prospective client would probably fall off the chair laughing his head off or turn blue trying not to laugh in the interest of politeness. You can't build a strong brand on a bad name.

In the long run, the name may be the single most important asset that you can have. The reason is very simple. In the beginning, what makes a brand successful is a unique idea that the brand can own in the mind. But in the long run, that unique idea or concept will disappear as competitors copy it. So what remains in the long run to differentiate a brand is just the name.

XEROX

Xerox was launched in 1959 as the first automatic plain paper photocopier. It was easy to sell a Xerox in the beginning because its copies were cleaner, sharper, easier to handle and easier to sort. Before Xerox came along, there were only thermal photocopiers available. If you have ever used a thermal fax machine, you will have an idea of how bad those thermal copiers were.

Today, all photocopiers are automatic plain paper copiers. In fact, you probably can't tell the difference between a copy made by Xerox and one made by its competitors.

We were once shown five photocopies made by different photocopier brands. We were asked to rank them in order of quality. It was difficult but we finally ranked them. And the one with the best quality was not a Xerox. The best copy was actually produced by a Toshiba machine. Second was Canon. Xerox came in third.

So all that is left to differentiate Xerox from the other photocopiers out there is the name. And in this respect, Xerox wins hands down because it has got by far the most superior name in photocopiers. A name that is short, unique, memorable, easy to pronounce and closely linked to the category called photocopiers. Is Xerox the best photocopier today? It is hard to tell. You can make up your own mind. We are no experts on photocopier technology. But we do know that Xerox has the best photocopier name.

NOKIA

Nokia managed to dominate the mobile phone category because, in 1991, it dropped everything that it was doing to focus on mobile phones. A Nokia phone used to be so much more superior than other phones in terms of user-friendliness, design, fit and finish, material quality and so on and so forth.

But the competitors have caught up with (and in some cases, eclipsed) Nokia in all those aspects. We are speaking as mobile phone users who have owned various brands of phones. From a consumer's point of view, Sony Ericsson's material quality and fit and finish outclass Nokia's. A lot of Nokia models today look cheap and flimsy in our opinion. A Sony Ericsson looks very expensive next to a Nokia even though it is not. And Samsung phones probably have the best colour LCD screens.

So why is Nokia still No. 1 in mobile phones although it no longer has a unique advantage over its competitors? Nokia's market share remains around 35 per cent globally. Nokia is a specialist. As we have shown earlier, people generally trust specialists more than generalists. Besides this relentless focus on mobile phones, Nokia also meets all the 10 characteristics of a great brand name that we are going to outline later in this chapter.

Incidentally, the Nokia name is derived from a black, furry weasel that is found in Finland's forests, according to Matt Haig in his book *Brand Failures:*

The Truth about the 100 Biggest Branding Mistakes of All Time. Nokia originally started out as a forestry company. Sony Ericsson is saddled with a line-extended name that stands for mobile phones and a thousand and one other things. The same goes for Samsung, Motorola and LG. Plus, those other brands somehow don't sound as good.

What about Motorola – the company that pioneered the mobile phone? Compared to Nokia, the Motorola name has two strikes against it. Firstly, it is not a name that is unique to Motorola's mobile phones. The company also uses the name on a lot of other things. Secondly, the name is longer than Nokia's. Perhaps that is why Motorola is trying to shorten it to just Moto. Hence, the "Hello, Moto" campaign.

LEXUS

Lexus made its name in the luxury car market by being the first Japanese luxury car. It created a new category. Lexus is known for its uncompromising build quality and refinement. "The Relentless Pursuit Of Perfection" is not just a marketing slogan for Lexus. It actually lives by this philosophy in everything that it does. Lexus has consistently topped quality and customer satisfaction surveys such as the influential J.D. Power and Associates 'Initial Quality Study'.

Can Lexus' capabilities be duplicated by another Japanese car brand like Nissan's Infiniti or Honda's Acura? Most definitely yes. But Lexus will still have an edge over its competitors because it has a fantastic name. It sounds expensive, luxurious and very premium. Infiniti is too long, bland and generic. Acura sounds more like a contagious disease in our opinion but you are free to disagree.

Plus, Acura did not go all out like Lexus. Acura still sells lower-end cars like the four-cylinder RS-X, which is actually the Honda Integra in other markets. Lexus started right at the top with the V8-powered LS400 targeted squarely at top-of-the-line German luxury cars like the Mercedes-Benz S-Class and BMW 7 series.

In the long run, Acura and Infiniti can catch up with Lexus in all the areas that made Lexus famous but they will be disadvantaged by their names. After all, if everything is equal among these three Japanese luxury car brands, which one would people choose? The one with the name that is synonymous with Japanese luxury cars – Lexus. You will also see that Lexus meets most of the 10 characteristics of a great brand name.

GOOGLE

Another fantastic name. So good that a lot of people no longer say, "I will perform a search on the Internet for the information." They just say, "I will Google it." It is a made-up name that is short, sweet, memorable and easy to pronounce. Google has become synonymous with Internet search engines the way Xerox is synonymous with photocopiers.

The Google name actually came about by accident. Apparently, when Larry Page and Sergey Brin first started the company, it was supposed to be called Googol but one of their earliest investors, Andy Bechtolsheim, one of the co-founders of Sun Microsystems, wrote a cheque wrongly to "Google" instead of "Googol". Instead of going back to Bechtolsheim to get the cheque amended – after all, he might have changed his mind – they decided it would be easier to incorporate Google and pay in the cheque. Great move, guys. And great name, no matter what.

WHAT MAKES A GOOD BRAND NAME?

1. Easy To Pronounce

If people can't even pronounce your brand, what are the chances of them buying it? It would probably take you two whole weeks to learn how to pronounce Tokyo Tsushin Kogyo. That is why, 12 years after it was incorporated, Tokyo Tsushin Kogyo changed its name to Sony, which comes from the Latin word *sonus* meaning "sound" and the English word *sunny*.

It is much easier to say, "I am going to buy a Sony DVD player" than to say "I am going to buy a Tokyo Tsushin Kogyo DVD player." Of course, Sony's success cannot be fully credited to its name but in a market that is so crowded, it certainly helped.

2. Easy To Remember

Creative Technology was the first to launch portable MP3 players but it has extended its line and does not have very memorable names. Creative ZEN, Creative MuVo, Creative NOMAD Jukebox and Creative ZEN Micro are not names that are very memorable compared to iPod. iPod is a made-up word. It is short. It is unique.

And it is memorable as it connotes a few things. The "i" in iPod alludes to the fact that it is intelligent and personal. The "Pod" in iPod tells people that this is something small and portable. Since iPod, many companies have tried to incorporate the "i" into their brand names. Look at some of the massagers that OSIM has launched – iSqueez, iMedic, iDesire, iSymphonic.

3. English-Sounding

It doesn't need to be an English word but it must work well in English. For some reason, English words are the easiest for people of other nationalities to pronounce. Perhaps that is due to the influence of American TV programmes or the wide availability of American brands or the fact that English is accepted as the international language of commerce (although we know of some French people who think that French is the international language of commerce). There are 6,912 languages in the world (yes, that's right) but English is still the generally accepted language of international commerce.

What do you think of the name Krating Daeng? Would you drink something that is branded Krating Daeng? Maybe not because you would be wary of anything that sounds like cow dung. Fortunately, the company changed its name to Red Bull. The brand took off and chalked up S$3.4 billion in sales in 2005. Today, it is the best-selling energy drink in the world.

There are many brands with non-English names but that is all right provided those names are easy to pronounce in English. Heineken, Porsche, Nike, Ya Kun, Nokia, Honda, Sikorsky, Häagen Dazs, Haier and Samsung are not English names but they work well in the English language.

What made Creative Technology successful was the sound card, a category that it has dominated since 1989. Besides setting the standard for the industry, Creative Technology's sound card was also blessed with a memorable name – Sound Blaster. Sounds memorable. The bottom line is this – if people can't remember your name, why would they buy your brand?

4. Short

From the examples that we have given above, you will have guessed that brevity is an important criterion for a good brand name. A good brand name must be short. Long names are harder to remember and pronounce.

Furthermore, a long name is very hard to turn into a generic for the category. People say, "Xerox a copy of this document for me", even if they are actually using a Minolta machine. If Xerox had used a long and convoluted name, it would have been hard to make people use that name as a generic for the category. That is why Federal Express changed its name to FedEx. Because it is easier for customers to say, "FedEx this to Tokyo" than "Federal Express this to Tokyo."

If you look at successful global brands, you will notice many of them invariably have short names like Google, Xerox, Intel, Zara, Oracle, Siebel, Cisco, Viagra, Yahoo!, eBay, Linux, Starbucks, Red Bull, Sony, Lexus, Hertz, Avis, Christie's, Palm, Visa, Linux, BlackBerry, Botox, Dell, Rollerblade, Kleenex, Playboy, Q-tips, Nokia, Kellogg's, Wrigley, Avon, Nestlé, Gucci, Chanel, Kraft, Nike, Rolex, Prada, Nivea, Porsche, Boeing, Amway, Compaq, Apple, Kodak, Pixar, Disney and so on.

If you look at *BusinessWeek*'s '100 Best Global Brands' list every year, you will see that about 48 per cent are two-syllable brand names and 31 per cent are three-syllable brand names. So, if you are creating a new brand name for your company or product/service, it might be worthwhile to remember this. We are not sure why the two-syllable brand names seem more successful but they seem to work very well.

5. Unique

Having a unique name is very important because you do not want to share your name with other brands. You want that name to belong only to your brand so that it stands for one thing and one thing only. iPod is a unique name. It stands for MP3 players. Starbucks is a unique name. It stands for gourmet coffee. Ya Kun is a unique name. It stands for *kaya* toast. When you mention Ya Kun, people will know exactly what you are talking about. There is no confusion because the name is unique to Adrin Loi's company.

Jacky used to work for a Singapore education software company with a name that was not unique. So it was hard to build a strong brand around it. But the company found a solution to that problem by giving its flagship product a unique name and then focussing its brand building efforts around the product and not the company.

That strategy worked very well until a few years later when the company found out that it actually shared its name with an American company that hosted pornographic content on its website! To make matters worse, a number of potential overseas investors and partners actually went to the other company's website by mistake. So, make sure you choose your name carefully.

6. No Generic Words

It is hard to build a strong brand if you use generic words. Generic words cannot be trademarked. One of the reasons Legend, the Chinese computer giant, changed its name to Lenovo was because the name Legend was too generic to be registered in most countries. So, it had to create a unique name like Lenovo to overcome that problem.

A generic word is also generally quite forgettable. Let's say that you have a company called World Trading Corporation. You can bet that there will be a lot of other companies in other countries that have the same generic name.

As a rule of thumb, try not to use words that you can find in a dictionary or thesaurus because it betrays your laziness and lack of imagination. Besides, there are millions of other people around the world who are already doing that. However, you can use a generic word out of context to build a brand. For instance, Mango, Orange and Apple are not really selling fruit. Mango is a Spanish fashion brand. Orange is a telecommunications company. And Apple is a computer company. But those generic words were used out of context so that is all right.

7. No Acronyms

Acronyms are close cousins of generic words. If you have a name like World Trading Corporation, you are in trouble as the name is not unique and it is way too long. As a result, you will eventually shorten it to WTC, which is equally as bad because acronyms are also not unique. What's WTC? It could be anything – Wild Tofu Company, World Tomyam Conglomerate, Web Transaction Corporation, Wet Teriyaki Chicken, etc.

What about IBM, BMW, KFC and GE – strong brands that use generic words that are then shortened into acronyms? Well, you are not IBM, BMW, KFC or GE. These brands got into the market long before many of you were born. IBM was incorporated in 1924, BMW in 1913, KFC in 1939 and GE in 1892. They have had a long time to establish themselves in the market and back in those days, competition was not as brutal as it is today.

If you try to launch your brand into today's crowded and ultra competitive market with a name that is generic or uses acronyms, you have already lost half the battle.

8. Linked To A Category Name

This is actually an area that many people overlook. So we will spend more time looking at it.

To be successful, a brand needs its brand name to be closely linked with a category. It needs to be seen as the leader or the "owner" of that category, like the way Coca-Cola is seen to own the category called cola. Quite a number of marketing people and branding consultants that we have spoken to are sceptical about having brands so inextricably linked to the categories they are competing in. The reason given is that if a brand is tied to a category, then it loses its ability to stretch into other products, services and categories.

We become very concerned when consultants and marketing professionals start talking about brand stretching because the more you stretch your brand, the weaker it becomes. The more you stretch your brand, the less meaning it has in the mind. And once your brand starts to become fuzzy in the mind, it becomes vulnerable to attacks.

What is a Hewlett-Packard? It used to stand for business computers. But HP's management, in an effort to grow the business, stretched the brand to cover various segments. Nine out of 10 businesspeople that we have come into contact with are very, very enthusiastic about HP's strategy. They hail it as a successful model that should be emulated by all. But if that model is so successful, why didn't former HP CEO Carly Fiorina last longer?

In order for a brand to be successful, it needs to own a powerful brand name and it also needs to have a good category name. Having a great brand name alone is not enough. Brand names mean nothing unless they can be immediately linked back to a category. If you study the history of successful global brands, you will find that besides owning a great name, these brands are also synonymous with a category.

You need to first set up and define a new category that your brand can dominate. And you need a simple and easy-to-remember category name. Next, you need to superglue your brand name to that new category. If that category grows, your brand will grow. If that category dies, your brand will die. That is the risk that you have to take. But that is the way strong brands are built. Strong brands are only strong when they are tied in to a category. Stretch that brand like HP did and you risk weakening it. Good thing that HP has refocussed its attention on PCs and printers.

Dell is strongly identified with a category called "PCs sold direct". If "PCs sold direct" as a category dies, then Dell will probably die along with it. Dell is strong only because its brand stands for a certain category. But in an effort to grow, Dell is now moving into other products like printers, ink, toners, TVs, software and other accessories. We are not sure how that strategy will work out in the long run but at least Dell is staying true to its direct-to-customer formula.

A good category name needs to be simple. Long, complicated category names won't fly with customers. The mind cannot store them well. Take a look at the brands that are listed below as well as their respective categories. Each one has a good brand name and a simple category name.

Brand Name	Category Name
Xerox	Photocopier
Google	Search engine
Intel	Computer chip
Zara	Just-in-time fashion
Oracle	Database software
eBay	Online auction
Linux	Open source OS
Starbucks	Gourmet coffee
Red Bull	Energy drink
Gatorade	Sports drink
Christie's	Auction
Hertz	Rental car
Visa	Credit card
Rollerblade	In-line skates
Kodak	Photographic film
Nokia	Mobile phone
Wrigley	Chewing gum
Kellogg's	Breakfast cereal
Kleenex	Pocket tissue
Boeing	Passenger plane
Gulfstream	Business jet
DeWALT	Power tools
Caterpillar	Construction equipment
Otis	Elevator
Pyrex	Fire glass
GORE-TEX	Waterproof fabric
Lycra	Stretchable fabric
Dri-Fit	Fast-drying fabric
John Deere	Farming equipment
Cray	Supercomputer
SKF	Ball bearings
Hyflux	Water treatment
OSIM	Massage chair
NVIDIA	Graphics chips
Gallup	Opinion poll
Yahoo!	Free e-mail
Skype	Internet telephony
AC Nielsen	Consumer research

Symantec	Anti-virus software
Trend Micro	Internet security
Leeden	Welding
Marshal Systems	Fire and gas detection
Shao Fook	Complex heavy lifting
Thermal Limitec	Passive fire protection
Plurotech	Rust converters
ParexDavco	Building materials
PS Fasteners	Fasteners
Hu Lee Impex	Vegetables
Mobile Gear	Laptop peripherals
Trek 2000	Mobile storage devices

Resist the temptation to give that new category a pretentious-sounding, bombastic name. It's very easy to fall into that trap. It must be a simple name – preferably generic, everyday words. When creating brand names, avoid the generic. When creating category names, try to be as generic as possible because if it is complicated, people won't know what the category is.

9. Has A Dot.com Suffix

On the World Wide Web, there are first-class Netizens and second-class Netizens. In this hierarchy – everything else being equal – a dot.com suffix is the first-class Netizen followed by a dot.com with a country suffix behind it. It does not mean that a brand without a dot.com suffix is not as good but remember Rule No. 1 of branding? Perception is reality. And people perceive a dot.com to be superior to the other suffixes including dot.biz and dot.net. Some Internet experts have told us that if you don't have a dot.com suffix, you are classified as an illegal immigrant on the Internet. Their words, not ours.

Perhaps that has to do with the fact that the Internet boom was driven by the United States, which made the dot.com suffix famous. A dot.com suffix is also more universal. In this age of globalisation, a dot.com allows you to set up shop in other countries with more ease.

The Singapore education software company that Jacky used to work for did not have a dot.com suffix initially. When the company started its regionalisation drive, it ran into some difficulty due to the lack of a dot.com suffix. Why? Because you cannot go into a market like Taiwan and use a dot.com.sg suffix. A dot.com would be more readily accepted by foreign markets. So, for every market that the company entered, it had to register a new domain name with the new market's country suffix. A tedious process and the suffix was not always available.

What if the dot.com suffix is already taken up? Then, you have three options.

Option #1

Attach something else to your brand name in the hope that the domain name is available. But that is not an ideal solution. Can you imagine if Google's domain name were www.googlegroup.com or www.googleinternational.com or www.googlesearch.com? It would impede the brand's progress.

Option #2

Buy the domain name. This is our preferred option but it can be costly. When Wilson started StrategiCom, www.strategicom.com was not available. So the company used www.sc-asia.com as a domain name. But that was not ideal so the company spent money and bought www.strategicom.com. We normally advise clients to buy the dot.com if they can afford it. Sometimes you get lucky and get the domain name really cheap. For example, one of Jacky's clients, Sei Woo Polymer Technologies, managed to buy www.seiwoo.com for only a few thousand dollars. Other clients are not so lucky.

Option #3

Change the brand name. However, most companies are resistant to this option because it involves a lot of work, especially if they are publicly listed companies. So make sure that when you create a new brand, the dot.com is available.

10. Language Neutral

Many brands have failed when they crossed borders simply because their names are not language neutral. The names actually meant something bad in other languages. That is why we always advise clients to test a new brand name in either 20 of the most commonly used languages or in their major markets before the name is launched.

The Ford Pinto did not do well in Brazil because *pinto* is a Portuguese slang word for "small penis". The Chevrolet Nova did not sell well in South America because *nova* means "it doesn't go" in Spanish. Clairol's Mist Stick did not do too well in Germany because *Mist* means "manure" in German. And there is a German brand of engine oil called Fuchs being sold in Singapore. We are not sure how well it is doing but we suspect that the name might hamper it because it sounds like the "F" word. That's why we use Mobil 1.

WHAT IF YOU DON'T HAVE A GOOD NAME?

You must first have the common sense to recognise a good name from a bad one. The above rules of naming should give you an idea. Next, if you have a lousy name like Sum Tim Wong, you must have the courage to admit that it is a lousy name. There is no shame in it. Then, change it to a better name! There are no rules that say that you cannot change your name. Don't get too sentimental about the name. If it's bad, it's bad. Change it. Otherwise, you will be saddling your brand with an unnecessary burden. Having a bad name is like trying to swim across the Straits of Malacca with a 7-kg bowling ball tied around your leg. Business is hard enough without having to overcome the negative perceptions a lousy name can give you.

We have consulted for many companies with Chinese names that are long and difficult to pronounce. The names make it difficult for these companies to compete internationally. Yet they are reluctant to change the name because it is the name of the founder. Even if the founder is no longer around, his sons or grandsons who are now running the business still want to keep the name. There is nothing we can do as consultants if clients insist on keeping a bad name.

However, it doesn't mean that if you have a Chinese name, it can't work in international markets. We have often been asked about Eu Yan Sang. We think Eu Yan Sang is a great name because despite being a Chinese name, it is quite easy to pronounce and more importantly, Eu Yan Sang is operating in a category known as "traditional Chinese medicine". You need to have a Chinese sounding name if you are selling traditional Chinese medicine. You better not have a name like Novartis, Pfizer, Glaxo or Johnson & Johnson.

Would you buy a cologne or a shirt from Ralph Lauren? Probably. But what if Ralph Lauren had kept his original name? In his own words, "My given name has the word 'shit' in it. When I was a kid, the other kids would make a lot of fun of me. It was a tough name. That's why I decided to change it." No kidding.

Would you wear a Ralph Lifshitz cologne? Or a Ralph Lifshitz polo shirt? We doubt it. That is why Ralph Lifshitz changed his name to Ralph Lauren. That probably upset his parents very much but it helped his brand make it big.

So if you have a name like Sum Ting Wong, what should you do? We would suggest that you change it to something like Wang De Foo, which reads like "wonderful".

In A Nutshell

The name is possibly the single most important branding decision that you can make in the long run because whatever you can do today that makes you an outstanding brand can and will be copied by your competitors. The scary thing is that your competitors can probably do it better and cheaper. However, the one thing that they cannot copy is your brand. They can but you can always sue them. In the long run, companies will tend to look more and more alike as they benchmark against each other. Therefore, the only thing that will differentiate you in the long run is nothing more than the name. That is why you have to make sure that you have a great name. Building a brand is hard enough as it is. If you have a bad name to boot, that is like shooting yourself in both feet even before competitors take aim at you. Some bad names are easy to spot – such as Ralph Lifshitz and Sum Ting Wong. If you have a bad name, don't hesitate to change it, even if it is your family name. Sure, your ancestors might roll over in their graves but if you are held back by a bad name like Lifshitz, change it. Some bad names are not so obvious. Xerox is a great name – for a photocopier brand. When Xerox tried to use the brand on something like computers, it became a liability. Kodak is a great name – for a photographic film brand. When Kodak used it on digital cameras, it became a liability. One brand to one category. One brand to one idea. That's the way it should be. Line extensions are generally bad for the brand, especially when you line extend into unrelated categories.

If you want to create a great brand name, the name must meet all the 10 rules of naming:

- Easy to pronounce
- Easy to remember
- English-sounding
- Short
- Unique
- No generic words
- No acronyms
- Linked to a category name
- Has a dot.com suffix
- Language neutral

CASE STUDY
You Better Have A Great Name Or Else – Gardyon

The Oil And Gas And The Offshore And Marine Industries

Names have a special place in the minds of those who operate fleets of shipping vessels and oil rigs; the same is applicable to the naming of power plants. There are conventions and meaning to them. Perhaps it is due to the fact that both industries have been the most vibrant and critical in the world in the last century. Or maybe it is because many industries around the world are powered by energy; the very energy powered by these industries. Although not a significant oil and gas market in itself, Singapore plays a key role in the sector through its status as a major refining and petrochemicals centre for South East Asia. Singapore, in fact, is unique and most unusual because it has an oil-refining capacity that is nearly twice its consumption of domestic petroleum products.

Industries such as chemicals, oil drilling equipment, petroleum refining, ship repair and offshore platform construction are key contributors to Singapore's economic growth. The latest Singapore Oil & Gas Report from Business Monitor International (BMI) forecasts that the country will account for 3.81 per cent of Asia Pacific's regional oil demand by 2014[47], while not contributing to supply. There is no domestic oil or gas production but there is an active downstream segment, with extensive involvement of international oil companies in refining and petrochemicals.[48]

Within the oil and gas industry, hydrocarbons are extremely dangerous products due to their highly combustible nature. Consequently, they need to be handled with extreme care. The offshore platform Piper Alpha, which was located in the British sector of the North Sea oil field, was engulfed in a catastrophic fire on 6 July 1988.[49] The disaster, which caused the deaths of 167 men, forced the oil and gas industry, as well as other industries, to rethink and re-engineer future risk management with regard to fire, especially ones involving hydrocarbons. One of the main problems at that time was the inability of the operators to focus specifically on fire prevention, something that did not seem to be at the forefront of the corporation's concerns in any case.[50]

Before the Piper Alpha disaster, industry regulations specified mainly water-sprinkler and deluge systems while passive fire protection, if there was any, was

---

[47] Singapore Oil & Gas Report Q4 (2010) from Business Monitor International

[48] 'Country Analysis Report: Singapore – In-depth PESTLE insights' published by Datamonitor in August 2009

[49] Department of Industrial Engineering and Engineering Management, Stanford University, California 94305

[50] Paté-Cornell, M. Elisabeth. 'Learning from the Piper Alpha Accident: A Postmortem Analysis of Technical and Organizational Factors', *Risk Analysis*, Vol. 13, No. 2, 1993, pp. 215-237

minimal. Reports on Piper Alpha and general research papers that followed in the wake of the tragedy focussed the attention of legislators, operators, designers and manufacturers to concentrate on a "safety case" to be the standard imposed on the industry. The safety case includes action to ensure a situation does not arise but is managed if it does. Standards specific to hydrocarbon-fire protection were also developed. It was stipulated that fire protection systems must withstand the effects of simulated hydrocarbon pool fires as well as the tremendous thermal loads and erosive mechanical forces following ignition of pressurised hydrocarbon gases. In other words, systems must be effective against jet fires.

Needless to say, the prevention of hydrocarbon fire is extremely important and, as a result, there has been a growing demand for passive fire protection.[51] Passive fire protection systems are used to protect structures from fire long enough for people to escape to safety and for the fire to be brought under control. In such situations, every second counts and could mean the difference between life and death.

The Birth of Gardyon by Thermal Limitec

Thermal Limitec inherited its reputation almost 50 years ago as part of one of the oldest and most respectable contracting businesses in Singapore and the region servicing the marine industry in the field of thermal insulation and refractory linings. The company serves many of the leading brands in the oil and gas industry from around the world. These clients range from oil and gas companies to builders of oil rigs, vessels and floating production, storage and offloading (FPSO) units. The company specialises in the manufacture of engineered passive fire protection products and engineered systems. The systems manufactured by the company are certified and used on onshore and offshore facilities owned by major global oil and gas companies including ExxonMobil, Shell, Total, ConocoPhillips, Petrobras and Pemex.

As Thermal Limitec is in a very specialised business, it has accumulated a wealth of experience over the years. Furthermore, to ensure reliability and safety, the company continually upgrades personnel skills and techniques in engineered passive fire protection. Given the increasing demand for passive fire protection in the oil and gas industry, it is well positioned in this high-growth sector.

However, Thermal Limitec's business has traditionally been in the trading and application of existing brands in passive fire protection systems. Company CEO Mr David Thomas knew that if the business were to grow to the next level, Thermal Limitec would have to focus on its innovation and marketing efforts. Thomas knew that in the engineering and technology landscape, the company needed to boost its

---

[51] Mather, Paul. 'Fire Protection Gets Passive', *International Hydrocarbon* (September 2001)

research and development activities in thermal science and technology. On the issue of innovation, Thomas was candid in an interview:

> *In terms of innovation, we must be aggressive in our R&D efforts. There is no other way to develop new products and solutions to the age-old problem of how to best protect refineries, onshore and offshore platforms in the most environmentally-friendly manner possible. Fire testing standards are also important in the industry, and we are aiming to be the first of companies in Singapore to be able to provide innovative passive fire protection products and solutions that can surpass high-level testing standards.*

Thermal Limitec has ambitions and inspiration to be one of the world's players in the area of thermal science and technology. At the beginning of 2010, Thomas realised that the company would have to go through extraneous measures to ensure that it achieves its broad strategic direction in moving up the value chain. However, this does not come without challenges.

The first of many challenges lies with Thermal Limitec being a victim of its own success – reputed as an application contractor for existing passive fire protection systems. The company has never been known by its customers as an R&D company, let alone with innovations. While the company is reputed as a specialist applicator, the first and perhaps most crucial perception challenge was the appropriateness of expanding its business model as an innovation company that is strong in R&D efforts.

The other perception challenge is related to its presence in the passive fire protection market. The reality is that it operates in a highly competitive market with many established players. Thus, Thomas was fully aware that the company had to be unique and differentiated from the competition.

The Strategy

CEO David Thomas is known to be a maverick in his industry. In early 2010, he commissioned a study to better understand the needs of the market and, at the same time, find out how Thermal Limitec was being perceived insofar as providing services to meet these needs. The findings made it clear that the brand was highly associated to application rather than innovative products. It clearly showed that Thermal Limitec was already deeply entrenched in the minds of its customers as a *trusted and specialist applicator* of existing and renowned passive fire protection systems. In the aspect of passive fire protection systems application, the technical ability and reliability of the vendor is crucial to ensure the safety of refineries as well as onshore and offshore platforms. Therefore, the competence and credibility of such vendors are the main factors in the purchasing decision. It is hard to build up trust that is established through such successful projects, and it is even harder to replace. As Thermal Limitec was already well established in the area of application, it was important not to create confusion of perception in the minds of its customers when it went ahead and created a new business model as a specialist in R&D. It was through this exercise that Thomas decided to create a separate entity so that the business as a whole could move up the value chain.

Equally critical to establishing a company is, indeed, the naming of it. Thomas knew that determining a great name was paramount to launching the brand properly from the get-go and this included the creation of customer perception. On this, Thomas had this to say:

> We worked very closely with a very established brand strategist firm and an extensive list of names was put through a systematic selection process that encompassed defined naming parameters and conventions before the corporate and product brand names were determined. The names selected were also tested for language and religion neutrality because we wanted this corporate brand to survive cross-cultural differences. After a thorough and structured naming process, the new name was validated to be suitable for use as the new corporate name. This is how GARDYON was born.

The name *Gardyon* is a combination of "guardian" and "beyond". It simply conveys the message that the company is guarding beyond approved standards of the industry.

The Execution

On 30 November 2010, a distinct corporate brand "GARDYON – Engineered to Protect Assets" was officially launched at one of the biggest oil and gas exhibitions in Singapore. With the launch of Gardyon, the company will be able to attract other global players that it can collaborate with on its future product developments. Thomas on the Gardyon brand:

> The name Gardyon conveys the message that the company is guarding beyond approved standards, suggesting safety and trust. The name in itself personifies

and sets the precedence for everything the company stands for. We are a trustworthy company that ensures peace of mind to our clients as we have an in-depth understanding of the oil and gas industry's dynamics, trends and challenges and provide time and cost-efficient solutions that meet our clients' specific needs. We want to grow and fully develop our technological expertise in breakthrough engineering in thermal science and technology, supported by a world-class turnkey service of providing a comprehensive execution plan from inception to commercialisation. The company is committed to pioneering engineered fire protection solutions that outperform conventional systems in terms of efficiency and, ultimately, sustainability. We have to develop people centred around recognising and fulfilling our clients' needs; a team made up of entrepreneurial people from diverse engineering backgrounds and extensive experience, all distinguished individuals in their fields, who are driven to ensure innovations are purposefully applied into commercial applications that create market dominance for clients. That's how we see ourselves in this new venture and our future. It is about "Going Beyond Borders As The Global Protector Of Oil & Gas Assets, Onshore & Offshore".

GARDYON
ENGINEERED TO PROTECT ASSETS

A robust brand strategy was devised for Gardyon so that it could spearhead its plans to enter the market as a global R&D specialist in thermal science and technology. This allowed Gardyon to leverage on its expertise and experience in the field.

The new strategy created by Thomas provided a new business model for Gardyon's activities in its overseas markets. Investment in innovation and marketing was part of a drive to strengthen Gardyon's position as a company that specialises in thermal science and technology. This gave Thermal Limitec the leverage and credibility to fully function as a downstream specialist applicator.

To operationalise the corporate brand, an IMC strategy consisting of a comprehensive set of stakeholder-specific brand messages was crafted and used to communicate the corporate brand in a consistent and coherent manner to all its stakeholders. On the whole, the execution provided the company with a powerful tool to penetrate its target markets, increasing the rate of success in its innovation efforts.

B2B

CHAPTER
15

Rule No. 8 –
The Power Of Consistency

WHY do you trust the people whom you trust? Because they are good people. People who have integrity. People, who have kept your trust. But that alone is not enough. In order for you to trust them, these people have to be good people consistently. They have to have integrity consistently. They have to keep your trust consistently. You wouldn't trust people who behave erratically in all the key areas that are important to you, would you?

Brands are just like people. In order for brands to earn your trust (and with it your wallet), they have to behave in a consistent manner all the time. People generally do not like to hang around schizophrenic people. They also do not like to patronise schizophrenic brands – brands that are not sure of who or what they are, brands with multiple personalities. In order to build a strong brand, you need to have consistency.

Contrary to what a lot of people believe, branding is a boring game because to build strong brands, you need absolute consistency, not just for the first few years but for as long as you have that brand. You need to do the same thing day in, day out. You don't mess with a winning formula. No matter how strong your brand is, inconsistency can destroy it. That is why if you are a person who is easily bored or the type who can't help tinkering with things, you probably shouldn't be in the brand management business.

We meet a lot of companies in the course of our work. Other than on a few occasions, the companies that we meet invariably want to expand the scope of their brand. It seems that management is naturally inclined to want to stretch the brand and line extend it. You will rarely find CEOs who say that they want to maintain a tight and narrow focus for their brand. Sometimes, CEOs will say that they need to focus the brand but very often that focus is so broad that it doesn't really count as focus anymore.

Everybody wants to grow. And to a lot of companies, growth means sexy little things like doing a brand extension, stretching the brand or implementing a master branding strategy. That usually means broadening the scope of the brand, which is usually the first step in destroying the brand's consistency. We often try to convince these companies that such strategies are detrimental to their brands but most people won't listen. Why should they? After all, everybody is doing it! Many marketing gurus recommend it. The companies' competitors are doing it so they cannot afford to be left out.

You know the saying, "A million people can't be wrong". If everybody is doing it, it must be the correct thing, right? Well, a million people can be wrong. One thousand five hundred years ago, everybody knew that the sun and the moon revolved around the earth. Five hundred years ago, everybody knew that the earth was flat. Five years ago, everyone knew that Pluto was a planet. Just because everybody is doing it or saying it doesn't mean it is right.

The only thing that brand extensions will do is extend the list of problems that your brand will face in the market, even if your brand is one of the most powerful brands in the world. The Mercedes-Benz case study is an interesting one.

WHY DO PEOPLE BUY MERCEDES-BENZ?

Mercedes-Benz owners will tell you it is because of the brand's engineering integrity, cutting-edge technology, quality, durability (you can drive a Mercedes-Benz to the moon and back and it will still be as good as new) and a whole lot of other things. Sure, Mercedes-Benz has all of the above but so does a BMW, an Audi, a Lexus, a Jaguar and even a Volkswagen. So why buy a Mercedes-Benz?

Prestige.

We know many Mercedes-Benz owners. Most of the high-tech functions in their cars are lost on them. They don't really need or use all those gadgets. All they do is get into the car and drive. So why buy a Mercedes-Benz?

Prestige.

There are plenty of good, justifiable reasons for buying a three-pointed star but prestige is still the overriding reason. It is prestigious. If a Mercedes-Benz owner is honest enough, he or she will tell you that above everything else, it is prestige that made them buy that brand of car. Prestige is intangible. Prestige is not something that can be copied easily by another brand. A Lexus is quieter. A Jaguar might ride better. A BMW might handle better. An Audi might be deemed as more elegant by critics. But none of them occupies that special position in your mind marked "Prestigious German Automobile".

Wilson bought one despite being a long-time Audi fan. When asked why, he thought long and hard before saying that a Mercedes-Benz does not cost a lot more than an Audi or a BMW but it is perceived as more prestigious. There you go! Confessions of a Mercedes-Benz owner.

Mercedes-Benz built this reputation by consistently over-engineering its cars. A Mercedes-Benz might not be the most fashionable car or the most generous with standard equipment but it is luxurious, it is built to last and it has a general air of superiority (some would say arrogance) around it that grows on you.

You know exactly what a Mercedes-Benz is because it consistently delivers on the brand's core attributes – right down to the way it smells! There used to be a time when you could enter a Mercedes-Benz blindfolded and know what car you were in just from the smell and the way the door shut with a solid thunk.

In the past, it used to take at least nine years to complete the development work on a Mercedes-Benz compared to the four years that most Japanese manufacturers take. Jacky used to read in car magazines that once a new model was launched, Mercedes-Benz engineers would immediately start working on its replacement because it took nine years to perfect the next model. By doing this, Mercedes-Benz set the standard by which all other luxury cars were judged.

SO HOW DID THE THREE-POINTED STAR GET RUSTY?

In an interview with *Inside Line* (21 November 2005), Dr Dieter Zetsche, the incoming chairman of DaimlerChrysler, made the following comment to the question of how recent quality problems had hurt the image of Mercedes-Benz:

> "A brand is like a savings account. For most of the past 100 years, Mercedes has paid into this account and built its brand equity. We have withdrawn from that account in recent years. But it is still a strong account and we certainly intend to build it up again in the future."

In other words, Mercedes-Benz hadn't been behaving in a consistent manner. Hence, the brand was damaged. Fortunately for Mercedes-Benz, it is a very strong brand and strong brands can weather shocks like these and bounce back provided they take corrective measures. With Dieter Zetsche at the helm, things have taken a turn for the better as he is a Mercedes veteran, having joined the company in 1976. Zetsche also ran Chrysler for five years and is widely credited for its turnaround at that time. But let us now look at how the Mercedes-Benz brand ran into trouble.

For a start, it expanded the brand in all directions. Somebody in Mercedes-Benz probably said that it should not limit the brand's potential by concentrating on the high end of the market. That was the beginning of the downhill spiral. It began in 1983 with the launch of the original Baby Merc – the 190E. It was a competitor to the BMW 3 series but that was still all right because the 190E was built solidly like a real Mercedes-Benz although it was cramped and did not have much road presence.

The real problem started in the early nineties when Mercedes-Benz shortened its development time to around five years instead of the usual nine. It rushed through the development of new models.

As a result, cars like the E-Class (W211 model) left the assembly line with a whole list of faults. That eroded customer confidence and sales went down dramatically. And that was Mercedes' bread-and-butter model. To make things worse, the E-Class began to be used widely as taxis in many countries, including Singapore! How prestigious is that? For the taxi company's customers, it may be fantastic, but what does that do to the Mercedes brand?

It even went downmarket with cars like the A-Class, considered too small to be a real Mercedes-Benz! Its interior was covered in low-grade plastics! It was a cynical marketing exercise that exploited the prestige of the Mercedes-Benz brand instead of building on it. Then, it launched the Vito MPV, which was nothing more than a glorified commercial van with seats. And the American-built M-Class SUV was so badly made that car journalists all over the world expressed shock. All these things were inconsistent with the Mercedes-Benz brand promise.

Then Mercedes-Benz merged with Chrysler. We are told by experts that 90 per cent of mergers and acquisitions end in failure. This one ended up destroying billions of dollars in market value. It was the mother of all mistakes to merge with Chrysler. What is a Chrysler? It is a cheap American car. Merging with such a company meant that the two entities needed to share components in order to cut costs. That was good news for Chrysler as it meant it could use Mercedes platforms, engines and gearboxes. For instance, the Chrysler 300C uses the platform from the E-Class and the Crossfire sports car is basically a re-skinned version of the SLK. In contrast, it was bad news for Mercedes' image as a prestigious car brand.

Furthermore, in an effort to boost sales, Mercedes-Benz started selling its engines to Korean car makers like SsangYong, who could then proudly claim that their cars were "Powered By Mercedes-Benz" – great for SsangYong but damaging for the three-pointed star's reputation.

But it didn't stop there. Mercedes-Benz went on to sell the W124 E-Class (launched in 1988) and its entire manufacturing facility to SsangYong. Granted, the W124 had been replaced by the W210 by then, but this move did not do Mercedes-Benz's image any good because SsangYong promptly launched the Chairman, a model based on the W124 and styled to look like an S-Class!

All these things were thoroughly inconsistent with what the Mercedes-Benz brand stood for. To make matters worse, scores of branding experts jumped to the conclusion that the Mercedes-Benz brand had been able to stand up very well to the brand extension exercise. They pronounced the brand extensions to be highly successful as they boosted sales substantially. What Mercedes-Benz executives and these branding experts missed out on is that the effects of inconsistency take time to manifest, just as the right marketing moves take time to bear fruit. And they also forgot that brand extensions will actually boost sales in the short term as you have more products to sell. But these extensions weaken the brand in the long run. When you extend a brand in all directions like Mercedes-Benz did, that brand no longer stands for anything concrete. That will hurt your sales eventually.

Mercedes-Benz used to top the J.D. Power and Associates quality surveys. However, by 2006, Mercedes-Benz had dropped to the 25th position on the J.D Power and Associates 'Initial Quality Study' with an average of 139 defects per 100 vehicles.[52] Twenty-fifth place is not the position for a premium brand. Mercedes-Benz has always been about luxury, prestige and engineering. How could a car so high in prestige be so low in quality? How did this happen? Inconsistency.

INCONSISTENCY ALLOWS COMPETITORS TO OVERTAKE YOU

Actually, BMW fared even worse with 142 defects per 100 cars and a No. 27 spot on the 'Initial Quality Study' rankings that year but a BMW is first and

---

[52] www.jdpower.com

foremost about the driving experience. A BMW has always been focussed on driving and, over the years, BMW has continued to create some of the best driver's cars in the world with clockwork consistency. In this respect, BMW has remained true to its DNA.

Despite BMW's worse quality ratings, it was still the more consistent brand and that allowed it to overtake Mercedes-Benz in sales. In 2004, Mercedes-Benz sold 1.06 million cars compared to BMW's 1.03 million. In 2005, BMW sales jumped 10.1 per cent to 1.13 million cars compared to Mercedes-Benz's 1.08 million cars.[53]

Don't get us wrong. We are not saying that Mercedes-Benz has become a lousy brand. On the contrary, Mercedes-Benz is a very strong brand but even strong brands can be damaged if treated inconsistently. Some people have argued with us that Mercedes-Benz's woes had nothing to do with inconsistency or brand extensions. They pointed out the obvious – the drop in quality. Yes, but why did the quality drop? Because Mercedes-Benz did not remain true to its roots of testing every component to destruction in the toughest real-world situations. Instead, it let its suppliers do the testing. Later, it admitted that this move was not ideal as it was necessary to see how these components interacted with one another in the real world.

Mercedes-Benz could be abused for so long before it started to crack under the strain precisely because it is a very strong brand. If you don't have a brand that is as resilient as Mercedes-Benz and you attempt to do what the Mercedes-Benz people did, you will be destroyed in no time.

MY STAR IS BIGGER THAN YOUR STAR

For a brand that trades on prestige, it is strange to find the Mercedes-Benz logo on the most unglamorous objects on the road such as commercial vans, buses and even garbage trucks. To make things worse, the three-pointed star on a garbage truck is much bigger than the one on the top-of-the-line S600 luxury model. How would that make the rich *towkay* (boss) who has just plonked down a few hundred thousand of his hard-earned dollars on an S-Class feel? How would that make you feel if you owned a Mercedes car? Not very good.

In our opinion, it should re-name its commercial vehicles division. You cannot have a luxury car and a garbage truck sharing the same brand. It's a recipe for disaster.

---

[53] Reuters UK, 9 January 2006

IS THERE A HAPPY ENDING?

By and large, yes. Mercedes-Benz realised its mistakes and put in place a new management team that refocussed the brand on its core values. If you are an avid reader of car magazines like Jacky, you will have found that reputable car magazines have commented on Mercedes-Benz's return to form in terms of quality. Not only that, the current generation of Mercedes-Benz cars also drives very well. Even Jacky was quite impressed with the ride and handling of new Mercedes-Benz cars. He was never a fan in the past. On top of this, Mercedes-Benz has even regained its sales lead from BMW.

	2008 (units)	2009 (units)
BMW[54]	1,202,239	1,068,770
Mercedes-Benz[55]	1,273,013	1,093,905

Once again, we are not saying that Mercedes-Benz is a weak brand. Mercedes-Benz, in our opinion, has one of the strongest brands in the world. However, even strong brands can be damaged by inconsistency. Imagine what could happen to you if you allow inconsistency to creep into your brand.

THE WAY TO DO IT

Among the top-tier luxury car makers, Lexus is by far the youngest. It was launched in 1989. But Lexus has been the best-selling luxury car in the United States since 2000, selling around 300,000 units a year. How did Lexus do it? It was the first serious Japanese luxury car brand – a new category. And it was resolutely consistent in delivering on its brand promise, "The Relentless Pursuit Of Perfection". Lexus might have been called boring and derivative in the past but in terms of quality, reliability, refinement and customer service (all the things that are critical for a luxury car), it has outpaced its rivals year in, year out. That is consistency. And you don't see a Lexus being used as a taxi. You don't see a Lexus commercial vehicle. You don't see a low-end Lexus.

BMW has also been very consistent to its brand promise of being "The Ultimate Driving Machine". Every single BMW that has left the production line was designed to be the ultimate driving machine. All of them handle superbly, even the X5 SUV, which weighs over 2 tonnes, although it would have been better if BMW had not built that behemoth in the first place. That level of consistency has built BMW into the brand that it is today.

---

[54] www.bmwgroup.com

[55] www.daimler.com

REMEMBER THIS: Inconsistency brought the powerful Mercedes-Benz brand to its knees. Inconsistency will destroy your brand. Maybe not overnight. The effects of inconsistency are insidious. They take time to manifest. But they will destroy your brand. Make no mistake about that. The next time you think of extending or stretching your brand, think again. If you insist on all these extensions, your brand will suffer eventually. Even Mercedes-Benz suffered and it is probably a far stronger brand than yours. So what makes you think you can pull it off?

Look at all the new, line-extended businesses that you have launched under your original brand. Have they done well? Have the extensions started to affect your core brand? They will very soon. It took many years for Mercedes-Benz to suffer the effects of violating this rule. It won't take that long for you.

WHY IS IT SO HARD TO REMAIN CONSISTENT?

Branding is boring because you need absolute consistency. Once people get bored, they will try to change things, tinker around with the formula. That is when trouble sets in. Plus, if you look at successful brands, the one thing that most of them seem to do when they become successful is to forget the thing that made them successful in the first place. Success breeds confidence. And also amnesia. Once a company becomes successful, it will think that it is invincible and start to line extend the brand into all kinds of things.

Mercedes-Benz isn't alone. Xerox was the most successful photocopier company in its time because it did everything right. It invented a new category called plain paper photocopiers at a time when everything else was a thermal photocopier. It promoted the category. It came up with a great name. It was highly focussed and consistent.

But some years later, buoyed by the success of its photocopiers, Xerox began to think that it could extend the brand into other high-tech areas like office automation and even computers. Xerox set up a lavish and cutting-edge R&D centre called the Palo Alto Research Centre, or PARC. It was the dream of every high-tech entrepreneur to get invited to PARC to peek at what it was doing.

In fact, that was one of Steve Jobs' dreams, according to the book *iCon Steve Jobs: The Greatest Second Act in the History of Business*. When he finally got his invitation, what he saw there blew his mind. PARC was doing things that were far more advanced than anything he had ever seen at that time. In fact, Xerox had a graphical user interface (GUI) for personal computers up and running five years before Apple launched its GUI, which then became the industry standard.

You could say that Steve Jobs was inspired by the research he saw at PARC. No one doubted Xerox's capabilities in high tech. It spent tens of billions of dollars on high-tech R&D but the only problem was that the Xerox name stood for photocopiers – not computers, not scanners, not fax machines, not even printers. So Xerox failed in this area and refocussed its attention on photocopiers. Xerox forgot what made it successful. Photocopiers. Xerox did not stand for computers or office automation. Launching all those other products was inconsistent with what people see Xerox to be.

Volkswagen also fell into this trap. Volkswagen used to mean "The People's Car". In fact, its name means exactly that in German. Volkswagen was very successful when it was making mass-market cars like the Beetle, Golf, Polo, Lupo and Fox. Then it moved up the value chain to compete in the luxury car sector, which was not a very good move. We are saying this not just as professionals but also as ex-Volkswagen owners. Moving the brand up the so-called value chain resulted in a lot of undesirable outcomes.

Firstly, it made Volkswagen cars expensive. Secondly, it eroded the Volkswagen brand equity because Volkswagen no longer had a consistent identity. Volkswagen is a mass-market brand. Maybe it is the premium mass-market brand but it is mass-market nevertheless. It is not a premium brand. As a result, the Phaeton, which was conceived to compete with the Mercedes-Benz S-Class, BMW 7 series, Jaguar XJ series, Lexus LS430 and Volkswagen's own Audi A8, was a flop.

Thirdly, it made things very difficult for Volkswagen's upmarket division, Audi. Why have two brands from the same group competing in the same sector? Volkswagen should take care of the mass market and Audi the premium sector. Fourthly, and probably worst of all, Volkswagen started sharing platforms and engines with Audi and even styled the face of its Passat, Jetta and Golf to mimic Audi's, which made things even more complicated. This inconsistent behaviour started to erode Volkswagen's sales and profits, even in its home market of Germany.

This should serve as a warning to anyone who thinks that they can pull off brand extensions successfully. Mercedes-Benz failed. Xerox failed. Volkswagen failed. Creative Technology, despite its leadership in sound cards, got burnt badly in the MP3 players sector. HP got into trouble because its brand was so heavily line-extended. Many, many others have failed. What makes you think you can succeed? We would hate to see your brand extension strategies put your company in trouble a few years down the road.

In A Nutshell

When we talk about consistency in branding, many people will tell us, "But that's common sense, right? No big deal." Yes, it is common sense. Yes, it is nothing new. Yes, everybody seems to know that. But it's still a big deal because many companies don't practise it. Consistency is something that is boring. It means that you have to do the same things day in, day out. It is not fun. It is not exciting. People are people, even people at the top. After a while, when things are going well, people will forget about consistency and then try to take their eyes off the ball. This is when problems start to creep in. When you are inconsistent, you project a schizophrenic image and nobody wants to buy from schizophrenic brands. We have shown in this chapter how inconsistency can damage even powerful and well-established brands. You probably don't yet have a brand that can be compared to these global brands and that is why you should tread even more carefully. If inconsistency can damage top brands, it can annihilate yours. Brands take a long time to build but a short time to damage. Rome wasn't built in a day. Oak trees don't grow overnight.

CASE STUDY
The Power Of Consistency – Leeden

The Engineering And Construction And The Offshore And Marine Industries

The outlook for the construction sector in Singapore is said to be promising with demand expected to reach between S$22 and S$28 billion in 2011, reflecting a continued and sustained workload. According to the Building and Construction Authority (BCA), public sector demand for construction in 2011 is likely to strengthen to between S$12 and S$15 billion, contributing about 55 per cent of overall construction demand. Private sector construction demand is expected to moderate from the previous year's level of S$17.4 billion to between S$10 and S$13 billion in 2011. The total construction output (payment made for work done) is estimated to moderate from a record high of S$31 billion in 2009 to about S$27 billion in 2010 as a result of the completion of a number of major projects including the two integrated resorts, Resorts World Sentosa and Marina Bay Sands.[56]

In similarly natured industries, the oil and gas and the offshore and marine industries are fuelled by the rising demand for energy due to the rapid development of China, India and numerous South East Asian countries. It is estimated that Singapore will account for 3.81 per cent of Asia Pacific's regional oil demand by 2014 and the demand for oil in the region will continue to outpace supply expansion.[57]

Within these industries, welding, gas and safety consumables and equipment are fundamental to their development. Welding is needed in all heavy construction and engineering work, especially when it involves mega-metal structures, while gas is a fundamental component to powering the welding process. While welding, the welder requires safety equipment to safeguard against personal injury and industrial accidents.

The Integration Specialist For Welding, Gas And Safety

Leeden Limited (formerly known as Ace Dynamics Limited) was incorporated in 1964 and listed on the Singapore Stock Exchange in 1975. Then, its core business was in providing welding solutions that included the supply of welding and safety products, industrial gases and other related services. It also provided a wide range of products used for welding and cutting machines, grinding wheels, pipe bevelling equipment, welding electrodes, gas regulators and welding accessories.

---

[56] 'Promising outlook for construction sector in 2011' published on 12 January 2011 on AsiaOne. Source: www.asiaone.com/Business/News/Story/A1Story20110112-257861.html

[57] Singapore Oil & Gas Report Q4 (2010) from Business Monitor International

At some point in its history, Ace Dynamics delved into other areas of business including property management services, residential property development, multimedia and entertainment.

In the industrial area of its business (which is its core business today), Ace Dynamics' business model was one of marketing and distributing well-known industrial product brands such as Miller, Flexovit, Hobart, OTC Daihen, Wachs, Red Wing and Nederman.

Over the course of time, it developed Auweld, its own proprietary brand. Ace Dynamics' customers have been mainly from the sectors of oil and gas, shipbuilding and ship repair yards, infrastructure, vehicle-related industries, metalwork fabricators, the electronics industry and gas dealers.

Its operations have been based mainly in Singapore. However, besides Singapore, its key markets include Malaysia, Thailand and Indonesia, with a distribution network covering Brunei, Vietnam, the Philippines, China and the Middle East.

One of the strengths of Ace Dynamics has been its strong expertise in welding, gas and safety equipment due to its long operating history in the business. This is sustained by its deep ASEAN network distribution reach and supported by a strong sales and marketing team.

Throughout the course of its history, there has also been a high reliance of the business on the Singapore market. This has prevented the company from growing to its fullest potential. This is a common phenomenon with many Asian companies. When domestic markets mature (short of going regional or international), and with the fervent quest for profits, diversification is one of the obvious routes. Diversification is both good and bad. While it gives a company width in terms of products and services in various industries, it will dilute the focus of the business and, further, its brand.

Aside from diversity, the other challenge that Ace Dynamics faced was in the operating of trade names for various markets. These different names were originally incepted to meet the needs of various markets. However, today, managing this host of different names is in itself a challenge to manage because it has caused customer confusion and led the company to a place where there is no clear focus in its brand and vision.

The Strategy

A company with over 40 years of history cannot arrive successfully without its fair share of good and bad decisions. The decision to diversify led the company to become diluted in terms of its focus and brand development.

On 1 July 2000, Steven Tham became Ace Dynamics' Brand Champion and CEO. Tham is a leader who embodies brand strategy efforts. As done by other world-class companies such as Sony, Virgin, Starbucks, Microsoft, Nokia, Giorgio Armani, Singapore Airlines, LVMH, L'Oréal and Nestlé, Tham began his organisational transformation journey from day one. He believed that to build the corporate brand, delivery must meet promise. In an interview with Tham, he had this to say:

> When I first took over the business, we were in many business interests, i.e. property, trading, multimedia and industrial consumables. This is not a business model; even if it is, I saw it as the wrong one for us from a long haul perspective. There is no credibility in diversity unless a company is a true behemoth; we are clearly not one. My first task was to look at all our businesses and decide which vertical could give us a fair chance of survival in the short term and sustainability in the longer term. The answer was in our industrial business. That said, Ace Dynamics was a brand associated to too many things; too many ideas. This clearly needed to change. In making the company a successful one, we first need to study our strength and weaknesses, the environment in which we operate and then decide a market position and a category that the company can occupy and excel in. Branding is very important in this aspect. We needed to develop a strong brand that is consistent with the business and a brand that all staff can eventually be proud of. Once decided, we must have the faith and commitment to carry it through.

Using his depth of experience, knowledge and insight, Tham took seven long years to build up credibility and respect as the company's CEO. Under his leadership, the various business development teams focussed mainly on chosen markets, essentially the oil and gas and the offshore and marine engineering and construction sectors.

The Execution
After seven long years of organisational transformation, the company found its focus in terms of its value proposition. In early 2007, the board took a strategic and bold decision to change the company's name. On 8 August 2007, Leeden Limited was born and Ace Dynamics became history. With this new name, it was also determined that its new business model was to develop a specialist group in the focussed area of welding, gas and safety. The board went even further to identify its market sub-segments of choice in the oil and gas and the offshore and marine engineering and

construction sectors. These were clearly stated in its trademark and, beyond, in its business model. Tham elaborated:

In building the Leeden brand, consistency is very important. Not only to the management, but all our staff needed to understand the brand concept, character and all the collaterals that come with it. Communication to management and the staff is important as there must be buy-in. We were also committed to promoting the brand in all its corporate and business activities. The day we identified that we were going to be an integration specialist in welding, gas and safety was the day we began divesting non-core businesses. We shut down a few and sold off the remainder as these had nothing to do with our new business model. We wanted to build a sense of preference among our clients because if our clients are prepared to stand up and state that they prefer Leeden, it is a powerful differentiating factor. What we offer had to be consistent with what we say in our brand up-front. We know that this can cause strong word-of-mouth behaviour among customers.

Leeden's rebranding and organisational restructuring exercise struck a chord with many of its customers. Its position of being the preferred brand in welding, gas and safety sets the company in an ideal place to strengthen itself to provide value-based solutions to customers in the offshore and marine and the oil and gas industries. This can only come about as a result of its focus on end-to-end welding solutions including specialised equipment selection, industrial safety (personal and workplace) and environmental protection programmes, all of which come complete with the integration of its industrial gas systems.

With its new brand, Leeden has now structurally transformed itself from providing a "selling" to a fully "integrated solution and services" proposition, with Asia being the primary market of focus.

Leeden aims to build greater customer mindshare through its singular and unique corporate brand as it strives towards its vision of "being accepted as Asia's foremost integration specialist in Welding, Gas and Safety". This is clearly one that focusses on being its customers' preferred service provider. Tham on the future of the business:

For Leeden, the next growth level is to carry the business to the region. A consistent brand is a big help and can quickly facilitate Leeden's expansion programme. Over the last five years, Leeden's expansion activities were mainly in Malaysia. For the next five years, Leeden will be expanding to the other South East Asian countries. We have incorporated companies in the region and are currently building resources to expand the activities. Having a strong corporate brand in Singapore as well as a product brand in Auweld will make the regional expansion much easier.

The Leeden brand position and its differentiation factor are the catalysts to radically drive the organisation's growth. Internally, they bring clarity to the strategic direction of the group in years to come and align the entire organisation to the shared vision. Externally, they differentiate Leeden from the competition, allowing it to compete successfully in its chosen markets and segments in the marine and oil and gas industries.

B2B

CHAPTER 16

Rule No. 9 –
Make An Enemy (Or Two)

WHEN you were growing up, your parents probably told you that you should play nicely with the other kids. They probably told you that you should make friends, not enemies. And for those of you who are now parents, you are probably telling your children the same thing. It is great advice and the world would be a much better place if we could all get along.

Unfortunately, if you want to build a strong brand, you will have to make some enemies. Strange as it may sound, you actually need to have enemies to ensure that your brand becomes successful. Yes, you need to beat your enemies in the marketplace but, at the same time, you also need them to help you grow. Nobody ever acknowledges their enemies for their brand's success but after reading this chapter, you might think differently.

We are not saying that you should go out of your way to antagonise people. That would just be silly. You still need to have friends in business. That's a given. You need good partners. You need supporters. Like quality, service and good employees, having friends in business is another hygiene factor – something that you need to have. But not everyone makes enemies. And you have to have an enemy or two to fight if you want to build a strong brand. But you have to pick the right enemy. In this chapter, we will give you some reasons why enemies are important and how you determine who your enemy should be.

ENEMIES GIVE YOUR BRAND A REASON TO EXIST

People love to see a good fight. It is human nature. And having an enemy to fight gives your brand a reason to exist. It also focusses and energises your brand, giving it a mission in life. You might think, "Hang on a second. My brand exists to fulfil a market need, not to make enemies." That is what you would like to think but if your brand does not have an enemy to fight, it will be quickly forgotten because it will become less interesting.

Let us give you some examples from the world of superheroes. One of the most successful and enduring superhero brands is none other than Superman. And why is Superman so successful? He has to fight a powerful enemy – Lex Luthor – and that gives Superman a reason to exist. Without an enemy to defeat, Superman would just be a super-powered weirdo who wears his underwear on the outside.

Why is Pepsi a strong brand? It has a powerful enemy – Coca-Cola. Fighting Coca-Cola gives Pepsi a reason to exist. Coca-Cola tells the world that it is the real thing. Everything else is an imitation. But Pepsi challenges that. Pepsi tells the world that Coke may be the real thing but it is also the old thing. Pepsi is the anti-Coke. Pepsi is the young thing. So Pepsi has a right to exist. To give the young and the young at heart an alternative to the old thing that is Coke.

When Duracell challenged Energizer in the battery category, it gave Duracell a reason to exist. By focussing on fighting a well-established enemy like Energizer, Duracell made its brand important in the eyes and minds of potential customers. Duracell exists to give customers an alternative – the alkaline battery – to what Energizer was offering at that time.

Burger King has a reason to exist because it is fighting the most powerful enemy you can find in the world of fast food – McDonald's. McDonald's is fast, clean, efficient and consistent. But McDonald's is all about standardisation and homogeneity. Burger King fought that with its "Have It Your Way" concept where you can customise your burger just the way you want it. Burger King exists to give customers an alternative to McDonald's.

Google has become a strong brand because it exists to fight a powerful enemy – Yahoo! – and everything that Yahoo! stands for including how Yahoo!'s search engine performs searches and ranks the results. Having a strong enemy like Yahoo! gives Google a reason to exist. At the time of writing this book (throughout 2010), we noticed that Google tried to pick a fight with a bigger enemy – the Chinese government. All we can say is, good luck with that, Larry and Sergey.

ENEMIES GIVE YOUR NEW CATEGORY CREDIBILITY

Creating a new category can be a great way to build a brand as we have shown you in Rule No. 3. However, in order for that category to have credibility in people's minds, it will need to attract more brands into it.

If you are the only brand in the category, then there is no competition. No competition means that the category will not draw the attention of the media as well as potential customers. And when you introduce anything new to potential customers, they will ask three questions that will determine whether your brand or category will make it or not.

1. Is This Something New?

People are interested in what's new – not what's better. If what you're offering is something new, people will show interest. If it is just a better product based on a theme that has already been established by someone else (usually the category leader), it will be seen as a me-too brand. Just calling something "new" doesn't make it so. It really does need to be new.

Here is an example of how language is upgraded but the meaning is not. You know how car manufacturers nowadays like to label a face-lifted version of an existing model as a new car? Well, people are not that stupid. They can tell that it is the old model with some cosmetic changes. So don't try to do something similar.

When Sony launched the Walkman, it was something new. Really new. The world's first portable cassette player. Naturally, people were interested. The MiniDisc was, likewise, a new category. Therefore, it also generated interest.

When Apple launched the iPod and iPhone, they were also regarded as new. MP3 players and touch screen phones had been around for a while when these two products were launched but Apple put a new twist on things. The iPod came with a rotary controller, was so easy to use that no user manual was needed and was supported by a vast store of digital music – iTunes. When the iPhone was launched, Apple gave it a really big and colourful screen, lots of applications and what really amazed us was the fact that to zoom in and out of the screen, you just use two fingers (pull the fingers together to zoom out and spread the fingers to zoom in). Really cool. New twists to existing products.

2. Who Is The Leading Brand?

The second thing that people will look for is the leading brand in this new category. When they saw that Sony was the leading brand in both the Walkman and MiniDisc categories, they thought, "Great! I know Sony. Great brand." So far, so good. People always look for the leading brand in any category because that is human nature and also because they need a reference point. If you know who the leading brand is and what it stands for and how good it is, then you have a benchmark upon which you can judge all the other alternatives within that category of products or services.

3. Who Else Is In This Category?

This last question is equally important. If people find that there aren't too many other brands in the category, they may get suspicious. They might think that there is something wrong with the product. When people asked who else was in the Walkman category, they found plenty of competitors like Aiwa, Philips, Panasonic, Samsung, etc.

If so many brands are in it, people will naturally think that the category must be important. In our opinion, this is the hurdle that the MiniDisc failed to cross. It never became as big as its predecessors – the Walkman or the Discman – because Sony's competitors didn't storm this category with the same gusto that they did in the Walkman category. Hence, the category never really made it into people's minds.

You need competitors in your category to give it credibility. You need competitors to attract attention to the category. The media and your potential customers will think the category must be important if so many brands are fighting for a slice of it.

Only if your category is credible can it grow. A lot of people think that having an entire category to themselves is a good thing. No competition. Actually, the reverse is true. When you start a new category, you will naturally have no competitors in the beginning. But as categories grow, competition will definitely show up on the horizon.

This competition will erode your market share from the 100 per cent that you enjoyed in the beginning to maybe only 40 per cent in the long run, depending on the intensity of the competition and the pace of technological changes in that category. It is usually difficult for a leading brand to maintain a market share of over 40 per cent in the long run. Not impossible but it is difficult.

In the mobile phone category, the leading brand is still Nokia. According to a report by Gartner that was published on pluggd.in, Nokia's market share in the first quarter of 2010 was 35 per cent. That's great. One in three mobile phones sold globally is a Nokia. It has hovered around this level for many years. It has been hard for Nokia to gain market share because brands don't operate in a vacuum. Every move that you make will be countered by competitors and Nokia has some serious competition.

When Coke first started, the market for carbonated soft drinks was almost non-existent so Coke had a 100 per cent market share. Coke promoted the category. The category attracted competitors. The Cola War between Coke and arch rival Pepsi helped the category gain visibility, credibility and growth. Today, Coke's market share is much less than before but Coke is still the leading brand in a multi-billion dollar category. Much better than 100 per cent of virtually nothing, isn't it? Coca-Cola as a company generated around US$31 billion (S$39.8 billion) in sales and had a net profit of around US$6.8 billion (S$8.7 billion) in 2009.[58]

So instead of engaging in a destructive price war with new entrants and trying to block competitors from entering, the category leader should concentrate on promoting and enlarging the category. It should also constantly remind the market of its leadership position and that it is the real thing. This will allow it to rise further above the crowd and cement its position as No. 1. As long as you promote the category, you will be perceived as the leader. And if you have perceptual leadership, it will be easier to maintain your market leadership in the long run. That is how things work.

A STRONG ENEMY HELPS TO PROTECT YOUR MARKET SHARE

When you have two strong brands fighting each other in a category, and each one is taking the opposite position from the other, then it forms a barrier that makes it difficult for other brands to eat into the top two brands' market share. Yes, you need competitors to jump into a new category in order to give it credibility but, at the same time, you do not want this slew of competitors to eat too much into your market share.

For decades, the battle between Mercedes-Benz and BMW left no room for other luxury car brands like Audi, Jaguar and Cadillac to really grow in that segment. That is another reason to make enemies. If Mercedes-Benz is the leading brand and BMW is the challenger brand, then in the minds of car buyers, there is no room for anything else. It keeps other brands out of the game.

When you pick an enemy, it is good to pick the leading brand and then position yourself opposite that brand − provided, of course, that the opposite position has not been occupied. You must take the opposite position from the leading brand because with two brands occupying different spectrums, it will be difficult for other brands to establish a foothold in the category.

---

[58] www.wikinvest.com/stock/Coca-Cola_Company_(KO)

If Coca-Cola is for old people and Pepsi is for young people, that covers almost every cola drinker in the market. There is very little room for a third brand to thrive in this environment. That may explain why the No. 3 brand, Royal Crown Cola, is so small.

If McDonald's is for kids and Burger King is for adults, that just about covers every potential customer in the market. As a result, there is very little room for a No. 3 brand to thrive in such a market. But Burger King abandoned its position in the nineties and that allowed other brands to make inroads into the fast-food industry.

If Mercedes-Benz is about prestige and BMW is about driving, that covers almost every potential luxury car buyer in the market. That is why Mercedes-Benz and BMW are still the two biggest players in this market – the only luxury car brands to sell over one million cars a year.

WARNING: IF YOU ARE NOT NO. 1 OR NO. 2, YOU WILL PROBABLY BE SMALL

Competitors are good for growing a category but keep the following in mind: In most categories, the top two brands will usually command the lion's share. If you are launching a new category or entering someone else's category, make sure you are among the top two. Otherwise, you will probably have a very small market share.

- Oracle and IBM have 72 per cent of the database software market. (Source: IDC)
- PlayStation and Nintendo have 85 per cent of the gaming console market. (Source: Hoover's Inc.)
- Coca-Cola and Pepsi have around 75 per cent of the carbonated soft drinks market. (Source: *Beverage Digest*)
- Intel and AMD have 98 per cent of the microprocessors market. (Source: ArnNet)
- Nokia and Motorola have 52 per cent of the mobile phone market. (Source: Gartner)

If you are not No. 1 or No. 2 in your category, you will probably have to be content with a much smaller market share than the category leaders.

WHEN IS BEING NO. 2 NOT ACCEPTABLE?

Microsoft is No. 1 in PC operating systems. Who is No. 2? No one. Because this is a standards game. When you are trying to get the industry to adopt your product as the industry standard, there is no place for No. 2.

As Microsoft has become the industry standard for PC operating systems, there is very little or no room for a No. 2 in this category. So, if you are battling to be the industry standard, it is winner takes all.

Therefore, despite Apple's superior Mac OS X operating system, it is unlikely that Apple will ever make much inroad into the OS market because the industry has already accepted Microsoft as the standard. In fact, Microsoft is so dominant that people used to tell this joke: "How many Microsoft engineers does it take to change a broken light bulb? None. They will just declare darkness as the standard."

THE PROBLEM WITH BEING NO. 2

The only problem with being No. 2 is management's attitude. Management doesn't like the idea of playing second fiddle. Management doesn't take too kindly either to people who suggest that they should settle for No. 2. Everybody wants to be No. 1 but what a lot of management types don't understand is that to be No. 1, you need to get into the mind first. If you are not first in the mind, it is hard to be No. 1 in the marketplace.

But then, not many business executives are keen on creating a new category whereby their brand can be the No. 1 because it is not an easy task. So what they try to do instead is muscle in on an existing category by sheer brute force. Let's outspend the leading brand in advertising and marketing, goes the conventional thinking. Well, you can try to outspend Nike in sportswear but how do you think that will pan out? Nike already spends over US$650 million (S$835.1 million) annually in advertising. Even if you can outspend Nike over the next five years, do you truly believe that you can overtake Nike?

Management has to understand that if it is not willing to create a new category in which it can be first, the best it can do is stake out a strong No. 2 position provided there isn't already a strong No. 2 in that category. There is nothing wrong with being No. 2. There are so many No. 2 brands in the market that are highly profitable and doing very well. In fact, one of the advantages of being No. 2 is that you can still move up. Once you are No. 1, there is nowhere to go but down.

The other thing is that for the No. 2 to climb up, No. 1 will have to lose sales. Conquest sales are not easy to get. Like we said earlier, for every move that you make, your competitors in general, and No. 1 in particular, will make a countermove. It's like playing chess. Move, countermove, move, countermove. The dance goes on. Unless the No. 1 makes a gigantic mistake or becomes totally complacent, it will be difficult for the No. 2 brand to gain market share at the expense of the leading brand. Sometimes, the No. 1 brand makes mistakes and succumbs but even then, it might take decades. General Motors used to own about 50 per cent of the American car market and despite all the product and marketing mistakes made by the General, it took decades before it lost its No. 1 spot.

THE STRATEGY TO USE IF YOU ARE NOT NO. 1

If there is already a clear No. 1, then you just have to take the opposite position. Hertz was No. 1 in car rentals for as long as people could remember. Avis cleverly staked out the No. 2 position with the tagline, "We Are No. 2 So We Try Harder". That was an excellent strategy but not because of what most branding experts think. Avis was often applauded for trying harder but that wasn't what built the Avis brand.

What built the Avis brand was its declaration that it was No. 2! Everyone knew that Hertz was No. 1 but until then, the No. 2 brand had been a bit fuzzy. The strategy that Avis took allowed it to be the clear No. 2. Hertz is No. 1 in car rental but if you don't want to rent from Hertz for whatever reason (maybe you don't like white rental cars), then what do you do? You go down the ladder to the No. 2 brand, which is Avis.

But that strategy wasn't as solid as most people thought because trying harder is not really a powerful differentiating idea. Customers expect you to try harder no matter what. If you don't try harder, they simply go somewhere else. Enterprise Rent-A-Car – although it was nowhere near Hertz – came up with a strategy that was even better than Avis'. It took the opposite position from Hertz. Hertz can often be found at airports. That is where Hertz is strong. So Enterprise avoided airports. Enterprise located its rental offices in suburban areas where Hertz is weak.

By taking this opposite position, Enterprise managed to become a real enemy to Hertz. Not by trying harder but by being different. Enterprise now has a reason to exist. Hertz serves the airports. Enterprise serves the suburban areas. Opposite positions. This strategy allowed Enterprise to overtake Hertz. Surprised? So were we. Although Hertz is still perceived as the king of rental cars, Hertz trails Enterprise in terms of revenue. In 2009, Hertz had US$7.1 billion (S$9.1 billion)[59] in revenue while Enterprise chalked up US$12.1 billion (S$15.5 billion).[60] Although Enterprise wasn't regarded as No. 1 or No. 2, it became – and continues to be – a serious enemy to Hertz. While Avis was trying harder to match Hertz in the areas where Hertz is strong, Enterprise attacked Hertz where it was weak – in suburbia.

TURN THAT WEAKNESS INTO A WEAPON

According to one of the world's leading military strategists – Karl von Clausewitz – in war, the big army will beat the small army. This is known as the principle of force. The army that can concentrate the most amount of force in the battlefield will prevail. It is not that much different in the business world. The big fish eats the small fish because the big fish is stronger than the small fish.

. And the bad news is: You Are The Small Fish.

You can't fight the big fish head on. You can't outrun the big fish. You can try to hide and pray that the big fish doesn't come into your playground and muscle you out. But there is something else that you can do. Instead of trying to hide or shield the weakness that you have, you can turn it into a weapon and use it to attack your bigger competitors. It may sound incredulous but it can be done and it has been done.

We want to share with you three examples, of which two happen to be our clients.

Danovel

Danovel is a relatively small furniture maker that has been making very high-quality sofas since 1960. The furniture market is a brutally competitive one and Danovel faced three challenges. One, it is the small fish. Two, its factories are located in one of the most expensive places in the world to manufacture furniture – Singapore. Three, it still makes furniture mostly by hand which means it is slower.

How can these weaknesses be turned into strengths? Well, Danovel repositioned itself as "The Handcrafted Fabric Sofa", which immediately tells customers that it is premium and it should be very comfortable. Being

---

[59] www.hertz.com (under Investor Relations)
[60] http://en.wikipedia.org/wiki/Enterprise_Holdings

handcrafted, customers are willing to forgive you for taking a longer time to make the sofa – hey, it is handcrafted after all.

By positioning itself as "handcrafted", Danovel is seen as a specialist and people have the (wrong) perception that specialists are small. And they are okay with specialists being small! They kind of expect specialists to be small players. What people tend to overlook is the fact that many of today's giant global brands became that way because they were specialists. GE was a light bulb specialist. Intel was a computer chip specialist. IKEA was a flat-packed furniture specialist. H&R Block was an income tax preparation specialist. The list goes on.

By the way, Jacky dislikes fabric sofas because they are hard to clean. And when he was studying in the States, he had a fabric sofa in his apartment. During winter, sitting on that sofa generated a lot of static electricity. That is probably how he got his electrifying personality. Jokes aside, however, when Jacky first sat on one of those Danovel fabric sofas with its feather sandwich construction, he sat for three straight hours. It was that comfortable!

Listerine

If you are old enough to have used Listerine in the sixties or seventies, you will know that Listerine used to taste really, really, really horrible. We imagine that it probably tasted a lot like the floor cleaner they use in hospitals. And Listerine has a very smart competitor called Scope. Scope took the opposite position and became the good-tasting mouthwash. It called Listerine the mouthwash that will give you "medicine breath". It attacked Listerine where it was weak. What did Listerine do?

Well, Listerine basically admitted that its mouthwash tasted really bad. When you admit something negative like that, what happens? People think you are honest. They become a bit more forgiving. Then, what do you do? You take it one step further. You try to turn that weakness into a strength. What Listerine did was bold – but it did it right.

Listerine used this tagline in its communications – "The Taste You Hate. Twice A Day." Brilliant! When people saw this tagline, they thought:

1. Yes, that is right. It tastes like poison. At least there's truth in this advertisement.
2. But if it tastes that bad, it must be really good at killing germs, right?
3. Yup, it's probably better than those minty-fresh, namby-pamby mouthwashes. I should use it twice a day.

And the phrase "Twice A Day" in the tagline was equally genius. It became a call for action. It encouraged customers to use more Listerine – and this was equally good for the bottom line. This strategy helped Listerine turn its weakness into a strength. Listerine managed to maintain its market leadership in mouthwash. And it also bought the company some time. Time to do what? To develop better tasting mouthwash! Way to go, boys.

VibroPower

VibroPower is a maker of power generators that are typically powered by diesel engines. Some of these diesel-power generator sets are powered by 16,000cc engines and they are as big as three master bedrooms joined together. What was VibroPower's weakness? It doesn't manufacture its own diesel engines. It buys diesel engines from Cummins, Perkins, Volvo Penta and many other generator manufacturing giants around the world. This could have been a problem for VibroPower because these engine suppliers also make their own brands of power generators. Consequently, customers would be in a position to say, "Hey, you are not the real thing. So, you have to sell it to me much cheaper or I will just buy from Cummins."

How do you overcome a weakness like that? What VibroPower did was to reposition itself as "The Custom Power Specialist". This is like saying, "Yes, we don't manufacture our own diesel engines but so what? This simply means that we can use whichever engine suits your needs best. We won't force anything on you. We customise based on your needs."

WHO IS THE ENEMY?

When you define your enemy, it is easy to think of another company but it doesn't have to be. As long as the enemy is clearly defined and perceived to be worthy by others, then it is a good enemy to fight.

For example, one of our clients, Enviro-Hub – a leading electronic waste recycling company in Singapore – didn't define its enemy in the traditional sense. Yes, it does have competitors, both in Singapore as well as overseas, but it chose an even bigger enemy to fight and that is *environmental destruction*. In the red corner is the enemy – Environmental Destruction. In the green corner is Enviro-Hub. Is that a worthy enemy? Yes. So, Enviro-Hub has a reason to exist. Enviro-Hub can become a stronger brand by fighting this enemy relentlessly.

This fight is captured in the company's new tagline, or the battle cry as we call it – "Let's Restore The Environment".

You can define the enemy any way you like. But just make sure that the enemy meets these conditions:

1. It is perceived to be dangerous. No point picking a fight with an enemy that other people view as a harmless kitten because the brand then has no reason to exist.

2. The enemy's defeat benefits your customers. If you pick a fight with an enemy and that enemy's destruction does not benefit your customers, then they won't care too much about whether you win or lose. As a result, they won't care too much about your brand. And the brand then has no reason to exist.

3. The enemy must be larger than you. People love it when David takes on Goliath. Although they might bet on Goliath, they always cheer for David. That's how we operate. We root for the underdog but we still buy from the leading brand. Why? Risk. Unless the underdog wins. When Google picked a fight against an enemy called "evil", it gave the brand a reason to exist. Google vowed to be a company "that does no evil". Hence, it is declaring war on evil and that is an enemy that is big.

YOU CAN GET IN THROUGH THE BACK DOOR, YOU KNOW?

What do you do when you are driving down a street and suddenly a brick wall looms ahead of you? You try to go around it if you can, right? No point driving straight into the brick wall unless you happen to be in a 70-tonne Sherman tank.

The same with branding. Not everyone has a brand that is the equivalent of a 70-tonne tank but almost everyone faces entrenched competition that is like a solid brick wall, especially if you are a new kid on the block. But surprisingly, most brands do the equivalent of driving straight into a brick wall. They try to take their entrenched competitors head on, which is suicide! Maybe the management of these brands watched too many *Rambo* movies. The *Rambo* approach is macho. It is sexy. It sounds so noble, so valiant, so heroic but in the marketplace, the *Rambo* approach gets you killed.

We have often written about the need for a brand to be differentiated in order to be strong. If you are not differentiated – if nobody can tell the difference between you and your competitors – people will just buy from whoever is cheaper. If you can sell cheap forever, then go ahead and compete on price. Companies with structural cost advantage that can sell cheap can become very successful brands as well. But most companies don't have structural cost advantage so they have to find a way to differentiate. We suspect this applies to most of you.

One of the easiest ways to differentiate your brand is to take the opposite position from the leading brand, provided, of course, nobody has done that already. This is great for brands that are not the first in the market. If you are first into the market like IBM in computers, Microsoft in operating systems, Coca-Cola in soft drinks and Mercedes-Benz in cars, you have many options on how you want to position the brand. If you are not the first, and the first brand has built a strong position, then the best thing to do is take the opposite position. But taking the opposite position is sometimes not very attractive or lucrative. Let me give you an example.

Selling To A Market Nobody Wants

What is Dell? One of the most successful computer companies in the world. Dell has been No. 1 or No. 2 for the longest time. What made Dell so successful? You probably know that Dell invented a new category – the first computer company to sell directly to consumers. This cut out the expensive middlemen and, in turn, resulted in great savings for consumers. But Dell's strategy goes a lot deeper than that.

Now, when Dell first entered the market, it was faced with two categories of computer users – businesses (corporate users) and consumers (home users). Everybody was going after the corporate users because they represented a much more lucrative segment. One account could generate hundreds of thousands to millions of dollars in sales. In contrast, one consumer account would probably give you a few thousand dollars in sales. It's a no-brainer. Go after the big corporate accounts first.

So, why did Dell target the consumer market? Dell understood the need for differentiation and it understood that the best way to differentiate yourself is by taking the opposite position. IBM & Gang were all going after the corporate sector so Dell took the opposite position by going after the consumer sector. IBM & Gang had (and still have) multiple layers in their distribution channels, which add to complexity and cost. Dell took the opposite position by selling direct to consumers. All the middle layers (distributors, agents, retailers, etc) were cut out. Those efforts in differentiating Dell made it stand out from the crowd. It generated a lot of attention from the media and from the public. Dell became successful.

Dell's Back Door

But the most amazing thing is that by targeting the consumers, Dell actually found a back door into those big corporate accounts! Today, Dell sells a large percentage of its computers and servers to corporations around the world because of this back door – something nobody else was aware of at that time. We are not sure if Dell itself realised how brilliant its strategy was or whether the company stumbled across it by accident. But it was brilliant nevertheless, not just in those early days when Michael Dell was working from the garage of his parents' home but even by today's standards.

You see, consumers actually live double lives. They may be consumers but they most likely work for an organisation somewhere too. Now, in the organisations that they work for, they are either decision makers or influencers. Dell's early customers bought its computers probably because of the tremendous cost savings. After all, in those days, people probably thought that you needed a better computer at work than at home. (These days, most people we know have better computers at home than at work.) So, they bought a cheap computer for home use. They bought Dell.

And somewhere along the line, they discovered that Dell was actually a very good computer and they also found that Dell's customer and technical services were excellent despite the fact that they had to get help over the phone instead of having a technician to help them in person. (We know Dell's service quality has been criticised a lot lately but it must have been pretty fantastic in the past or people wouldn't have bought Dell.) This positive experience with Dell made these consumers think that maybe they could use Dell computers at work. So, they either made the decision to buy Dell for the workplace or they recommended Dell to the decision makers in their companies. Because of this, Dell computers gradually found their way into companies.

Dell didn't go head on with IBM, Compaq, HP, Texas Instruments, Acer and the rest. Dell did the sneaky but smart thing. It entered through the back door. If it had gone head-to-head with IBM, it would have been clobbered. That's what 800-pound gorillas do when they are annoyed with you.

Don't Pick Somebody Your Size To Fight

Walmart is the world's largest retailer with a turnover of over US$408 billion (S$524.2 billion) a year. Walmart also found a back door into the retailing market. When Sam Walton first started, he decided that Walmart would not go into the big cities where there were many entrenched competitors who could have easily kicked the young company around like a rag doll. Instead, Walmart took the opposite position. It initially set up in towns that had populations of 50,000 and below. This had many advantages.

Firstly, the big boys at that time couldn't be bothered with small towns like the ones that Walmart targeted. Secondly, the main competition was the Mom-And-Pop stores that Walmart could easily beat. This will smack of bully-boy tactics to some of you but as Jacky's business ethics professor used to say, "Treat what is legal in business as ethical. If it is legal and you don't do it, your competitors will and they will win. Why allow them that luxury?"

Because of this strategy of taking the opposite position, Walmart managed to build up its economies of scale quietly over time, giving it tremendous bargaining power with suppliers. That drove its costs down so much that when it ventured into the bigger cities, the established players could not match Walmart's "Everyday Low Prices". They couldn't block Walmart because Walmart had done the sneaky but smart thing. It had found a back door into the big cities. In fact, Walmart found a back door that opened up to the whole of the USA.

WHAT BACK DOOR CAN YOU FIND TO ATTACK THE ENEMY?

What Dell did provides some valuable lessons for management and marketing managers everywhere. Don't drive straight into that brick wall. Try to find ways around it. If there is a segment of the market that you cannot access because it is dominated by powerful players, try to find a back door. That back door could be anything. You have to find it.

1. Start thinking of which market you actually want to end up with.
2. Then, start thinking about all the roadblocks (competitors) that are in the way.
3. Finally, try to think of a back door that you can use.

This is something that we do on a daily basis – we try to help our clients find back doors because no matter how big our clients are, they always face somebody bigger when they venture into international markets. That is why they have to find back doors sometimes. You may find it hard to believe that clients with a turnover of over S$1 billion might need a back door but that's what happens when your international competitors are S$6-billion giants.

In A Nutshell

Enemies are important because they give your brand a reason to exist. If you are not here to fight someone or something, then customers will not see the reason for your existence. Yes, at the back of their minds, they know businesses all exist to make money but if you show that you are picking a fight with an enemy, then that battle becomes the focal point of their interest (and belief) in your brand. When you pick a fight, much attention will be focussed on your brand. When two brands fight tooth and nail, it leaves no room in the middle for another brand. In categories where there are two brands (usually No. 1 and No. 2) that fight each other very hard, the top two usually command more than 50 per cent of the market share combined – sometimes much more than 50 per cent. When you set up a new category, having an enemy or two helps to give credibility to that category. If you have a new category and nobody is interested in challenging you in this category, then customers will think that the category can't be very important. When Sony launched the Memory Stick, a portable flash-based storage device, no one jumped in to challenge it. When Trek 2000 – a highly innovative Singapore company – launched its ThumbDrive, many companies jumped in to compete. That category grew. Now, the "thumb drive" is the de facto portable storage device.

CASE STUDY
Make An Enemy Or Two – Marshal Systems

Offshore And Marine Giants Need Protection Systems

On 27 March 1980, in the Ekofisk Field on the Norwegian Continental Shelf, a massive wave hit one of the legs of the *Alexander L. Kielland* (a Pentagon-type semi-submersible), causing it to break and send the 208 people on board into the sea, ultimately killing 123 at around 6:30pm GMT.[61] On 6 July 1988, about 190 kilometres north-east of Aberdeen, there was an explosion on the Piper Alpha drilling rig, which killed 167 people in total (either in the explosion or when being rescued). Among the various factors that contributed to the severity of the incident were the breakdown in the chain of command and lack of communication to the platform's crew.[62] On 3 November 1989, in the Platong Gas Field in the Gulf of Thailand (around 430 kilometres south of Bangkok), the drill ship *Seacrest* capsized, killing 91 people in heavy seas during Typhoon Gay. No distress signals were heard from the *Seacrest* and none of its lifeboats was found, suggesting that the accident had occurred too quickly for the crew to respond.[63] In the last 50 years alone, there have been 184 fatal incidents recorded on oil rigs around the world according to Oil Rig Disasters.[64] On August 2010, the Health and Safety Executive (the UK's national independent watchdog for work-related health, safety and illness) and Oil and Gas UK (the trade association that represents the oil and gas sector) issued a safety warning to the offshore oil and gas industry, after a year that saw a big rise in injuries to workers and other serious incidents.[65]

Protecting Offshore And Marine Giants – Marshal Systems

Since the 1980s, South East Asian countries like Vietnam and Singapore have seen rapid growth in their offshore and marine sectors. As a consequence, this expansion has caused a rise in the demand for integrated systems that protect offshore and marine capital assets and the lives of those working on them. In Singapore, initiatives such as the 2006/2007 ASMI Safety Agenda were incepted to create a safer working environment for workers in the offshore and marine industry through safer work practices. There is also demand for integrated systems that prevent hazardous industrial accidents at sea. These integrated systems cover communications, fire and

---

[61] http://news.bbc.co.uk/onthisday/hi/dates/stories/march/27/newsid_2531000/2531091.stm

[62] The opinions of Lord Caplan of the Inner House in Caledonia North Sea Limited vs London Bridge Engineering Limited and Others ("Piper Alpha") handed down on 2 September 1997 in reclaiming motions (i.e. appeals).

[63] '97 Missing in Capsizing' published in the *New York Times* on 4 November 1989

[64] www.oilrigdisasters.co.uk/

[65] 'Oil and gas industry offshore safety warning issued' published by the BBC on 24 August 2010

gas detection and control and instrumentation, providing a holistic approach towards safeguarding offshore and marine assets.

This global growth and demand for offshore, oil and gas vessels and rigs as well as the large-scale accidents experienced on a global scale were the driving force behind the birth of Marshal Systems. Founded in Singapore in 1993, Marshal Systems Pte Ltd ("Marshal"), formerly known as Marshal Technology Marketing & Engineering, is today a leading systems integrator preferred by internationally renowned companies in the offshore and marine industry. The reality of this industry and the simple nature of the business are in themselves hazardous and carry high risks. That is why Marshal provides its customers with seamless connectivity solutions that cover communications, fire and gas detection and control and instrumentation. As a one-stop solution provider, Marshal offers a full suite of services that include design and engineering, procurement and sourcing, manufacturing and assembly, and testing and commissioning.

The Strategy: Offshore Accidents – Marshal's Enemy No. 1

For almost two decades, Marshal has amassed a track record that has enabled it to refine its processes, people and ability to value-add beyond the principal products it represents. Traditionally, Marshal focussed on the domestic market of Singapore, which is bolstered by an extremely robust shipbuilding industry and an equally healthy oil and gas sector. Marshal has attained substantial success serving the Singapore market, having built strong relationships with global powerhouses such as SembCorp Marine and Keppel FELS.

Instead of manufacturing its own products, Marshal focusses on its core area of expertise – systems integration. By partnering with global brands that are synonymous with uncompromising quality, Marshal chooses principal products that are worthy of the systems it designs. Having built an effective and efficient network of systems, processes and people domestically, Marshal established its first office in China in Shanghai in 2009 as part of the company's long-term strategy to grow its business abroad.

In view of its internationalisation plans, the company deployed a Perception Audit of its corporate brand. The findings revealed various challenges that Marshal has had to deal with. The fundamental perceptual challenge the Marshal brand faced was that customers perceived Marshal as a simple supplier of products rather than a systems integration services company providing reliable solutions covering communications, fire and gas detection and control and instrumentation. In essence, customers were buying from Marshal because of what it sold rather than the services it provided. Such a perception is an inherent risk for Marshal because the company does not manufacture any of the products it sells. Instead, it sells products that carry principal brands, thus increasing its dependence-value ratio.

Another brand perception challenge was found in the company's name – Marshal Technology Marketing & Engineering. This did not reflect the company's core expertise in the area of systems integration. Furthermore, the company's trademark did not bear a descriptive tagline that best described the company's value proposition.

In order to appreciate the repositioning of the Marshal brand, you need to clearly understand that brands operate on the principles of adversity and competition. In order to dispel the perception that Marshal was a simple supplier, chosen customer segments needed to understand the critical importance of integration. While each product brand is superior, technology and processes that drive these products are more often unique and proprietary. However, when being installed on a huge vessel like a semi-submersible, drilling ship or mega oil tanker, communications and detection systems need to converge for ease of control.

In partnership with a global brand consulting firm, Marshal decided that its brand strategy was to make offshore and marine accidents its number one enemy. While regularly keeping a close eye on its competitors, Marshal decided that its biggest enemy was the fatalities caused in a disaster on board a vessel or drilling platform. In doing so, it picked the right enemy to fight.

In warfare, as many soldiers would attest, it is the integration and deployment of resources, such as men, fire power, technology and systems, clearly supported by a battle plan that ultimately spell victory. The same approach was applicable to Marshal. The brand strategy was to position and communicate to its chosen markets that it integrates and deploys resources such as very skilled and competent people, best-in-class telecommunications, fire and gas detection and control and instrumentation systems technology and systems. All of these are clearly supported by an internationalisation plan.

The Execution

In a battle, soldiers need to know exactly what they are fighting for. Every soldier is required to know his/her role within his/her unit. Hence, a clear mind embedded with the reason and cause is important to his/her fight. In Marshal's case, the corporate name "Marshal Technology Marketing & Engineering" was not an accurate representation of its new strategy – the superior integration of products rather than simply selling them. This led to a repositioning of the corporate name from "Marshal Technology Marketing & Engineering" to "Marshal Systems".

Next, in the execution of its battle plan, it was important to communicate its "specialist force" against offshore and marine accidents by protecting the assets of its allies, i.e. owners of offshore and marine assets. There is no better way to do this than by dramatising it in a tagline and pegging the same tagline onto the trademark.

With regard to the trademark, while a new strategy was formed, a new symbol was needed too. Many "soldiers" felt that the current trademark was good but for a bygone era. Hence, a new trademark was designed, this time bearing a tagline that clearly communicated the battle plan.

MARSHAL
PROTECTING OFFSHORE & MARINE GIANTS

In a rare interview with Mr Jeffrey Tay, Managing Director of Marshal Systems, Tay had this to say about its new brand position:

The Company adopted a brand position of "Protecting Offshore & Marine Giants" and this reflects a setting where our customers are assured that their assets are being protected when equipped with systems that are integrated by Marshal's specialists. This is clearly reflected in our track record and clientele. This new brand position provides a higher competitive status which conferred upon our people the pride of the company. Here, the mission and goal is no longer fragmented. It is unified in the sense that the common mission is to prevent offshore and marine accidents on the assets that our clients own. With this broad mission in view, we all can better serve our customers more effectively and efficiently.

The subsequent stage of execution was to ensure that its soldiers and allies knew the company's battle plan and what it had to offer. Here, Marshal's unique selling proposition, found within its superior integration capabilities, had to be made known. Hence, every stakeholder and all possible touch-points were mapped. The company further ensured that the common messages of "Excellent Processes To Achieve Zero Error", "Value-Add Beyond Products" and "Customer-centric and Competent People" were clearly communicated, first to all its staff, then to existing and potential customers.

This brand strategy provided Marshal with a blueprint to differentiate it from its key competitors in its chosen markets by positioning it as a systems integration specialist preferred by offshore and marine giants. It also allows Marshal Systems to better manage perceptual gaps that existed. The brand strategy project also paved the way to repositioning the company's name to Marshal Systems – one that best communicates the value proposition towards its chosen markets. Today, Marshal serves an international clientele in more than 10 countries around the world on large international projects.

On 18 October 2010, Viking Offshore & Marine Limited, a leading integrated offshore and marine solutions provider listed on the Singapore Exchange, announced it had bought a 100 per cent stake in Marshal Systems.[66] The press aptly described Marshal Systems as "a leading integrator of marine communication, fire and safety equipment and control and instrumentation systems". The acquisition is part of Viking's strategy to build up a suite of complementary capabilities for its parent company to transform the latter into a leading offshore and marine integrated services provider.

It would be insufficient to say that the new brand position made Marshal Systems more appealing as an investable company than prior to it having clearly articulated its brand strategy. But suffice to say, the new brand position has clearly communicated what Marshal Systems does, how it does it, its unique selling proposition and, most of all, its brand position. This is indeed supported by comments made by Viking's Chairman Mr Andy Lim on the acquisition of Marshal:

> "Marshal represents a significant piece in the bolt-on strategy of Viking in the offshore and marine businesses. Our range of services is now very compelling, offering economies of scale and increased opportunities for cross-selling as we step up our overseas expansion…to emerge as a leading one-stop offshore and marine specialist".[67]

In summary, Marshal Systems made offshore and marine accidents its number one enemy and its customers its allies. Therefore, its new mission is to protect its allies. This provided the platform to transform Marshal Systems from a successful business into a focussed and highly differentiated brand that provides the company direction in its marketing and innovation activities. Ultimately, a stronger Marshal Systems corporate brand will enable the company to withstand both local and foreign

---

[66] Media release "Viking buys offshore and marine specialist for $17M" dated 18 October 2010

[67] "Viking buys Marshal Systems for S$17M" extracted on 12 January 2011 from www.channelnewsasia.com/stories/singaporebusinessnews/view/1087776/1/.html

competition more effectively, bringing long-term sustainability to the business. Here is what Tay had to say on bringing Marshal Systems to the next level:

> *Our next level is defined in a significant increase in revenue double of what Marshal Systems currently achieves. We also want to experience global market penetration into the economies of China, Vietnam and Brazil. While the quantity of business is to increase, and we are already seeing early signs of this, we also have to grow qualitatively. Our engineers should be world-class because the nature of our clients' assets is world-class. In this new business collaboration between Marshal and Viking Offshore & Marine, Marshal Systems is better and stronger. We are now poised to provide better integrative solutions not only in systems but also bigger turnkey packages that include HVAC, accommodations and hydraulics.*

B2B

CHAPTER
17

Rule No. 10 –
Know When To Launch
A Second Brand

ONE of the biggest mistakes that a company can make is to think that its brand can stand for everything under the sun. But that is what many business executives think the moment their company becomes successful. Success naturally breeds confidence. And because they have made it in one category, many business executives think they can use their brand name in other categories. Very often, they forget what made them successful in the first place and start to line extend their brands into other products or services.

The typical argument that management puts forward is that the brand is already well known, therefore it will be easier and less costly to launch a new product or service under that name. Plus, the marketplace is so crowded with brands and their marketing messages that it would make better sense to use an already well-known brand to launch that new product or service. That way, the new product or service will be able to rise above the clutter by leveraging on the parent's powerful brand name.

We are sure many of you have made this argument before and we know it seems to make a lot of sense but doing that could turn out to be a very costly mistake – not just for the original brand but also for the new products or services launched under that line-extended brand. New products and services, especially in a pioneering category, need new brand names.

Management can usually point to increased sales to justify this move but here is the danger. Branding mistakes don't immediately hit you on the head. They build up over time. The problem with line extension is that it may give your sales a boost in the short term simply because you are now selling more products! But in the long run, line extension damages both the core brand and the new products launched under the core brand.

The reason is simple. With line extension, the core brand is weakened because it no longer stands for the one thing that made it strong in the first place. It now stands for several things and when you stand for several things, you end up standing for nothing. And the new product or service using the line-extended name is also disadvantaged because it is using a name that stands for something else. In branding, there is no such thing as being neutral or having the best of both worlds. You are either this or you are that.

DO YOU BRUSH YOUR TEETH?

One of Jacky's clients was debating with him endlessly on the merits of using line extensions as a way to build brands quickly. After a while, Jacky suddenly asked the client, "Do you brush your teeth?", prompting everyone in the room to glare at him for being so rude.

The client looked puzzled. He must have thought that Jacky was implying that he had bad breath. Nevertheless, the client regained his composure and said, "Yes. At least twice a day."

Jacky then asked the client, "What brand of toothpaste do you use?"

The client replied, "Colgate."

Jacky asked, "Why Colgate? Why not Oral-B? I hear that they make excellent toothpaste and Oral-B is a well-known brand in oral care."

The client paused before answering, "I see where you are going with this. Well, Oral-B is known for toothbrushes, not toothpaste."

Jacky pressed on, "Would you buy a Colgate toothbrush? After all, Colgate is a famous brand for toothpaste so why not make use of that famous brand and extend into toothbrushes? It is the same thing after all – toothbrush and toothpaste both fall under the category of oral care, right?"

The client said, "Actually, I would buy Colgate toothbrushes. I have bought them before so it would seem to me that Colgate can be line-extended into something other than toothpaste."

Jacky asked, "If the Colgate toothbrush is priced the same as the Oral-B toothbrush, would you still buy it?"

The client answered with a shrug, "I've never thought of it that way but if they are the same price, then probably not."

Toothbrushes and toothpastes are two very low-interest categories, don't you agree? They are not something that most people spend a lot of time thinking about. Even then, most people would make a clear distinction between what the Colgate brand is and what the Oral-B brand is. Colgate stands for toothpaste and Oral-B stands for toothbrush. If Colgate wants to compete with Oral-B in the toothbrush category, it would need to have a lower price because as famous as the Colgate brand is, it is not famous for toothbrushes.

Even in the toothpaste category, Colgate still can't stand for everything. Colgate stands for protection toothpaste – protection against cavities, plaque and tartar. Colgate also makes toothpaste for sensitive teeth. But when toothpaste for sensitive teeth is mentioned, most people would think of Sensodyne. And Colgate also makes whitening toothpaste but when whitening toothpaste is mentioned, chances are, most people would think of Pearlie White or some other brand.

Colgate needs a second brand if it wants to enter another category effectively but even with a different name, it will still find it hard to compete against entrenched competitors like Listerine in mouthwash, Oral-B in toothbrushes, Sensodyne in sensitive teeth toothpaste and Pearlie White in whitening unless it can find a useful point of differentiation.

So, do you still think that just because your brand is famous in one area, it can be successfully extended into other categories? Even if it is a related category, you might still have difficulties as illustrated by the Colgate example.

DISPOSABLE CONTACT LENSES

Bausch + Lomb is one of the top contact lens makers in the world. It started to focus on contact lenses after the US Food and Drug Administration (FDA) approved its soft contact lenses in 1971. If you started wearing contact lenses in the eighties or nineties, chances are you would have bought a pair of Bausch + Lomb. In those days, you couldn't talk about contact lenses without the optician recommending you a pair from Bausch + Lomb.

Today, the contact lens category has grown a lot and it has even divided itself into new categories. Today, you have general vision contact lens, colour contact lens, astigmatism contact lens, multifocal contact lens, daily wear contact lens, flexible wear contact lens, extended wear contact lens and daily disposable contact lens. And probably some other categories that we are not even aware of.

If you walk into an optician's today to buy daily disposable lenses – which is a new category – the brand that comes to mind first is 1•DAY ACUVUE, a Johnson & Johnson product. Focus DAILIES from CIBA VISION is the other brand that might come to mind. Why not Bausch + Lomb? Because daily disposable contact lens is a new category and you need a new brand to go along with it. Using an old brand that is well known for something else in a new category will hamper its chances of success. The next story is probably one of the best examples of this.

WHO INVENTED DIGITAL PHOTOGRAPHY?

Canon? Nikon? Olympus? Sony? Nope. It was Kodak. Surprised? We were when we first found that out. Yes, Kodak pioneered this category way back in 1976. So, it should have dominated this category with an iron fist, right?

Polaroid pioneered a new category called "instant photography" and dominated it. Of course, Polaroid is no more because digital photography has made it obsolete but when the category was still relevant, Polaroid was king of the hill in instant photography. Nikon was one of the pioneers of the single lens reflex (SLR) camera and, today, Nikon is one of the leading brands of SLR cameras. Carl Zeiss is a pioneer in camera lenses and today is a leader in this category.

So, Kodak should be No. 1 in digital cameras but it is not. What happened? Kodak is a brand that is known for photographic film so launching a new category called "digital photography" would have meant going head-to-head with its own photographic film business. Despite this, Kodak should have still launched the digital camera. After all, most things that used to be analogue eventually went digital and Kodak would have known that cameras would eventually go that route too. But Kodak waited too long to get into the game, giving Canon, Sony and the rest a head start. When Kodak eventually did enter the digital camera category, it made a big mistake by not launching a new brand for its digital cameras. It insisted on using the Kodak name because it is a well-known name. However, the problem was that the Kodak name was not known for digital cameras – or any type of camera for that matter.

That mistake probably cost Kodak the lead in this sector. Look at the market share of the various brands of digital cameras. There was an article on Your Photo Tips on 10 December 2009 by Damien Franco that talked about the Top 10 best-selling point and shoot digital cameras on Amazon.com.[68] Take a look at the list below:

#1 Canon PowerShot SD1200IS
10 MP Digital Camera with 3x Optical Image Stabilised Zoom and 2.5-inch LCD

---

[68] www.yourphototips.com/2009/12/10/the-10-best-selling-point-and-shoot-cameras-of-2009/

#2 Nikon Coolpix L20

10 MP Digital Camera with 3.6 Optical Zoom and 3-inch LCD

#3 Canon PowerShot A1100IS

12.1 MP Digital Camera with 4x Optical Image Stabilised Zoom and 2.5-inch LCD

#4 Canon PowerShot SD780IS

12.1 MP Digital Camera with 3x Optical Image Stabilised Zoom and 2.5-inch LCD

#5 Panasonic Lumix DMC-ZS3

10.1 MP Digital Camera with 12x Wide Angle MEGA Optical Image Stabilised Zoom and 3-inch LCD (Black)

#6 Canon PowerShot SX20IS

12.1 MP Digital Camera with 20x Wide Angle Optical Image Stabilised Zoom and 2.5-inch Articulating LCD

#7 Nikon Coolpix S620

12.2 MP Digital Camera with 4x Optical Vibration Reduction (VR) Zoom and 2.7-inch LCD

#8 Canon PowerShot D10

12.1 MP Waterproof Digital Camera with 3x Optical Image Stabilised Zoom and 2.5-inch LCD

#9 Fujifilm FinePix J28

10.2 MP Digital Camera with 3x Optical Zoom

#10 Canon PowerShot S90IS

10 MP Digital Camera with 3.8x Wide Angle Optical Image Stabilised Zoom and 3-inch LCD

We see Canon, Nikon, Fujifilm and even the odd Panasonic on the list but no Kodak. Why not? After all, these are digital cameras bought on Amazon.com and Amazon.com has a big base of users in the United States (it is American after all) and Kodak is an American icon. Could it be that the Kodak brand is strong, but strong in photographic film, not digital cameras? One brand for one idea. Kodak's brand stands for photographic film. Kodak's brand does not stand for digital cameras.

Some CEOs have told us before that sometimes having such a strong brand is a negative because it does not allow you the flexibility of expanding into other categories. That is nonsense. You should want to have a strong brand like Kodak. Do you know how much money Kodak made in photographic film over the many decades that film cameras were still relevant? But products have life cycles. Categories sometimes have expiry dates. When that happens, you need to launch a new brand or create a new category (but park it under a new brand).

Kodak could have learnt a lesson or two from the likes of Procter & Gamble and United Technologies Corporation. Procter & Gamble is a highly successful company that many people know and admire. And it has got the right idea. It owns different brands that stand for different things. Each brand is targeted at a particular category. Procter & Gamble doesn't make one brand stand for many different things. These are some of the brands that the company has: Braun, SK-II, CoverGirl, Gillette, Head & Shoulders, Olay, Vidal Sassoon, Crest, Oral-B, Pringles, Vicks, Tampax, Charmin and Pampers. That's the way to do it in the B2C market. United Technologies Corporation also owns a portfolio of successful product brands such as Otis (elevators), Carrier (air conditioners), Pratt & Whitney (jet engines) and others. That's how you do it in the B2B market.

NEW CATEGORIES NEED NEW BRANDS

Have you ever wondered why those big luxury cars from mass-market car makers like Peugeot, Rover, Fiat, Citroën, Renault, Opel, Ford, Volkswagen and Mitsubishi don't sell very well despite the fact that they are very well-equipped and priced cheaper than the equivalent Mercedes-Benz, BMW, Audi or Lexus?

You don't need to be a genius to work this out. Who wants to buy a luxury car from companies that are known for making cheap mass-market cars? No matter how good the cars are, as long as they wear the wrong badge, they won't sell in the luxury car sector.

Now consider the watch category. Take two well-known brands – Rolex and Seiko. Rolex is a premium Swiss watch. Even entry-level Rolex watches cost around S$6,000 or so. Seiko is a mass-market Japanese watch. Seiko makes very good watches for the mass market. Its watches usually retail for a few hundred dollars. Even if Seiko comes up with much better, much higher-quality watches than Rolex, do you think it will be able to penetrate the high-end market if it uses the Seiko name?

If Seiko wants to go upmarket, it needs a new brand. Just because Seiko is successful in the mass-market sector doesn't mean that it can sell watches in the S$6,000-and-above category. Likewise, if Rolex wants to go downmarket, it needs a new brand – like Tudor, for example. If it goes downmarket with the Rolex brand, guess what will happen? It will destroy the brand equity of the upmarket Rolex watches. Why pay S$6,000 for a high-end Rolex when you can get a S$1,000 low-end Rolex that is still a Rolex? And that S$1,000-Rolex will probably not do very well either because who wants a cheap Rolex in the first place? When you buy a Rolex, you want people to know that you have paid for an expensive watch.

New categories need new brands.

That is why Toyota, despite being such a powerhouse in cars as well as being the world's most profitable car maker for decades, wisely chose to launch a new brand when it ventured into the luxury car segment in 1989. The rest, as they say, is Lexus history.

Take the drinks and beverage category for example. Each new category has been dominated by a new brand, not a line-extended brand. No matter how powerful a brand is, you cannot make it stand for a category that it is not known for.

- Red Bull was the new brand launched into the new category called energy drink.
- Gatorade was the new brand launched into the new category called sports drink.
- Evian was the new brand launched into the new category called bottled spring water.
- Dr Pepper was the new brand launched into the new category called spicy carbonated drinks.
- Snapple was the new brand launched into the new category called natural fruit drink.

None of these brands were line-extended from an existing brand. That is why they are strong. They were new brands that stand for the new categories they were launched into. When you launch a new category or enter a new category, make sure you do so with a completely new brand.

BUT WHEN DO YOU LAUNCH A SECOND BRAND?

There is a caveat to Rule No. 10. While it is necessary for companies to launch a second brand when they enter a new category, this doesn't mean that companies should launch brands indiscriminately. Before you run off and order a slew of new brands to be launched, you must understand that you need to do it at the right time. And the right time is when your existing brand has become a dominant force in its category or if the existing category is becoming obsolete due to technological changes.

There are too many small companies out there with more brands than they can manage. If you only have a fraction of your category's market share, don't launch new brands. Focus on getting your brand to the top. If you are too busy launching multiple brands while you are still a small player, you will waste a lot of time and energy managing a plethora of brands, none of which are significant players.

Many companies that we have met would rather have 5 per cent of 10 markets than 50 per cent of one market. When we asked them why, the answer was always the same. Growth and diversification of risks. But being a 5 per cent player in 10 markets is actually very risky. Look around you. The big, global brands are dominating even local markets. Everywhere you go, you see global brands dominating every category. So, if you are a small player in 10 categories, you will eventually have to come to terms with 10 global giants and if history is anything to go by, you will probably get steamrollered 10 times.

It is better to focus your energy on building a powerful brand in one category and then launch a new brand into a new category. But you need to be successful in one category first before moving on. If you cannot even grow in a category that you know well, how can you grow in a category that you know nothing about?

Toyota didn't launch Lexus until its Corolla model was firmly entrenched as the best-selling car in the world. And only after Lexus became the best-selling luxury car in its key market, which is the United States, did Toyota launch Scion, a US-market only brand aimed at the young, sporty types.

In A Nutshell

A brand is just an idea that exists in the minds of customers. A strong brand is one that owns a powerful idea in the mind. One idea. Not two. Not ten. Not a hundred. If you own a powerful idea in the mind, you have a strong brand. That is extremely hard to come by so don't throw it away by line-extending that brand and diluting that idea in the mind. Categories will grow and mature. When this happens, companies seeking further growth will usually try to extend their brand into other areas. Don't do that. Launch a new brand if you want to venture into a new category. If you line extend your brand, you will do two things – both of them bad. One, you will dilute the focus and the strength of the brand because the brand no longer stands for one thing and one thing only. The purity is gone. Two, you limit the growth opportunity for the new product because it is saddled with a brand that is known for something else. And if you use a line-extended brand on the new product or category, you will have to sell much cheaper than the leading brand.

Take a look at these items:

- Xerox. Computer.
- HP. Plasma TV.
- Oral-B. Toothpaste.
- Colgate. Electric toothbrush.
- Hyundai. Luxury car.
- Samsung. Family car.
- Honda. Private jet.
- Swatch. Compact car.
- General Electric. Insurance.
- OSIM. Vacuum cleaner.

Would you buy any of these products if they were sold under the brands they are attached to? You might – provided it were a lot cheaper. If a Hyundai luxury car is priced the same as a Mercedes-Benz, why wouldn't you just buy the real thing? You need to launch a second brand if you want to sell a new product or service. But you only launch the second brand once the first brand is already very strong. If you can't increase sales of your core brand in a category you know well, how can you possibly do well in a category you know very little about?

CASE STUDY
Know When To Launch A Second Brand – AlphaBeta's Ellaziq

The Food Manufacturing Industry

The Food and Agriculture Organization of the United Nations forecasts that global food production must increase by 70 per cent by 2050 in order to sustain a global population that is expected to be 9.1 billion at that time. This has a high implication on food companies within the South East Asian region. According to Statistics Singapore and the ASEAN Secretariat, Singapore's population has increased rapidly over the past two decades, from 3.047 million people in 1990 to 4.027 million in 1999 and to almost 5 million people in 2009. This trend of rapid population growth can also be seen in the regional population growth of ASEAN from 430 million people in 1990 to 514 million in 2000.

In Singapore, the food manufacturing industry, with help from the government, has begun implementing new initiatives to enhance the capabilities of local food manufacturers, increasing its ability to capture the potential of a growing worldwide demand for food. According to a report by Spring Singapore, Singapore food manufacturing companies are also leveraging on the country's expertise in food science and related technology by investing in R&D to develop novel products, bettering processes and improving food packaging. A rising number of food manufacturers are also adopting internationally recognised food safety certification in a bid to gain a competitive advantage over other global competitors.

AlphaBeta – Food For Thought

Established in 1986, AlphaBeta Foods Manufacturing (not its real name) produces a variety of Eastern and Western sausage products under in-house brand names such as "AlphaBeta" and "Karla's" (not the real brand names). It is currently a leading supplier and key manufacturer of a wide range of sausages as well as stuffed fish and seafood products in Singapore. Its sausage production plant was also the first in Singapore to obtain ISO 9002 and HACCP certification.

From a product range perspective and over time, the company has expanded its product portfolio to include sausages tailored to the taste buds of different consumers in different segments. Apart from selling its own brand of sausages to food outlets, supermarket chains and wholesalers, it engages in contract manufacturing for other food companies and supermarkets. Through the company's uncompromising quality, food safety and reliability, AlphaBeta is a preferred supplier.

A comprehensive demographic study of more than 200 countries shows that there are 1.57 billion Muslims living in the world today, representing 23 per cent of an estimated 2009 world population of 6.8 billion.[69] Of this figure, 20 per cent resides in Asia. From a food perspective, this presents an attractive market opportunity for AlphaBeta. Situated close to predominantly Muslim countries such as Malaysia and Indonesia as well as the Middle East, AlphaBeta decided to expand its business and capture the halal food market by offering halal sausages produced by a newly set-up halal food company with its own halal production facilities.

The Strategy: Journey To The Inception Of Ellaziq

In AlphaBeta's journey to capture the halal food market, the first, and perhaps most crucial, brand perception challenge it faced was its success as a non-halal food manufacturer. Traditionally a non-halal food manufacturer, the association to the parent brand would be undesirable for its halal food operations. That is why the company recognised the importance of devising a separate corporate brand for its halal food company, one that was differentiated from both its competitors and the parent company's corporate brand. Although the two companies were to co-exist in the area of management and share the same corporate services, they were to be operated as unique and separate entities. In a rare interview with AlphaBeta's CEO Mr Ong Chip, Ong shared his vision on developing a strong halal food company:

> AlphaBeta is the biggest process meat producer in Singapore and our success in providing quality food to the consumer is the most important mission. This is a reflection of our ability to achieve ISO 22000, HACCP and Singapore AVA grade "A" certification. On top of quality, innovation in introducing new products has also been a business philosophy for us. The halal food strategy is one such innovation in our business model. Singapore continues to hold a world-class status of quality, assurance and reliability in our food export business. Our halal business strategy rides on this reputation because as a company, our customers too are of the opinion that we bear the same attributes.

---

[69] 'Mapping The Global Muslim Population. A Report on the Size and Distribution of the World's Muslim Population' published by the Pew Forum on Religion and Public Life in October 2009.

Another brand perception challenge encountered by AlphaBeta was its relatively late entry into the halal food market. As a late entrant, the company faced a market that already has many established and entrenched players. As a result, it needed to not only provide halal food products of the highest standard but also have a brand that is unique and differentiated from the other more established players in the market. Without a strong and differentiated brand, it would be difficult for the company to successfully export its halal food products into these overseas markets. Furthermore, as a newcomer in the overseas halal food market, AlphaBeta did not have a clear and proper understanding of these overseas markets, including foreign culture, language and social norms, which could have consequently hindered its internationalisation efforts.

AlphaBeta's goal was to construct a corporate brand that represents the company's halal food business and product brands for the halal food products it seeks to offer. Due to the stringent regulatory and religious conventions that govern the halal food market, AlphaBeta had to ensure that its manufacturing plant and raw materials are acceptable to the Islamic religious council of Singapore that confers the halal certification upon qualified companies. (This certificate is known to be trusted, reliable and widely accepted.)

Failure to grasp the specific needs of a new market can be costly, both financially and in terms of damaging the corporate image. Therefore, to achieve AlphaBeta's goal, the assistance of a global brand consulting company was sought. The company and its consultants mapped out a positioning and differentiation strategy for this new entity that would help to enable the parent company to capture its desired market share overseas. In order to devise a suitable differentiation and positioning strategy, an analysis of factors that affect customers' purchasing behaviour was conducted via a perception audit.

To Ong, the most sensible option for diversification was to move his food manufacturing business into a segment or a market that was clearly parallel to what AlphaBeta is already doing, hence the choice of the halal segment. However, developing new products in this segment requires effective ways to reduce risk and exploit gain. New ideas need to be thoroughly tested and evaluated to reduce food hygiene risks and help fine-tune the marketing mix before any launch. Thus, an in-depth analysis of key competitors in the halal food space in AlphaBeta's chosen markets was also done. The results of the analyses on both customers and competitors led to the recommendation and acceptance of positioning a new halal food company – one that specialises in halal food products and differentiated through its unique specialisation in the area of halal food. It quickly became clear that the way forward was to create a second brand for AlphaBeta, a brand that would be independent from AlphaBeta and set up specifically to focus on halal food development. By choosing to create two separate brands, the company would be able to go after two different target markets, benefiting the corporation as a whole. It was clear to Ong that this second-brand proposition was probably the best way to address the halal segment of the food market.

The next, and equally important, phase was to create the corporate and product brand names of the new company. Since the name is the first thing stakeholders see when they encounter a brand, an extensive list of names was put through a systematic selection process that encompassed defined naming parameters and conventions before the corporate brand and product brands were jointly determined by the consultants and AlphaBeta. The names selected were also tested for language and religion neutrality to make sure that there was no conflict with local cultures in the targeted overseas markets.

After the corporate brand name and two halal product brand names were selected, a tagline was also created for each of the brands to dramatise the differentiation and positioning strategy. At the corporate level, the tagline reinforced the company's specialisation in halal food. For the product brands, the taglines served to dramatise differentiation and positioning that, apart from being coherent with the corporate brand, were relevant to the respective target customers.

The brand names were then structured in an easy-to-understand framework whereby the product brands were classified under the corporate brand. Using such a brand architecture facilitates the inclusion of new product brands in the future as the halal food company expands its halal food offerings.

The establishment of the positioning and differentiation strategy provided the direction and foundation for Ellaziq, AlphaBeta's fully owned subsidiary for its halal business.

ELLAZiQ
The Halal Food Specialist

The new product brands for specific market segments were developed as follows, namely El-Dina (high-range) and Kizmiq (low- to mid-range).

To operationalise the new halal food company's corporate brand, an IMC strategy consisting of a comprehensive set of stakeholder-specific brand messages was crafted and used to communicate the corporate brand in a consistent and coherent manner to all its stakeholders.

The Execution

While a well-known brand name does not guarantee a successful extension, extending the AlphaBeta brand in this instance would have been a very costly mistake. Simple brand extensions are more often than not unwise. Establishing a second brand was clearly the right decision to make in AlphaBeta's case. This is because AlphaBeta and its range of product brands are already established and strong in their own right within the non-halal food category. Consequently, it would have been extremely confusing, and perhaps even wrong, to have parked halal products under the same umbrella.

Given the evolving complexity of consumer demands and purchasing patterns, brands that offer consistency in terms of promise and delivery generally yield higher returns in loyalty. Ellaziq's focussed brand architecture for halal foods allowed the company to spearhead its plans to expand into halal food markets abroad, particularly in its market segments of choice in the ASEAN region. As market segments are often socially fragmented, the two product brands – El-Dina and Kismiq – were created to cater to different market segments, allowing the company to leverage on its expertise and experience in the halal food manufacturing industry while maintaining a clear distinction from the parent's corporate brand.

It should also be noted that the creation of its own halal food brands has reduced the parent company's dependence on various halal-certified manufacturers and allows Ellaziq more control over the quality of its halal products.

The brand strategy also provided direction for Ellaziq's innovation and marketing activities in its overseas markets. Resources invested in innovation and marketing have been part of a drive to strengthen Ellaziq's position both in terms of product development and expansion of its product range. Ellaziq was also able to execute the brand strategy in its overseas markets through a well-crafted integrated marketing communications strategy devised to achieve efficacy and consistency.

The journey to developing a second brand requires both corporate belief and the deployment of resources. As the global demand of halal food continues to grow, Ellaziq will widen its product range by exporting to its chosen markets through participation in international trade missions and exhibitions. As a burgeoning second brand, developing Intellectual Property through the establishment and protection of its trademarks is and will continue to be serious issues for the company. Ong sees these efforts as clear and important statements to its customers and, indeed, an offensive strategy to force competitors out of the market. Ellaziq's business philosophy is to build its reputation as a maker of premium-quality halal food products and achieve its market position by maintaining world-class standards of safety and quality by using premium-quality ingredients in the production process. In other words, it strives to be the first company to bring value innovation products to the marketplace by maintaining its premium-quality position as a "Halal Food Specialist".